summum of the cinema in such terms.

There follows, since cinema is an infant of technology, a review of some of the implications of transforming one medium, that of letters, to another which is both technological and variform. The end of this section treats an eighteenth-century epistolary novel and the questions raised by translating a personal, nontechnological form into its very opposite.

Next, the nature of the relationship between art and photography is investigated, along with the aesthetic responsibilities of the cinema. Then considered are the psychology and the "grammar" of film, insofar as that term obtains, with inspection of how conventions of the cinematic mode affect the subconscious motives involved in presenting a narration—in short, how a film is recounted.

The last section proposes three principal ways by which novels to date have been adapted for the screen, with a number of illustrations for each. These ordering devices, says Professor Wagner, may have varied in intensity at different times, but all serve to show something of the resilience and fertility of the human mind in accommodating those visions that pass and repass before it.

THE NOVEL
AND
THE CINEMA

THE NOVEL
AND
THE CINEMA

Geoffrey Wagner

"The time of the image has come."
—Abel Gance

RUTHERFORD • MADISON • TEANECK
FAIRLEIGH DICKINSON UNIVERSITY PRESS
LONDON: THE TANTIVY PRESS

© 1975 by Associated University Presses, Inc.

Associated University Presses, Inc.
Cranbury, New Jersey 08512

The Tantivy Press
108 New Bond Street
London W1Y OQX, England

Library of Congress Cataloging in Publication Data

Wagner, Geoffrey Atheling.
    The novel and the cinema. See S1₱·

    Bibliography: p. 358-364.
    Includes index.
    1. Film adaptations. I. Title.
PN1997.85.W33   809.2′3   74-20939
ISBN 0-8386-1618-6

SBN 0-904208-80-X   (UK)
PRINTED IN THE UNITED STATES OF AMERICA

Contents

Acknowledgements

I particularly need to thank Mrs. Elizabeth Lippoth and her staff of the Audio-Visual Department of the City College of New York for their tireless help in locating source material and arranging screenings. My research was also facilitated by a grant from the City College English Department for which I am grateful. Acknowledgement is also made to Alfred A. Knopf, Inc., for permission to quote from the works of Thomas Mann and H. L. Mencken, and to Farrar, Straus & Giroux, Inc. for permission to quote from Alberto Moravio, *A Ghost at Noon*.

G. W.

Introduction

Sound cinema is literate. It therefore partakes of literature. Whether it must consist of narrative literature is a disputed point. In any case, the term narration is an insecure one here: a verbal survey, backwards or forwards, of a scope of life, inner or outer, is not the same as a succession of images passed before the eye in time. There are those who argue—at first hearing, convincingly—that motion pictures have been forced to be "verbally" narrative by virtue of their market place. Commercial cinema has generally required a story.

Such critics might point out patches of films that are purely "poetic," passages of *Le sang d'un poète, Le grand Meaulnes,* even the abstract flight sequences of *2001* wherein little action is advanced. Some documentaries, travelogues perhaps. The "action" in Flaherty's *Louisiana Story* is quite slight. *Citizen Kane* begins with its ending, as does Welles's 1955 rephrasing of *Othello.* Starting with an ending has now become a cliché and can often confuse rather than clarify—*Serpico* (1973) was far easier to follow in its printed than in its filmic version. This was not only be-

9

cause chronology was abandoned, but since the characters were undefined and stereotyped and the story-line had little progression (in the film the various meetings to establish that Serpico wants to reach the Police Commissioner could have been compressed into one). Where, therefore, lies the virtue of what is called narrative advance? Should we not see that such narration is an artificial straitjacket imposed on motion pictures by financial adventurers?

By logical extension of this argument we should not see films in cinemas at all; we should see them, rather, in galleries, like paintings. Perhaps the most appropriate venue might be in some atemporal situation, in which the viewer elects to watch a series of dislocated images, as in the peepshow paradise of the pornography addict who drops his coin in the slot for a set of scenes, some of which, if he is unlucky enough to start with the last section, he sees backwards. He is hardly interested in what we know as narrative.

It is then further argued that narrative fiction is but one aspect of *lettera scripta,* which includes poetry among other forms. It is true that, to an extent, you can conduct a poem in a set of images which are not intended to lead in a linear direction but rather endeavour to expand a central metaphor. Some of Shakespeare's sonnets, if read without the epigrammatic clincher in the final couplet, would answer to this approach; much vatic poetry—Hart Crane, Dylan Thomas, Allen Ginsberg—would; and anyone who has over the years tried to teach Rimbaud's "Le bateau ivre" must at some point have been aware of the hungry sheep looking up in expectation of a narrative, and there shall no narrative be given them.

This book will not set out to prove or disprove any hard-and-fast theory concerning the novel and the cinema. For this very reason it is important to be clear about certain terms from the start. For film to become "poetic," as some critics require, it might have to make as craven a capitulation to literature as it is said to have in following the novel, which is anathema to the same group! We must bear in mind that image[1] is not image.[2] Sir Herbert Read once wrote:

> If you ask me to give you the most distinctive quality of good writing, I would give it to you in this one word: VISUAL. Reduce the art of writing to its fundamentals and you come to this single aim: to convey images by means of words. But to convey *images*.

At first glance this seems persuasive enough. Conrad's famous Preface to *The Nigger of the 'Narcissus'* tells us: "My task which I am trying to achieve is, by the power of the written word to make you hear, to make you feel—it is, before all, to make you *see*." D. W. Griffith's echo seems now equally well-known: "The task I'm trying to achieve is above all to make you see." The comment seems close to a copy, yet visual literacy is not literal literacy. The written image, the metaphor on the printed page, is altogether distinct from the physical existence conferred by throwing a picture on a screen.

In *The Cinematic Imagination,* which treats some of these matters thoughtfully, Edward Murray maintains that neither Balzac nor Tolstoy could cause us to "see" a face "as vividly as a movie camera can" (for which I would want to substitute "as physically"). He then proceeds to maintain that this direct "palpability" of cinema confers on it a superiority: "Watching a film story is ordinarily a less reflective but a more moving experience than reading a novel." Anyone who concludes the present book with the impression that one mode or the other is "superior" may be said to have emerged with but a dim idea of its author's intentions. A literary image does not require *per se* a sequence or continuation (beyond that demanded by grammar) in the same way as a physical image thrown on the screen. "In the cinema," wrote André Levinson nearly half a century ago, "one extracts the thought from the image; in literature, the image from the thought." So strongly is this the case that I. A. Richards once protested what sounds like the complete contrary of Sir Herbert Read's dictum:

> For words cannot, and should not attempt to "hand over sensations bodily"; they have very much more important work to do . . . language, well used, is a *completion* and does what the intuitions of sensation by themselves cannot do. Words are the meeting points at which regions of experience which can never combine in sensation or intuition, come together. They are the occasion and means of that growth which is the mind's endless endeavour to order itself. That is why we have language. It is no mere signalling system. It is the instrument of all our distinctively human development, of everything in which we go beyond the other animals.

These are golden words, indeed, for if properly heeded they suggest another sort of narrative, one which need not be a going-after but rather a going-with, as a part of "our distinctively human development." Such is how one writes a serious novel rather than a detective mystery. Murray's position seems to take it that the novelist sits down, imagines a scene in his mind's eye and approximates as closely as possible to it with words. If not a real falsification, this is a vulgarisation, the property of those who exclaim delightedly, "I can just *see* that character." Some of Dostoyevski's characters are extremely hard to "see," but they are great and real characters nonetheless.

They are so because language is a completion, an entelechy, and film is not. By its nature it cannot be. Film is a diffusion. The activity of extracting thought from a concretion (as Levinson suggests) has to be so. Borderlines become unclear. This is not to denigrate cinema in any way, though it certainly is an admission of a difficulty in reaching norms about such a plural form. As Murray himself concedes, when we hear Othello delivering his famous speech to the Senate, we strain to catch the words rather than watch the back of Orson Welles's head. Again, I. A. Richards hits the nail of this particular dilemma on the head:

> The school teachers are forgetting everything that matters most about language in treating it as just a stimulus to visualisation. They think the image fills in the meaning of the word; it is rather the other way about and it is the word which brings in the meaning which the image and its original perception lack.

This, therefore, is the point of departure here: to take Eisenstein's celebrated demonstration of Dickensian origins in Griffith in an epistemological context. It was simply that the great American director was aware he was handling a different *kind* of image, one from which thought had to be forced rather than vice versa. The problem of narrative is perhaps a red herring in this matter. The main problem is to dramatise this imagery, as indeed the initial concept of the image (Dickens's "The kettle began it . . ." at the start of *The Cricket on the Hearth* which Griffith filmed). Film saw in narrative fiction, rather than in poetry or drama, imagistic techniques and strategies which contributed to its own rapid development. In this sense only does the present book propose any dependence of cinema on fiction.

Having said as much, however, one realises that the debt is very large. The novel had been moving away from the "omniscient" point of view long before Griffith is said to have separated film from theatre. Since Balzac and *Madame Bovary* the novelist began to fade as a presence within the fiction. There is usually a time-lag in the commercialisation of a technique, and the technique by means of which, in a fiction at least, the author *becomes* his characters, refines himself out of existence ("paring his fingernails," in Stephen Dedalus's parody of the operation) and employs style as vision, became pre-eminent before commercial cinema really developed, and was immensely congenial to it. It is true that in the theatre also the audience cannot detect the author's presence, but the notion of style as vision, so dear to Flaubert, of style as telling you something (indeed, everything) is borrowed by cinema from the modern novel rather than the theatre.

The emphasis on style was congenial to cinema since it engaged technics. The technical ability of Flaubert and Joyce was so great that their influence still dominates the novel in a culture committed to technological advance. Stendhal's *Le rouge et le noir,* on the other hand, is altogether too intimate, there is too close a collaboration between the author and his effects, for it to find many direct successors today. Attempts to film this scintillating fiction to date, even one including a Julien Sorel as genial as Gérard Philippe, have proved dismal failures.

Authorial omniscience had left the serious novel, if not before Griffith, at least before the great era arrived of purloining fiction for films, of what Robert Richardson nicely terms "theatrical xerography." Percy Lubbock had systematised the Prefaces of Henry James by 1926, in *The Craft of Fiction,* no less than a handbook on how to manage "point of view" in narration so that the author was imperceptible, if not frankly invisible. Film, gifted with an even more formidable array of techniques, obviously felt it also had a right to these ruins, and fairly relished its new role. For in the theatre the author had never been present (with the exception of a few bizarre instances, mostly to be found in Shaw).

Stemming from the Eisenstein thesis, the approach offered in these pages might be further clarified by a diametrically opposed position, that advanced by Murray in *The Cinematic Imagination.* Here some recent effects (such as intermissions in certain long films, like *Lord Jim* or *Richard II,* or that "the average play today looks as though it was written and staged for the cameras") seem to have led the critic to suggest a semantic feedback, namely that most writers are today would-be scenarists, capable of that apogee of intelligence, the "cinematic imagination." But in verbal terms the latter must always be a borrowing, and therefore the prerogative of the inferior literary artist. Midge Decter writes of Leon Uris as follows:

> Mr. Uris's prose *writes* movie stars, which is no simple matter—especially in view of the postures these stars are given to assume. The muscles of every hero must threaten to rip through his clothing; adolescent heroines must awake to the stirring of strange new feelings within their budding breasts. . . . *

Yet with better writers the direction seems to be reversed, André Bazin estimating, in *What Is Cinema?*, that *Kane* "would never have existed" but for Dos Passos. Murray, however, concludes confidently:

> The history of the novel after 1922—the year *Ulysses* appeared—is to a large extent that of the development of a cinematic imagination in novelists and their frequently ambivalent attempt to come to grips with the "liveliest art" of the twentieth century.

It may be that some of the authors he cites (most of them American), men like Scott Fitzgerald, Dos Passos, Arthur Miller, did "react" to cinema and its new effects. It is also, unfortunately for this theory, the case that by 1922 the whole of Proust—together with the non-narrative intention of that great *oeuvre*—had appeared, the whole of James, and most of Conrad. Alain-Fournier had written his major fictional work; Huysmans had turned his back on time; Gide had begun his experiments in contrapuntal fiction, Dujardin completed his in stream-of-consciousness. Kafka, who detested the cinema, had written everything of consequence in his canon. Hamsun and Mann had both arrested the narrative and shown cross-cutting, parallel ac-

---

* On the other hand, Agnès Varda would "make a film exactly as one writes a novel."

tions and other techniques said to be the purlieu of the "cinematic imagination." Moreover, there was by this time a considerable body of theory on how to direct fiction, in the Prefaces and Journals of such writers. Finally, by 1922, *Ulysses,* which contains every trick of the "cinematic imagination" for at least three decades in advance, *had been written.* Conrad was mildly interested in films at the end of his life but to characterise Joyce's interest in the Bucharest Cinematograph Volta during his Trieste period as an infatuation with cinema (as do Murray and other critics) is little short of absurd. The entire Volta episode is summarised in the chapter of Richard Ellmann's biography of Joyce dealing with the years 1909–1911. It was obviously far more an infatuation with the idea of making some money for a change.

However, the showing of inept Italian films (even about Beatrice Cenci) in Dublin was hardly conducive to the latter, and Joyce's dream of glory as a film magnate soon expired. When, much later on, Joyce met Eisenstein he told the Russian director that *Ulysses* was not amenable to the screen. Certainly Joyce went to *Potemkin* but, since it was silent and he was at the time blind, the experience must have been distinctly nugatory. In brief, Murray's theory strikes me as fairly preposterous and just about the opposite of what is offered here. As Bertolt Brecht said in "The Film, the Novel and Epic Theatre," "The mechanisation of literary production cannot be thrown into reverse."

A culture obtains the art form it desires. Film is the art of a technocracy, and a technocracy is ineluctably narrative. In his valuable *Literature and Film* Robert Richardson suggests that "if science and technology have become the forms for much of the creative energy of the twentieth century, then we should not be surprised to find the motion picture, that child of the machine, of the physics of light, and of the chemistry of film, one of the most vital if indeed not the most vital of the modern arts." Arnold Hauser is brought to the bar in support—"The film is, moreover, an art evolved from the spiritual foundations of technics."

In his admirable survey of realist fiction, *The Gates of Horn,* Professor Harry Levin tells us that "epic, romance, and novel are the representatives of three successive estates and styles of life: military, courtly, and mercantile." To this one now adds that the cinema is the representative of the technological "style of life," television (in fact or fiction) still being for the most part diluted cinema. It is seen on a box rather than in an auditorium, that is all.

It has been a feature of each new form to assimilate the characteristics of its predecessors. Poetry, travelogues, etiquette books were all superceded by the first novels, their effects duplicated. The cinema has by now so manipulated images of travel that that element of the novel which supplied local colour is now quite supererogatory. The novel, however, never tried to be poetry itself. Technology is a mirror situation. One of the grosser penalties of being the representative of the technological "style of life" has been the erosion of Joseph Joubert's maxim that illusion is a necessary part of reality. Too many films have been too literal to be art: they involved actual faces, landscapes, things; the reality was inescapable. It is for this reason that a section of this book investigates the technological playback in early cinema; for by now cinema has sophisticated itself to the point of acknowledging Joubert's maxim and of allowing illusion to show reality, while, on the other hand, one part of the novel seems to strive to become motion picture *avant le jour.*

Yet Richardson, who concurs that "film is a branch of literature," also calls it "this remarkable new medium." It is convenient to talk about film as such, but in truth it is many. Ingmar Bergman's likening of the construction of a film to the collective building of Chartres cathedral ("I would play my part in the collective building of the cathedral") attests as much. Film is a collaboration of discrete forms. Any film editor knows as much. It is customary for literature professors to intone the proposition that a good poem cannot be put in novel form. Joyce would not have written *Ulysses* as a fiction unless the experience he was handling had demanded that particular literary form for its expression. But the experience was always there, at large in the world. One could scarcely argue that prior to Defoe, for instance, the experiential content of the novel could have had no outlet, since the only such were poetry and drama.

The cinema is a number of media, and a collocation of forms. Joyce's "viewing" of *Potemkin* came vividly to mind when, in October 1973, a town in Rockland County, New York, appointed a blind man to head an obscenity committee for screening films, cabaret acts, and the like. Under press questioning this individual admitted that other members of the committee would "fill me in when the screen goes silent." A homosexual porno like *Bijou* carries a soundtrack almost wholly composed of classical music; one wonders how its prurient content is gauged by one blind.

Cinema's quality is that it binds within one experience a variety of human reactions to media. Eisenstein is today generally detested by auteurist critics for his thorough realisation that film, by its very plurality, can never be considered an autonomous form ("It is only very thoughtless and presumptuous people who can erect laws and an aesthetic for cinema, proceeding from premises of some incredible virgin-birth of this art"). It is for this reason perhaps, cinema's plural and elastic nature, its Protean guises, that man has tended to triumph against the technological content within it—of which narrative is undoubtedly one aspect. (One thinks of the errand of the great early comedians, Chaplin, Keaton, Lloyd.) In other words, cinema is so arrogantly technical that human principles are asserted within it, as if from survival's sake.

Having cleared away some of the debris, we are obliged to characterise our line of approach. It stems from Richardson's belief "that literature had already achieved some unusual and purely visual effects before film even arrived," and by literature we here mean the novel. Accordingly, the first section of the book will review some of the origins of the two forms—the advantages and penalties of any art manifested by appeal to the populus in the first instance. *Citizen Kane* is considered at the close of this section almost as a *summum* of cinema in such terms, and this is the only full-length consideration of an original screenplay offered here.

Next, since cinema is an infant of technology, there will follow a review of some of the implications involved in transforming one medium, letters, not originally technological and requiring very little "extra equipment," to another which is several and does. The Eighteenth-century epistolary novel treated at the end of this section seems the acme of a personal, non-technological form and its translation into a film raises many pertinent questions.

Having then reviewed the social genesis of the two modes, and having conceded the highly technical nature of the cinema, we will try to understand something of the way in which the latter mechanically reproduces, and thereby qualifies, reality. To this end problems of "visual thinking" will be resumed, and the nature of the relationship between art and photography investigated. Something of the aesthetic responsibilities inherent in any work of this kind with the camera will be examined.

Finally, we shall move on to consider the psychology and the "grammar" of film, insofar as the latter term may obtain in this field. We will inspect how conventions of the cinematic mode affect the subconscious motives involved in presenting a narration, as also how that narration is achieved—how, in short, a film is recounted. The analysis of a film at the end of each section is offered more as an exercise in what that section is engaged with, rather than as an extended review.

The last part will propose three principal manners by means of which novels have to date been adapted for the screen, with a number of illustrations in each regard. These ordering devices, of which we have selected three, may have varied in intensity at different times, but all serve to show something of the resilience and fertility of the human mind in accommodating those visions that pass and repass before it.

THE NOVEL
AND
THE CINEMA

One:
ORIGINS

The Problem of Popularity

Both the novel and the motion picture grew up as modes of entertainment. To a large extent both still are such, but they offer wide differences in the transmission of meaning. Man is thought to have been speaking for over 700,000 years. He has practised alphabetic script for perhaps 3,500 of those years and punctuation for but a fraction of that time. The motion picture has been with us for less than eighty years.

As a new literary form, perhaps the last in the West, the novel was from the start dependent upon receipts and sales. It was by contracts and accountings that the bourgeoisie was to free itself from feudal fetters; and literary patrons were not conspicuous for providing such. While Lord Halifax was proposing "improvements" in Pope's Homer, the new novelists were watching the market. We cannot disallow cinema the dignity of art simply because it has relied on the box office; as a matter of fact, prior to the major successes of Griffith and the early American comedians it did not truly do so. An actors' strike in 1900 seems inadvertently to have first demonstrated the poten-

25

tial popularity of cinema; some theatre managers stayed open by showing moving pictures, which proved a surprisingly palatable replacement—at least for vaudeville. A subsequent shot in the arm was given by the First World War which lent the U.S. a virtual movie monopoly.

It is important, therefore, to begin with an admission that film shares with the novel a dependence on commerce which, in turn, links it closely with a commercial society. Even if, as in Russia, the cinema was put to the service of national prestige rather than the cash register, it had to be popular. Which is to say that—*pace* Locke and Hume—public sharing was a precondition of meaning. Or at least of a meaning we already possess.

Today the theatre is more or less commercial in this sense, but it was not always so—Shakespeare's altering considerably with a change of venue. Some of the greatest drama was produced when an aristocratic employer—even a king—acted as aesthetic arbiter. No film of Shakespeare has done much more than reproduce its original or render what Sartre called, when discussing what film gives us of fiction, "a more or less faithful commentary"—Richardson's "theatrical xerography." This can hardly be said to be the case when the audience for the adaptation is limited or eclectic. *MacBird,* running off-Broadway, merely used the Shakespearean original as a point of departure for another form—raucous contemporary political satire; Humphrey Richardson's *The Sexual Life of Robinson Crusoe* utilised Defoe for aphrodisiac effect.

The Shakespearean transposition points up the very different conditions at the source of each form with a new intention. Part of the thesis of the present book is that cinema is at its most convincing when it declines to be a dramatic mode and leans, rather, on its immediate antecedent in the aesthetic representation of reality (or irreality) — namely the novel. Peter Robeck's *The Great Director,* produced by John Boorman for BBC West in 1966, demon-

strates that, like Joyce, Griffith anticipated almost everything available to his new medium—even, at one point,
CinemaScope or the wide screen, a purely visual emphasis.*
Seen today, much of the Babylonian material in *Intolerance* appears indebted to the paintings of Jean-Léon
Gérôme, but in general all the close-ups, angle-shots, flashbacks, and other devices of narrative are already in the
novel.

Film has been bedizened by this ancestry, it is true. The
percentage of filmed novels over given periods has been
assessed in a now famous doctoral dissertation by Lester
Asheim, a book by Hortense Powdermaker, and *Variety*
magazine. A 1934 survey, "prime time" indeed for the pil-
laging of fiction for film, shows one-third of the total output of RKO, Paramount, and Universal to be derived
from novels (short stories being excluded). More recent es-
timates of total studio production taken from novels—let
alone "fiction," which would include short stories—have
gone over fifty per cent.

The received opinion that Griffith, the enthusiast for
Dickens, turned the film towards the novel needs much
closer inspection. At one point (1909) he got Biograph to
let him make a film based on Browning's poem "Pippa
Passes." Over in France Zola's canon had already been
plundered for film: the commodious pages of *Germinal*
alone elicited three works in the decade before *The Birth
of a Nation* and *Intolerance;* in 1903 Ferdinand Zecca made
La Grève from one slice of *Germinal,* Lucien Nonguet his
Au Pays noir from another two years later; and in 1912
Victorin Jasset made *Au Pays des ténèbres* from the same
book. It is clear that only relatively recently has the orig-

---

* In the Paris film exhibition of 1900 there was a screen 53 feet high and
70 wide; it is said that Henri Chrétien anticipated CinamaScope by design-
ing an anamorphic lens (with a 180 degrees range) for use in the periscopes
of World War One tanks. Looking out of a tank, however, proved different
from looking in on a theatre screen.

inal screenplay been envisaged as the true genesis of cinema. *Citizen Kane* struck its blow in that direction, if only via biographical parody. It was on the set of *La Règle du Jeu* in 1939 that Jean Renoir hinted at this second phase of literary values in cinema. Freed from the tyranny of the novel (he had made a *Nana* in 1926, a fairly boring *Madame Bovary* with Valentine Tessier in 1934, and a brilliant *La Bête humaine* from Zola again in 1938), Renoir is quoted as saying:

> It used to be the era of the actor: the film was equivalent to its star, and so we had the Mary Pickfords, the Douglas Fairbankses, the Greta Garbos. Then we had the age of the directors: and the films of King Vidor, Sternberg, Feyder, Clair. Now a new epoch is beginning: the epoch of the writers; because from now on it is the scenarist who will create the film. . . .

The dependency of film on fiction has been such that it has clearly exasperated so-called *auteur* directors. Godard, who has adapted Maupassant and Moravia, suggested showing a book's pages, one by one, on the screen. This, in fact, was how many classics used to begin in the Thirties: a hand turned a page and a dissolve introduced the action. Godard's remark was reminiscent of the experiments made at fictional literalism in France of late—in Marc Saporta's *Marienbad*-like *Composition une* whose pages can be shuffled like a deck of cards, or Lionel Chouchoun's "novel" where artifacts of the story (a bus ticket, a hairpin) are stuck on the pages. "Film and literature," Norman Mailer has said in a recent interview, "are as far apart as, say, cave painting and song." Elsewhere, in an essay entitled "A Course in Film-making," Mailer added, "Great novels invariably make the most disappointing movies, and modest novels . . . sometimes make very good movies." Bergman, who has used more literary sources than many imagine, has been equally categorical on this score:

Film has nothing to do with literature; the character and substance of the two art forms are usually in conflict . . . We should avoid making films out of books. The irrational dimension of a literary work, the germ of its existence, is often untranslatable into visual terms—and it, in turn, destroys the special, irrational dimensions of the film.*

The statement is a sweeping one and, as such, assumes that we treat "the two art forms" as equipollent. They cannot be so, and it is in our interest to recognise this, just as, if we are to enjoy both forms to the full, we must see their similarities. A talking film can partake of literature, and the tragedy is that so few have done so. A shooting script can be compared, on the printed page, with a drama, but the comparison might work to the detriment of any argument for cinema as art, since so few screenplays can be said to have literary value.** When Alan Bates spoke Lawrence's dialogue verbatim in parts of *Women in Love*, one realised sharply this lack. Nevertheless, most forms of entertainment share art's concern for rendering reality and, in Siegfried Kracauer's term (borrowed from Nietzsche), to redeem it.

The library of treatises we now have on the genesis of the novel shows that in common with any healthy art form it began its own tradition. In this the cessation of patronage was a prime ingredient. In common with the cinema the novel turned its back on the aristocratic employer and sought popular support: this is not simply to say that popular themes were sniffed out—they were, and *Cla-*

---

* In *Cries and Whispers* Bergman has a character, the dying Agnes, put to sleep by the reading of *Pickwick Papers;* he makes an amusing comment thereby, yet somewhat disturbs the rhythm of his film, since no Swedish translation of this work was available until after the action depicted seems to take place.

** The first screenplay to be commercially published in America was *All about Eve* (1950), in which Marilyn Monroe had a small part; it was re-issued in 1973.

rissa Harlowe was one of them. Primarily it meant that a large extension of liberty had been effected in the public consciousness. Marshall McLuhan is right in saying that "It would be difficult to exaggerate the bond between print and movie in terms of their power to generate fantasy in the viewer or reader." To drive home his contention he cites Cervantes, beside whom one could here ask Fielding to stand:

> Sophia was in her chamber, reading, when her aunt came in. The moment she saw Mrs. Western, she shut the book with so much eagerness, that the good lady could not forbear asking her, What book that was which she seemed so much afraid of showing? "Upon my word, madam," answered Sophia, "it is a book which I am neither ashamed nor afraid to own I have read. It is the production of a young lady of fashion, whose good understanding, I think, doth honour to her sex, and whose good heart is an honour to human nature." Mrs. Western then took up the book, and immediately after threw it down, saying— "Yes, the author is of a very good family; but she is not much among people one knows. I have never read it; for the best judges say, there is not much in it."—"I dare not, madam, set up my own opinion," says Sophia, "against the best judges, but there appears to me a great deal of human nature in it; and in many parts so much true tenderness and delicacy, that it hath cost me many a tear."—"Ay, and do you love to cry then?" says the aunt. "I love a tender sensation," answered the niece, "and would pay the price of a tear for it at any time."

The Richardson/Osborne film of *Tom Jones* faithfully included this incident, though more from fraternal sentiment, it seemed, since Mrs. Western's censorship was never explained. It was directed against what both René Clair and Quixote realised, that to accept an unreal world for reality, to suspend disbelief for an extended period, is to fracture and split open society. It is also to turn man into a symbolist.

Perception is not simply the receipt of so much information, visual or other; its work in conception is greatly aided by fantasy, and children have sometimes been found to have fewer difficulties of comprehension than adults in this regard. There is a visual literacy in seeing cinema. In a section of *Visual Thinking* Rudolf Arnheim refers to the famous Forsdale experiments with Eskimo and African tribesmen confronted with a screen—even, in some cases, with a photograph—for the first time. They did not look at the shapes symbolically—"when a film showed persons going off the edge of the screen, the audience wanted to know how and why they had disappeared." We shall return to the role of visual thinking in viewing a film; this Arnheim describes as "the ability to see visual shapes as images of the patterns of forces that underlie our existence—the functioning of minds, of bodies or machines, the structure of societies or ideas."

The cinema usurps reality in a particularly potent way. We may smile at the Forsdales' "savages" running in terror from a flat image on a screen, but we are not always aware of that divorce of consciousness effected in film's basic semantic. Its relationship with reality is quite different from that of language, yet the two are often treated as the same. With language we store a past, protect a present, and hope to confer some stability on a future. Hortense Powdermaker tells us that "A low-income group of workers, for instance, were very critical of part of one movie which touched their own experiences, saying, 'That's just Hollywood!'—but in the same movie they accepted as completely true the portrayals of a successful girl artist and her two wealthy boyfriends, the counterparts of whom they had never met."

The semantic ratio to our lives of, first, cinema and, now, television has modified behaviour in a new way, the latter being unlike the former in that it shows or can show events happening concurrent with the viewing. Most of us are unaware of how within even a short life-time the cinema can grossly qualify what we accept as the past. The modest and touching *Brief Encounter* (1945) was made close to events for a British audience and is a far more responsible picture of feelings in Second World War Britain than many films made since. Those of us who lived through that war—in North Africa, Italy, Europe, as well as Britain—have by now seen its simulacra on the screen so often that memory yields to fantasy out of sheer fatigue (Robert Mitchum on that Anzio beach-head). Travesty—as in nearly all the Rommel films—can be discounted and dismissed; but with its accretion of insidious deposit the lava of cinematic legend builds up and destroys the remembered past. Dresden simply was not like *Slaughterhouse-Five*, even by standards of the speediest shorthand, any more than North Africa was like *Patton* (to say nothing of Sicily). Possibly many Americans will think of the Fifties via *The Last Picture Show*, until another visual reading takes place. It is not merely that the picture is false; it is rather that the imagination has not been allowed, in such cases, to fulfil its office. McLuhan is right: we accept a depiction of reality so long as it generates fantasy. It was Picasso who remarked that it was useless to stick a real moustache on a collage to portray a real moustache: it might be much more effective if used to represent an eye.

The reflex on reality, or feedback from the cinema, was perhaps never better demonstrated than in the much praised American western. Anyone who has ever motored through the great Southwest and seen the scimitar shape of a western hat over a knotted kerchief silhouetted against the mahogany hillsides can understand the cliché's appeal. The myth was magic and perhaps America's greatest contribution to fiction.

Photos of genuine westerners, west of Kansas City that is ("Beyond Fort Scott, no God"), taken in the last century, show scroungy types in sober garb. It is said that William S. Hart, brought up among the Sioux, complained in some disgust at the bowdlerisation of the true Old West. His Ince films began to lose popularity during the Twenties to those featuring Tom Mix, two-reelers that put a slice of costume romance into the knight of the plains. This spread back locally, after which the mythologising of the cowboy as a clean-living hero rather than a scruffy drunk, a development symbolised by his singing ability (Gene Autry) or general showmanship (Ken Maynard), proceeded apace. The myth was then rewritten as fact on the screen. In the year 1970 *Butch Cassidy and the Sundance Kid* won as many Academy Awards as *Hello, Dolly,* while John Wayne earned the Best Actor award for *True Grit.* This is not to mention the dozens of releases of old westerns on both the circuits and TV, including epics like M-G-M's successful *How the West Was Won,* with its 1,200 buffaloes, twenty-four name stars, and herds of yelling extras. It is singularly instructive to see a film like this in Southern Colorado, in an audience mainly composed of Indians.

The American West has now imitated what Hollywood created as the West through the Twenties. There is a very American kind of pilgrimage made these days, from the locations for *The Outlaw, High Noon,* and *Shane* down to the patent parodies of the order of *Butch Cassidy, Willie Boy,* and even *Cat Ballou.* Such sight-seeing makes a truly bizarre comment on the communication media, as *The Big Trail* and *Cimarron* appear on TV again in a second childhood of celluloid, while the West itself sets up and sells simulacra of the impersonated West:* phantom towns, ghost Main Streets, bad man's gulches and head-'em-off passes. There are said, in fact, to be more Tombstone Cities in Italy these days than in America, thanks to the vogue of the so-called spaghetti western. Once, twelve miles out of Tucson, I found Old Tucson, which is in fact New Tucson, being for the most part a mock-up of the stagecoach, bar-room brawl, and white-hatted, pony-trotting good guy

---

* It is estimated, for instance, that the filming of *The Alamo* cost ten times as much as the actual military operation involved.

stereotype created by Columbia Pictures in 1940 for *Arizona*.

This stumbling block of syntax in the film medium has even caused Mexican censors of late to refuse to allow the importation of films showing, south of the border, an exclusivity of sombrero-ed villains alongside hoop-earringed *cantina* girls eternally masticating roses. The true reverberation of Marcel Ophüls's *The Sorrow and the Pity* was that it made a head-on assault, via the purloined immediacy and contemporaneity of TV, on an iconic picture of the war in France, one now sedulously set out in French schools: that upon the German occupation everyone became a member of the Resistance, embraced Jews and finally, led by General de Gaulle, liberated the land. As William Kuhns says in *Movies in America*, "The stars soon began to imitate their movies."

It was this power that put the Mrs. Westerns on guard. They saw that the novel, written in the medium of the business note and everyday affair, would develop hand in hand with political franchise, which was predicated upon imagining what might be better for you. In *Candide*, made into many films as well as an American operetta, Voltaire parenthetically envies the liberty of thought and publication permitted in Britain through his hero's hilarious visit to Pococurante. The latter may reply, "I should applaud the liberty which inspires Englishmen of genius if passion and party spirit did not corrupt everything estimable in that precious liberty," but Voltaire knew that England had killed its king in 1649 and that a prelate had never since held political power there. Paradoxically, the replacement of the patron by the printer-publisher meant an increase of literary liberty all around. In Voltaire's lifetime a resident of Montmartre was burnt alive for publishing blasphemy and a bookseller sentenced to the galleys for life.

In France and Germany during the early Eighteenth century literature was still essentially a court art. The protection of a patron was essential. Throughout his lifetime Rousseau received next to nothing for *La nouvelle Héloïse,* despite its popularity with women. When twenty years later a young Army officer called Choderlos de Laclos, who had read and admired Rousseau's famous paean to human virtue, reversed it in a picture of sexual vice, the selling of books had become more of a trade in France and *Les liaisons dangereuses* went through fifty editions during its author's lifetime.

That both the novel and the cinema grew up as mass arts seems today an easily-received platitude, yet one whose implications are not always understood. Clement Greenberg has reminded us that a wide spectrum of literary sources, from the *New Yorker* onwards, are involved today in diluting high art for mass consumption ("Kitsch is a product of the industrial revolution which urbanised the masses of western Europe and established what is called universal literacy"). As for film, mass appeal only seems to have become a feature after, at the earliest, Porter's work in 1903 (*Uncle Tom's Cabin; The Great Train Robbery*). Edison himself, for whom Porter had worked as a mechanic, does not appear to have realised the public potential of the kinetoscope of the 1890s, and creative film-makers like Ferdinand Zecca and Georges Méliès continued in blissful ignorance. The work of both these men, interspersed with drawings, seems much closer to Dadaist photo-montage than what we call cinema today.

Yet there is a difference to note. From its inception the film began to be visited for entertainment, and this eventually ended in the pernicious front-office notion that quality was knit into audience size (by 1931 fifty million Americans were going to the cinema each week). This was not invariably the case with the novel, which was read for other purposes—as travel or etiquette books (*Paul et Virginie*). Hardy's Tess wishes she could have read novels in order not to have fallen into a social trap. Even today, as

C. P. Snow has remorselessly reminded us, we read fiction for sociology (if not vice versa).

Moreover, a short stretch of a novel can be read, then put aside and revisited. The film must hold its audience, or else. Hitchcock's reputation rests to an undeniable degree on his ability to keep bodies vertical in auditoria. This property was not an essential of fiction, though it undoubtedly helped when serial publication came to be required by magazines, as was the case for Dickens. It was not necessary, however, to complete even a Dickens fiction in a compulsive two hours. In this connection, it is interesting to note that Hitchcock was never originally admired by Anglo-Saxon critics. It was the French magazine *Cahiers du cinéma* which created his "intellectual" reputation—his own writings are extraordinarily down-to-earth—and Alain Resnais, in a typically French tribute, imposed a photo of Hitchcock standing, somewhat elevated, by a lift in *L'année dernière à Marienbad*.

France has always had a culture in which aesthetic values have located themselves in enjoyment and entertainment. This has permitted their intellectuals the liberty of rarefied logic. Enjoyment is culturally coded and, like humour, often highly subjective. Eric Rohmer reminds us that "Slowness is relative. What some consider slow may seem eloquent to Indians. If you talk about slowness, what about Ozu, Bresson and Dreyer?" He could have added Eisenstein. Boredom may not necessarily be an aesthetic deficiency, but it certainly affects an entertainment vehicle for which money has been paid. This is not merely philistinism's loud-voiced charge. The critically-esteemed Hitchcock outsells at the box office all the directors Rohmer mentions, while some of Bresson's *longueurs,* as in his tedious *Les Dames du Bois de Boulogne* (1944), seem due more to incompetence than anything else.

Today the critic Richard Schickel suggests that we may be returning to the pre-popular era: "It's important to understand that only a very few movies are of interest to the masses." At the time he wrote those words the highest grossing films of all time were, in order of box-office ranking, *The Sound of Music* (which had to date earned $112,481,000), *Gone with the Wind,** *Airport* and *Love Story.* All four were critical disasters in their time and it is possible that readers of this book may have seen none of them. *The Godfather* and then *The Exorcist,* far more intelligently-made films, overtook these figures for a while, probably due to shock value, but Schickel is reminding us of a prevailing tendency, and observing that today those who go to the cinema on a regular basis are probably far more critical, in the sense of liable to reject, than their predecessors of the pre-television era. *The Exorcist* played in five theatres in Manhattan to childish television audiences beside whom it was genuinely hard to hear what was going on.

Shock value is good box-office, but it need not be aesthetic. In a novel we are not always permitted to form discrete images. In Friedkin's film we were scarcely permitted to form thought. An image of a girl masturbating with a crucifix or urinating at her mother's party is likely to be shocking to the eye. Seated in front of the printed page we exercise a certain control. When the demon speaks through the young girl Regan, the voice is simply described by Blatty as "guttural." Although *The Exorcist* was an example of a fairly faithful "transposition," its filmic errand was to provoke fright rather than convey meaning. Such can be seen in episodes involving desecration of the Church, of the fouling of the crucifix, and Father Karras's guilt; Friedkin stages these for immediate shock effect, which is high, though no higher than the same trick effects in *The Legend of Hell House* (discussed below). The religious

---

* *Gone with the Wind* (1939, Victor Fleming) grossed $77,900,000 from its opening to its 1967 re-release; NBC-TV paid $5 million to license the film for one showing in 1976.

meaning of these scenes is secondary. For Blatty they had been primarily religious—Karras had felt guilty of losing his faith. Friedkin emphasises his desertion of his mother so that he can have Regan turn into her for a moment, on her bed. The clue to the murder of the director Burke Dennings, a lonely alcoholic in the book, is the swivelling of heads on necks, as Regan at one point speaks with his British accent. The reflection of evil is lost, while the cash register ticks on.

It is from the ranks of critics that some of France's most interesting directors have lately come (Rohmer among them). Schickel himself has collaborated on a screenplay with his wife. Peter Bogdanovich was originally a film critic as was, in England, Karel Reisz. Screenplay writers now increasingly number former critics: though admittedly at a distance from the parent studio, Penelope Gilliat wrote *Sunday Bloody Sunday*, a fairly unfriendly dig at the lifestyle of another British critic, and Penelope. Gavin Lambert is yet one more case in point.

In the development of the novel mass appeal carried both its privileges and its penalty. Sophia's illicit reading was representative of what a large, and largely female, readership, of the type excoriated at the start of Jane Austen's *Northanger Abbey*, was turning to and indulging in; suppressed classes, sexual and social, were seeing themselves and, in a clandestine form, freeing themselves.

If on a slower scale, the playback may not have been unlike that effected by iconography a century later. For instance: a leading authority on feminine attire tells us that women did not have sloping shoulders in mid-Nineteenth-century England but that novelists said they did, and illustrators agreed they did, whereupon they did. Siegfried Kracauer showed that "No social whole existed in Germany" immediately prior to Hitler, and what he calls "the swastika world" was visibly latent in a large number of films of the era, many now lost. In conceiving of man as a passive digit, easily manipulated, Hollywood for Hortense Powdermaker "represents totalitarianism. Its basis is economic rather than political but its philosophy is similar to that of the totalitarian state."

High-speed technology today effects a similar reality-fantasy feedback via the American "protest" films of the Sixties. The reiterated depiction of mindless "revolutionaries" simply cemented the Nixon regime in power. When thought through in peace and quiet, subjected to the analysis of a Kracauer, such native works were soon seen to have few social insights and often to have disguised, by their visuals, a virulent form of proto-fascism—from *Easy Rider* and *Alice's Restaurant* to *Medium Cool* and many others, now mercifully forgotten. In their day they were immensely popular. A contra-cultural film like *More* collided with its anti-hedonist criticism of drug abuse. The refraction had its result. In such depictions all police were vicious reactionaries, and in life some became so. A dissident and insecure youth saw what it took to be itself on celluloid and parroted back the image; old wives of both sexes and all ages came to gawk at the result.

The symbolic ratio suggested by putting Eldridge Cleaver's wife into *Zabriskie Point* narrowed further in the rock documentary, where a real attempt was made to force reality to be fantasy and one of which, *Gimme Shelter* (1970), showed an actual murder at a concert by the Rolling Stones while to the side promoters were urging youths to get off the scaffolding and make the general exploitation a little simpler for all concerned.*

D. A. Pennebaker's *Monterey Pop* (1968) seemed to try to make meaning itself dependent not only on popularity, but also uniquely that of youth. This was then called youth

---

* "In the spotlights you could plainly see the Angels chasing someone through the screaming, stampeding crowd . . . soothing words came from Jagger: 'We always have something very funny happen when we start this number.' " Sol Stern, 'Altamont: Pearl Harbor to the Woodstock Nation,' "Scanlan's," I: 1, March, 1970, p. 46.

culture. A year later *Woodstock* performed a similar reversal of Methodist revival meetings, or musical super-bowl
games, if with much the same values as both, this time
with bongos and frisbees and the usual boringly orthodox
villainry in short hair and/or wearing ties. A couple makes
love while the promoters (Lang and Kornfeld) are inter-
viewed about dollar receipts. "Financially this is a disaster,"
complains Kornfeld; however, as Marsha Kinder and Beverle Houston remark in *Close-Up*, "the audience is aware
that the promoters have sold the exclusive film rights for
more than two million dollars and that, in many places,
tickets to see the film cost as much as five dollars." Apparently the adulated Janis Joplin declined to take part in the
film not for artistic reasons, but in a quarrel over cash.

The feedback involved in popularity was certainly an important element in the birth of the novel. Defoe's fantastic
last years testify to as much. No longer did the writer have
to listen to a patron, he went out and put his ear to the
soil of society in order to ensure sales. Both Defoe, who
wrote a sympathetic tract on girls' education as well as
Moll Flanders (which Virginia Woolf saw as evocative of
women's rights), and Fielding interested themselves in social rejects or outcasts, in the so-called *picaro*, a Chaplin-
esque figure. For the life of the rogue-*picaro* was whimsical, subject to chance, to the laws of this world, rather than
the next. Recommended by Rousseau, and made into a film
by Buñuel among others, *Robinson Crusoe* presents us with
a literal outcast who must form his own pattern of life,
declare his own mastery of the world's material, and does
so via contracts and documents well backed up by gunpowder.

All films made of *Crusoe* to date, including Buñuel's,
have either skirted or omitted this essential ingredient,
principally because it is hard to make it visually exciting.
Nonetheless, a substitute could have been found. Crusoe's
computations have been shown to be absurd, even para-

noiac, but they are the stuff of the novel in that they accurately predict the end of a class via contracts as against inheritances (de Sade, another representative of this manic arithmetic, suffered embezzlement of his). The identical monomaniacal objectification occurs again in Balzac. Flaubert felt himself to be completing Cervantes in a mercantile era. Yet the even earlier English scandal novelists, much more loosely structured, strove hard to serve the needs of a new reading public—as any Hollywood magnate later tried to serve his.

It may be that Mary de la Rivière Manley, arrested for writing *New Atalantis* in 1709, and her admirer Eliza Haywood turned out a form of semi-licentious trash. So did Hollywood. Mrs. Manley's *Secret History of Queen Zarah* of 1705, a fairly full-blooded blast at the Duchess of Marlborough, carried a preface which was, as J. J. Richetti remarks, "not so much literary criticism as market analysis." Mrs. Haywood emulated her predecessor's popularity with some success. Bonamy Dobrée tells us that both ladies "may well remain unread." They may indeed, but in the first decades of the Eighteenth century they were pre-eminently popular, and considerably formative of taste. Professor Richetti reminds us that "the changes which take place in prose narrative are partly the result of the changes in the market brought about by the needs of an expanding female audience." The new form of entertainment, in other words, externalised social problems. The cinema was to do the same.

Schiller soon saw this in Germany. In France Marie Antoinette owned a copy of *Les liaisons dangereuses* under a plain cover. In the Nineteenth century novels were taken as social tracts, Zola's *Germinal* becoming a text-book on how to organise strikes in coal mines, while his *L'argent* was used as a minor stockbroker's manual. The famous literary persecutions that ensued, all over Europe, only lent strength to the feeling that the novelist held a certain power. If the new medium could function as a social lever, then the novelist ceased to be what too many writers had been in an aristocracy, namely so much polite decoration. In Vincente Minnelli's 1949 *Madame Bovary* James Mason plays Flaubert at the trial in an entirely unnecessary, indeed thoroughly distracting, frame for the whole. Nonetheless, many of the sentiments uttered by this Mason-Flaubert could also be put to stand behind the new medium of cinema.

Popularity carried its penalties then as now. By the end of the Eighteenth century England's population was of the order of six million, with a novel readership estimated at around 80,000. Not large, yet apparently, by the standards of our time, discriminating. In 1765 the library of a shoemaker's hand included *Paradise Lost,* Gay's *Fables,* translations of Epictetus, and Pomfret's poems. Lackington's autobiography, or *Confessions,* tells us that he started bookselling with five pounds and was soon selling 100,000 volumes annually. In a way it was a little Hollywood.

These books were not cheap. Ian Watt cites income statistics. Most novels were coming out at this time in two volumes duodecimo, for the readership had leisure. The daughters and wives of the richer farmers, shopkeepers, tradesmen, parsons, were not spending their days bent over the sink; prior to public libraries and serial-including journals the new novel was somewhat costly.

At the turn of the century there is Wordsworth's celebrated dictum that "of two descriptions, either of passions, manners, or characters, each of them equally well executed, the one in prose and the other in verse, the verse will be read a hundred times where the prose is read once." This remark seems a fossil today. An authority on fiction like Irving Howe virtually reverses it when he writes, "the majority of readers in the last two hundred years have found in the novel the literary form which most clearly satisfies their wishes for a close correspondence between life and art."

In the year that Howe wrote this (in a preface to a textbook) Pauline Kael called films "the most total and encompassing art form we have." One is uncomfortably reminded that today the novel is often regarded as no more than an adjunct to or advertising medium for the film. Writers like Uris, Wouk, Wallace would seem to see the novel as an irritatingly essential step towards the eventual gold of the major studio production. Much is said by the fact that Tom Tryon, a successful film actor, wrote both the novel and the screenplay of *The Other* for the film of which he was also executive producer. Erich Segal's 1970 *Love Story* was a novel written subsequent to a film scenario (by no means as uncommon a practice as some critics assumed). According to one journalist writing that year, the contempt of art was such that movie companies helped to fabricate book best-sellers out of *Love Story, Rosemary's Baby,* and *The Godfather* by supplying employees with cash to buy copies in bookstores monitored by the leading best-seller lists. The perfidy is perhaps less than what was for so long the reverse, the debasement of a classic fiction by transposition into film, since most of the writers involved in the above were so mediocre.

If the novel lacked definition at the start, so does the film now. This puts an onus on both. Nietzsche saw the Socratic dialogue as the principal pattern of fiction, "viewed as the Aesopian fable raised to its highest power." Narrative fiction soon came to assume the terms of all previous written matter, eventually including the poem itself. André Gide, claiming the rights of literature to destroy itself, put the form finally in question by stepping out of *The Counterfeiters* and asking, in a word, quite what the point was in continuing. At the inception of fiction we find a host of imaginary voyages, travel diaries, pirate romances, picaresque tales, so intermingled that it is becoming increasingly hard to sort out the fiction from the fact, or vice versa. If fact was fabricated in narrative prose of this time, source studies are now abundantly documenting a feedback in the operation as pedants carry off, ant-like in their jaws, prize morsels of fact from the fiction (A. W. Secord and J. R. Moore from Defoe, for instance). The early scandal or slander narratives also seem to have been Gordian knots of *romans à clef.*

The cinema has been equally beset by this width of reference, one which is knowingly reported, for its day, in *Citizen Kane.* Poetry, travel, the newsreel, interview, now the rock documentary, plus drama, the comic strip, history, science-fiction—all press to be accommodated in the going public medium. There has even been a recent mirror-image attempt by Woody Allen to duplicate TV techniques in cinema. Nor is it always realised that film has to put on, without "putting on" as it were, the new and ever more ardent sexuality. Few filmgoers were aware that in the year *The Godfather* was so successful the pornographic *Deep Throat,* despite handicaps of outlet, surpassed it at the box office (a $3,000,000 income in its first year on a $25,000 investment).

An initial problem to acknowledge, therefore, is that both novel and film involved popularity. Coming relatively late in a fast-developing technology this was particularly the case with film, as the facts show. In 1907 there were only six American film-making companies, producing about one short film a week for store-front theatres; by 1914 the new motion picture industry was the fourth largest commercial interest in the United States. By 1912 Mary Pickford had appeared in some 105 Biograph films, nearly all under the aegis of D. W. Griffith. Until Miss Pickford herself bought the negatives of a majority of these flammable prints and gave them to the American Film Institute for preservation, it did not seem likely that much would remain of such nitrate stock. But it was a testimony to the rapid growth of popularity. By 1918, thanks to Thomas Ince, mass distribution arrangements had been made throughout the country.

Later in the century television was to supersede the cinema in sheer popularity. The box-office decline began in the U.S.A. after the Second World War; the drop in audience attendance was conservatively estimated as 13% in 1948, 7% in 1949, and another 10% the following year. Statistics show, however, that the decline had already started: in 1944 there were 442 feature-length pictures made in the U.S. In 1945 there were only 389. Short pictures dropped from 567 to 521. In 1947 the so-called majors amortised costs amounting to $290,000,000. Gilbert Seldes saw the sharpest attendance drop in the older, or more discriminating, groups. "Except for the makers of baby foods," he wrote at the time, "no industry in the United States has been so indifferent to the steady falling away of its customers as the movies has been." His *The Great Audience* of 1951 illustrated Will Rogers's celebrated adage, "Nothing will kill the movies except education."*

The film must hold its audience here and now, or else. If it does not, you will be reluctant to spend hard-earned cash on another. There are those who argue that far from being a limiting criterion this feature actually liberated directors. Writing on "B" westerns, William K. Everson notes: "The director of the 'B' western, working away from the studio, his product not important enough to warrant supervision or interference during or after production, was literally free to do as he liked. As long as he brought in a saleable product on time and on budget, nobody cared whether he made a poetic masterpiece or five reels of fisticuffs." Popularity means audience appeal and television fortunately thinned the cinema audience just in time. Hollywood moguls were surely the slowest in history to realise this. The attitude of a director like Mervyn LeRoy began to seem hopelessly anachronistic—"if Mona Lisa looked

---

* The same desertion of the cinemas by a mass public took place in Britain, where cinema admissions were 1,514 millions in 1948, only 1,430 millions in 1949.

like Hedy Lamarr, more people would go to the Louvre."
Absurd millions were lost because of this imperception. As
H. L. Mencken forever put it:

> If the experts who profess the subject are to be credited, it is
> because every movie, before it gets to the screen, must be filtered
> through a dozen intelligences—and many of them are not in-
> telligences at all, but simply vacuums. It is because the con-
> fection of movies is not entrusted to artists, but to gangs of
> blacksmiths. These blacksmiths decide what is to be played,
> and then they decide, in detail, precisely how it is to be played.
> The result is the aforesaid garbage.
>
> No art, however sturdy, could conceivably survive such mur-
> derous sabotage. If any opera librettist had to submit his work
> to a committee of trolley conductors, and the composer had to
> write every note under the eye of a church choir tenor and an
> auctioneer, and if the resultant composition had to be pro-
> duced by a designer of hot dog stands and the singers re-
> hearsed by an oyster shucker, then opera would be what the
> movies are today.
>
> In brief, they are idiotic because their production is mainly
> in the hands of idiots—with a few cynics interspersed to watch
> for the times when even idiots show some sense.

CITIZEN KANE (1941)

It is perhaps appropriate to begin any close examination of films with one that was not taken from a fiction. This seminal work provides precisely the right "fictional" experience for its time, and also turned its back on a long train of major films based on novels. Indeed, Welles himself was shortly afterwards to play an eye-rolling Rochester in *Jane Eyre*.

A great deal has been written about *Citizen Kane*, and its indebtedness to earlier films almost too eagerly charted (e.g. the alleged debt to Carl Dreyer's innovative use of the wide-angle lens in his 1931 *Vampyr*). These minutiae need not concern us here, being rather the province of the film historian. *Citizen Kane* can be looked on as a model of cinematurgy to that time, and indeed well beyond it. Its illision of styles (a mobile camera) was the basic pattern of its brilliance, and precisely what novelists had evolved— style as vision. Thirty years after it was first shown, to collective withdrawals, the shooting script and cutting continuity (roughly speaking, the before and after) were published in a lavish volume, almost instantly remaindered.

CITIZEN KANE (1941, Welles): one of many shots emphasising ceilings (thus creating lighting problems at the time); here the composition serves the domineering nature of Kane's character behind the charm.

When assessing a film, even more than when evaluating a novel, the critic must be permitted the liberty of what one can call the *achieved intention*. Ernest Hemingway once spent too much time indulging in an irritated correspondence with an English professor after the latter had detected latent homosexuality in the master's works. The professor took the position that, whatever Hemingway's intention had been, he himself, as a reader, was entitled to his own evaluation.

For an object, a filmic image, to be symbolic it must be actual. Erwin Panofsky's early article on "Style and Medium in the Moving Pictures," first published in *transition* in 1937, stresses the fact that what we encounter on the screen is first and foremost a physical reality. If it is not a reality, we cannot infer from it. In an early story by Joyce a character goes into a bar and orders some ginger beer. With it he orders a plate of peas. An American literary critic, interpreting this story as parallel to the Esau-Isaac legend, tells us that the peas stand for a "mess of pottage." They do not stand for a mess of pottage; they stand for a series of internal compulsions and elements of social sequence. The point is: did or did not the character order a plate of peas? Joyce's first observation is that he did so, in common with other drinkers of his day, and he embeds some social history therein. You could not order peas in a Dublin pub of the kind today, and that you could do so then is evocative commentary. At the beginning of the century most Dublin pubs were also grocers (the publican's assistants often known as "curates"), and a plate of peas was a cheap dish to fill the belly. That such a drinker may make a recondite pun with Esau, or Isaac, or Nebuchadnezzar, is secondary symbolism, so much ornamentation grafted on reality. But some form of reality has to be there. As George Bluestone puts it, "The sled in *Citizen Kane* must first be recognizable as a sled before it can be contrasted to the fantastic cluster of art works upon the lawn. If the cinematic eye can link diverse spatial images, the images themselves must be meticulously arranged." This ability to sense out "the cinematic eye" was Welles's great gift.

One more example will be necessary. Recently Alain Resnais was kind enough to come to one of my own cinema classes which had just seen *Last Year at Marienbad*. An intense student asked him why a chair was facing a particular direction in a particular shot. The youth was able to dilate on the symbolic meaning of the positioning of this chair. At first Resnais, one of the most modest of men, was puzzled, genuinely searching his memory to help—he had not, it transpired, seen the film for many years! Then he recalled that in a previous take the actor occupying that chair had simply left it turned that way, and they had been pressed to go on shooting. The "accident" might arouse legitimate speculation, but for this to be true *interpretation*, for the chair to be symbolic, the director rather than the actor would have had to approve or arrange the direction of its seat.

In a similar way there have been dozens of studies on that screaming cockatoo at the end of *Citizen Kane*, when Susan Alexander finally decides to leave Xanadu, and Kane (in a nicely-written line) objects that "You can't do this to me." In a particularly elaborate analysis of the film and a comparison with Karl Freund's recently rediscovered *Mad Love* of 1935 (a re-make of the 1921 *Sappho* starring Peter Lorre and Colin Clive), Pauline Kael noted the similarity between the bald Lorre, with his "spoiled-baby face," and the ageing Welles-Kane; she thereby received the cockatoo's screech as one of sexual frustration, a shorthand for Kane's feelings at the time. Much in the same spirit another critic called it "an unforced metaphor arising naturally out of the action." Yet another heard it as "Kane's impotent rage." The point is that the cockatoo screeches rather than does not screech. Its cry consists of sound waves, its image exists in space. The evident photographic accident that one can see through the cockatoo's eye reads today, on re-viewing, like a knowing parody of the celebrated "iris" dissolve, already a cinematic *cliché* by this time and scarcely used at all by Welles. Typically, Welles retorted to a question by Peter Bogdanovich that he had made the bird shriek to "wake 'em up." Invited to elaborate, he continued, "Getting late in the evening, you know—time to brighten up anybody who might be nodding off." In the same vein I have heard a scenarist asked why a script ended at such-and-such a point; he answered that by then everyone in the story had been killed off. If

we want to examine cinema seriously, we shall have to dis-
count a good deal of this mischievous philistinism. As viewers, as readers, we must be concerned with the received
result.

It is quite clear that the now celebrated dying word of
the megalomaniac Kane—"Rosebud!"—has been exaggerated
as a clue to character. It is at first no more than the
name of a sled, and then it stands for those dreams ideal-
ised in the purity of snow stirred up by a glass paperweight. All will finally be lost in the furious flames of the
concluding pyre.

Kane loses everything: sled, parents, mother-love, wife
and son (in a car accident too little covered later), lover,
newspaper, best friend, money. Rosebud becomes a succinct
statement of that romanticism which is reality, in an indifferent century and a pecuniary country, as well as that
reality which is romanticism. The entire *motif,* the quest
for a catalyst established in the news organisation's projection room at the start, signifies what cinema is . . . or was
laying claims to be at the time: the restructuring of reality, the imposition of some abiding pattern, however arcane, on life's *membra disiecta* in an activity analogous to
art. Perhaps film will one day focus these several parts for
us, for it is by film, and its allied media, that man is being
so tragically fragmented and dismembered today.

No one hears Kane say the magic word. As the camera
approaches the Poe-ish Xanadu in the first shots, and then
draws up to the last symbolic light, "there are revealed"
(in the words of the Mankiewicz-Welles shooting script)
"rare and exotic blooms of all kinds. The dominating note
is one of almost exaggerated tropical lushness, hanging
limp and despairing—moss, moss, moss. Angkor Wat, the
night the last king died." The light then goes out and
cuts the music and thus, we feel, ends Kane's life . . . significantly, at the beginning of the film. The fact that the
work begins with its end is not of consequence in itself,

only in the use Welles made of it; many other films of no value (such as William K. Howard's *The Power and the Glory* of 1933) had begun with the death of their heroes. The idea is carried over from fiction, where the masterpiece of the form is Tolstoy's *The Death of Ivan Ilych*.

After this opening we enter Kane's bedroom, the window frame having been used as a true cinematic "frame" in a nice verbo-visual pun. In passing, Kane's bedroom seems small, and that of Susan Alexander later even smaller, by comparison with the almost expressionist proportions of the other interiors of Xanadu.* We are surprised to find Kane's bedroom lit. However, the shooting script noted "Faint Dawn" only; in the cutting continuity we read "light comes on softly in b.g." There is then the superb close-up of Kane's lips as he utters the symbolic word. Next we have the dropping of the paperweight and the nurse's entry seen convexly through it, echoed later when Kane bursts in on Susan Alexander's attempted suicide, the visual emphasis being her bedside glass. Kane's hands are folded over him as the soundtrack conveys its suggestive run-down, like some defeated phonograph. We then fade out and in to the shadow of the body lying on the bed with "light shining dimly through window in b.g.," doubtless the shooting script's dawn, hopefully that of a non-Kane era.

The Rosebud element is maintained consistently, for what it is, at various points in the film, and it seems the "space" in the story since no one in the narrative had ever heard his last word. Kane is on his way to a warehouse, presumably containing (from what he says) the effects of his childhood—including the sled—when he is spattered with reality (the world's mud) and so meets Susan (romanticism), the sled's substitute. In her room he tells her,

---

* It has often been said that *Kane* is a film of ceilings: the celebrated Assembly Room at Hearst's San Simeon was of a size dictated by a Sixteenth-century wooden ceiling imported from Italy.

"I was on my way to the Western Manhattan Warehouse—
in search of my youth . . . You see, my mother died too—
a long time ago. Her things were put into storage out West
because I had no place to put them then. I still haven't.
But now I've sent for them just the same. And tonight I'd
planned to make a sort of sentimental journey—and now—."
Later, Susan, when she takes her bow after *Thaïs*, singles
out from the piles of flowers heaped in front of her one
representative. The shot down on the stage renders her
selection indiscernible; only in the cutting continuity may
we learn the identity of the flower, that Susan "backs away
to right b.g. with *rose,* exits behind curtains . . ." (my
italics).

Perhaps this scarcely matters. What does matter, or dis-
turb more perhaps, in a film in which the make-up artist
was so consummate in ageing characters, is that Susan
barely seems to grow old at all. Luckily, Welles made few
such concessions to convention. We recall that when the
reporter, Thompson, has read the semi-ecclesiastical document, militarily guarded, in the Thatcher Library, he
turns to the parody of a "butch" lesbian who has let him
in and mockingly asks her, "You're not Rosebud, are you?"
The librarian, Bertha, was very much of this world, notably in Germany—and we had seen Kane cavorting with
Hitler in Berchtesgarten. We are everywhere throughout
this remarkable work confronted with an achieved work of
cinema. No one to my knowledge has yet mentioned that
the Rosebud Reservation in South Dakota is still the heart
of the Sioux nation, viz. of that elemental America men
like Kane raped. John Houseman has told us that the script
was first titled *American.*

What results from this confidence of vision is a supreme
mastery of existing style. The first twenty minutes of *Kane*
are still a stunning romp through media, by which a human being of consequence can be dissected, deformed and

destroyed. Like any film *Kane* will date,* but seen as many as thirty years after its release those first minutes remain fresh, even uniquely contemporary.

It must be admitted that much of this vitality relies on parody, a form in which one is compelled to be ahead of one's target. This is instanced in the obvious skit on Busby Berkeley musicals during the office celebration for Kane (who, like his model Hearst, was an abstemious man). Welles is here cocking a snook at the whole financial structure of Hollywood—*Sally, The Desert Song* and *The Gold Diggers of Broadway* all in a single year at Warners (1929) ; but he may have been doing more. In 1935 there had been two big Berkeley successes, *Bright Lights* and *I Live for Love;* the latter had starred Dolores Del Rio with whom Welles was having an open affair during the scripting of *Kane.* More than one critic discerned a form of latent Fascism in those goose-stepping chorus lines—and Kane had been seen with Hitler at the start of the film. Berkeley himself seems to have worked intuitively. "I'm completely at a loss to explain my 'method,' " he once said and, when asked if he had been influenced by Expressionism, he retorted, "I never heard of it." Naturally, in the case of the Welles parody, since the effects were visual rather than verbal, the cameraman Gregg Toland must take considerable credit (as Welles himself has graciously enough admitted). It was perhaps Toland who saw in advance the diverse ways in which a human being was to be fractured, misquoted, taken out of context and the like by media.

In the flamboyant rush of the first part of *Kane,* done with unmatched panache for its time, we see the following media lampooned: newsreel (in all its vacant pomposity and with a brilliant impersonation of Westbrook van Voor-

---

* The Thirties films of Renoir and Marcel Carné (*Le Jour se lève, Quai des brumes*) , so touching at the time and often informed with significance by the young Gabin, have dated today in a way no great novel of the period has.

is's *March of Time* accent); documentary (plus jerky silent screen, the effect of cranking slowly); animated cartoon (of Kane's publishing empire); Fascist photography (the typical shots from beneath at "Berchtesgarten"); early equivalents of the flash-bulb; the grossly-inflated political poster; handwriting—even the manuscript (in the Thatcher/Pierpont Morgan Library); telephone; radio; typewriter (Jed lying drunk over his review); split-screens; letters (Jed's to Kane with its visually established torn-up check); candid camera (a fine shot of Kane as an old man in a wheel-chair propelled by a Negro filmed with a shaky hand through grillework). In a sense, even book illustration of the time is parodied, in the obviously stylised depictions of the exterior of Xanadu. Its original, San Simeon, was quite as ridiculous.

When we reach the film's prime symbology, the medium of newsprint, on which the whole Kane-Hearst-Luce reality rested, the opening sequences are splendidly telling.* McLuhan maintains that the newspaper is like cinema in that it is a collective art, like the symphony orchestra (which is not an art at all but an interpretive agent). Yet he elsewhere derides something he calls "print"—and the modern newspaper is certainly such. Let us follow McLuhan for the moment, however, and accept the newspaper as a "mosaic" medium, not invariably read from left

---

* In the light of recent events they are more. Both Hearst and Kane were only children born in 1863; both were expelled from Harvard. Hearst's father, a farmer, made his millions by investing in the Comstock Lode; Kane's fortune comes from a deed to the Colorado Lode, and is attributed to whim. The film's Susan Alexander was based on two women in Hearst's life, Marion Davies and Sybil Sonderson (whose later alcoholism is followed in the movie). But the feud between Hearst and Welles (and, less directly, George Schaefer, President of RKO) derived more from the damaging political comparisons made by *Citizen Kane*. For example, the telegrams between Hearst and Frederick Remington, covering the Cuban war, are virtually duplicated and their innuendoes enraged Hearst. It is ironic today to note that Marion Davies played a wealthy girl kidnapped by gypsies in *Runaway, Romany* (1917).

to right (or right to left, or up and down, as with Arabic or Chinese). In common with the newspaper, theorises McLuhan, "the TV mosaic image demands social completion and dialogue." Our inquiry here must remain normative. *How does the film pass information?* We cannot pause to complain that the newspaper page is not really a "mosaic" to the eye at all, nor whether it is true for most of us that "It is not pleasant to turn on TV just for oneself in a hotel room, nor even at home." Many of us have frequently turned on television in a hotel room, with qualified satisfaction.

Viewed post-McLuhan, *Citizen Kane* certainly suggests knowing allusions, perhaps via Toland's artistry, to the revolution proceeding apace in our reception of information. Like the overlapping dialogue, the film's wipe dissolves— both vertical and horizontal—were not only daringly successful but openly suggestive of the turning of a printed page; they remind one of the many "frame" sequences for the presentation of classic novels throughout the Thirties. More than once Welles confronts us with newspaper pages. By implication he asks us how we do our breakfast reading, a critique pressed home in the series of breakfast shots of Kane and his first wife denoting the degeneration of their relationship (her dress gets higher above the bosom). We see runs of newspapers going out like so much sausage meat, and wipes that totally dissolve their intentions. Nearly all the techniques of transition, however, are clever and apposite. There is one fine dissolve via rain prior to an El Rancho restaurant sequence and another, beautifully executed, from the diary to the snow of childhood. There is an apt cycle formed (from photo to reality back to photo again) when we see a picture of the news staff of the *Chronicle*—the camera pulls back and we see the same men in the same positions posing for a photo of the *Inquirer* staff, which then turns into the photo itself. This is so visually complete that we hardly need Jed's comment on the morality of switching journalistic sides thereafter: Welles was here pointing up the amoral implications of story journalism. ("Let him roar," the press photographers had said of King Kong when warned that their flash-bulbs were infuriating the beast. "It makes a swell picture.") There is another telling verbal transition when Thatcher wishes his ward a Merry Christmas, to which is appended "And a Happy New Year," coming twenty years later when he is dictating a letter to Kane.

In this way, by shrewd use of technique, the film teaches a basic essential of cinematurgy, that we select far more with the camera than we do with the human eye, which is blessed with what is sometimes called "continuous vision" (Welles showed ceilings in *Kane*). This selection, and its composition to convey meaning, is *Rosebud* to cinema, its style, its jigsaw puzzle which must be put together for a meaningful pattern. It is not really the narrative that interests us in *Kane*. We know what is going to happen. It is, rather, the overwhelming sense of reality—and this task required art.

Yet *Kane* is finally far more than so many assembled particles of technique. Any pseudo-*Kane* will bring this out. *The Candidate,* which achieved critical and popular success in 1972, was similarly inquisitive of media's ability to dislocate and distort a man's personality, principally by means of television. Though technically able, *The Candidate* remained empty. It contained stretches as non-narrative as parts of *Kane,* but these segments could have been shuffled in any direction, at will; one cannot say the same of *Citizen Kane.*

In Welles's one great work—and his first if we except his 1934 one-reeler, a fragment called *Hearts of Age*—form is made to marry content in ideal harmony. A film like *The Candidate* had no content to force into form, so that one was simply left with tricks. The ultimate *reductio* of the *Kane* assemblage, or documentary satire, might be Norman Mailer's *Maidstone*, shot by D. A. Pennebaker, best known until then for his films on Bob Dylan and *Monterey Pop*. The comparison is truly odious since the standard of art in *Maidstone* is almost non-existent. Even an enthusiast like Hal J. Seldes, writing in *Avant Garde*, concedes that the Pennebaker literal approach "can produce abysmal depths of boring self-indulgence."

Again, the novel had prepared non-narrative. Conrad, Ford, Gide and Proust had all abandoned linear stories prior to Griffith's major successes. Conrad, whose *Victory* was first made into a film as early as 1919, subsequent versions appearing in 1930 (as *Dangerous Paradise*) and 1941, sensed a fraternal medium in cinema. Any teacher, hurriedly preparing the story of a Conrad novel for a class, knows how difficult it is to grasp the facts by sequential dips into the book. A fiction like *Lord Jim* really begins, as we shall see, about halfway through.

The Trials of Technique

Myrna Loy is said to have expressed sorrow when she heard, in July 1934, that John Dillinger had been shot shortly after seeing her starring in *Manhattan Melodrama*. Bela Lugosi developed delusions about being Dracula and asked to be buried in the same way.

The relationship between technology and human nature is a complex subject. It has been depicted by masters of what the French call *anticipation* from Plato, Bacon, Kepler and Cyrano to Verne, Wells and the moderns. It is significant that the erstwhile conjuror Georges Méliès's most famous film was *A Trip to the Moon* (1902), in which he was able fully to liberate his fantasy since it was based on a Jules Verne story that invited such. Technological advance is something quite different from the change that took place in society prior to the industrial revolution. Radio, the car, and television have altered the world for the ordinary man and woman more immediately than any religious or political change of the past. The science-fiction writer Isaac Asimov theorises that in this a turning-point for Europe came at the French Revolution, after which society was condemned to constant change, and politics to be subservient to technology:

> Probably the first single event in history which affected the general population in a fundamental manner with sufficient quickness and intensity to be unmistakable to all was the French Revolution of 1789–1799. This phenomenon differed from previous rapid changes, such as Alexander's blitzkrieg against the Persian Empire, in that the alteration that resulted applied not to a thin Macedonian aristocracy, but to the entire French population from King Louis to Jacques Bonhomme . . . Before 1789 human society didn't change as far as the average man was concerned and it was silly, even wicked, to suppose it could. After 1815, it was obvious to any educated man that human society not only could change but that it did.

This change of rate (or rate of change) in industrial and scientific development has made of politics the handmaiden of technique. Certainly, this seems to be the case in modern America and will probably become increasingly so in all the developing countries. As Asimov speculates, even in contemporary Russia it would be more radical for the common man to lose the car than Communism. An American worker would blench less if informed there were no more Democratic party, or Christianity, than if told that television were to be denied him. So with the camera, and eventual moving picture. It is essential to understand from the start that the cinema is a discrete industrial invention. When Louis Daguerre exposed an image on a chemically-coated plate, he was not duplicating the relationship of print to fiction. Novels have been printed, it is true, but they have nearly all been written by a human hand and even today many novelists continue to shun the typewriter for their first drafts. If Defoe were reborn tomorrow he would have all the equipment necessary to produce a novel. Méliès or Porter, or even Vertov, would at first be lost on a set today; they would have to relearn their craft. Already the helicopter in *La Dolce Vita,* a striking image of modernity at the time, seems a little dated today, in need of reinforcement.

Any study of the growth of fiction tends to become dogged by this relationship. In England what novels preceded Defoe, Fielding and Richardson were heavily feminine and erotic. The form then became more general and skilful so that we look on it, as so much else today, teleologically. The novel is asked to improve in a given direction, like a motor. The film undoubtedly profits, as we have seen in the case of *Kane,* by any spectacular "aheadofness" since the rapid turnover of industrial trends is now duplicated in our artistic life. Artistic change ceases to be organic and becomes artifically stimulated. A victim of teleology, the artist becomes his own executioner by enjoying only a technical freedom. Or so it too often seems. Too many studies of the novel invite the view that it is a technological artefact, forever "advancing," but as T. E. Hulme remarked, works of art are not eggs.

It is still perfectly possible to enjoy anew the novels of Dickens, Thackeray, Tolstoy, the Brontës or Jane Austen, but from the filmic past it is only the unusually innovative work, like *Kane,* which still gives more than the pleasure of a curio. For leisure reading novels of the past stand up as ready to be bought as those of the present. It is simply not possible to say the same of the film. The classics of cinema—*Potemkin, Caligari, Mother, M*—exist for the most part by their technique and are generally less enjoyable to see, on an afternoon, than equally inventive contemporary works. Indeed, they are run chiefly for the film buff or cinema historian.

The two forms do share, however, the same communicative process—that to be operative a message must have a source, a destination, and a channel. As you read these words I am the source, you are the destination, and the channel is the white page on which certain black marks have been printed. For sound the channel is the air. In telephony it is the wire. It is necessary to clarify these elementary points since the popular communications writer Marshall McLuhan created much stir with a theory that "the medium is the message." Despite the fact that McLuhan slipped out from under any definitive task by claiming that his system was "probing" (evidently a meliorative activity) rather than "packaging" (pejorative), it remained unclear whether he or his followers understood what a medium was at all, and in inspecting the relationship between film and fiction one must have certain guidelines.

The medium of a radio programme is its "carrier" frequency, measured in megacycles. The message is the music or whatever is "modulated" or superimposed on the carrier. Radio theory had long stressed this distinction, and any licensed radio operator (or ham) could rhapsodise on the subject for hours. If I get a letter from my Auntie Loo, the medium is not the postman, it is the written word. Similarly, if a screen shows me the words "Three weeks later" the temporal transition has been effected verbally. If I see, instead of this, leaves dropping from a tree, it has been accomplished visually; the riffling of the numbered leaves of a calendar, once a stock device on the screen, might be placed somewhere between the two. It is unfortunate that McLuhan confuses an effect with the cause of that effect without incurring challenge—he has provoked the liaison, he replies, and is simply asking questions. This is seriously shirking the duty of the intellectual. Until recently, at any rate, McLuhan does not, to judge from his writings, understand the difference between electric and electronic (the first the grosser, power-carrying aspect of electricity, the second the finer, sensory, or switching aspects involved) ; his discipular Druids, in America at least, merely made confusion worse confounded.

This semantic sleight-of-hand, generally received as "scientific" in the popular mind, is raised here since, though McLuhan is now back in Canada licking his wounds, it was genuinely damaging to those interested in communicatory events that involve, from our first years, a response to environment. "With the telegraph came the integral insistence and wholeness of Dickens," McLuhan would write, or again, "print created individualism and nationalism in the 16th. century."

Yet which came first, the chicken or the egg? If you make no difference between nervous and physical functioning, you run the risk of becoming glib. Indeed, when you follow the Toronto sage more carefully, you share with Kenneth Burke the feeling that the man is dealing less with words than with matters of "terministic policy." For, as regards the relationship between literature and film, the reverse of McLuhan's "theory" could be put forward, just as his argument that TV is a medium stirring participational desires in the young backfires when you consider the general disgust with TV prevalent among the more educated youth of today (that the world is watching television hardly proves that the world is right).

It could be proposed that the film emerged in literature before it did on the screen. The contrapuntal techniques of *Kane* are long anticipated by Hamsun, Joyce, Conrad and Gide; and in comparing his approach with that of Kurosawa in *Rashomon*, Welles said no more than that both derive from fiction. For *Rashomon* Kurosawa used Ryunosuke Akutagawa's story "In a Grove." It was in camera technique—in Kurosawa's case, the brilliant tracking shots through the forest—that both directors excelled. The film emerges also in the early work in Germany of Willy Busch (also a photographer and draughtsman), in "Bonaventura" 's *Nachtwachen*, to say nothing of Alain-Fournier's *Le grand Meaulnes*, sensitively translated by Havelock Ellis and made into a visually beautiful, yet totally empty, film in France in 1967—a model instance that colour cannot carry meaning by itself. The "Circe" episode in

Joyce's *Ulysses,* written as an early expressionist unit, seems far ahead of *Kane,* let alone *Caligari,* in its fracturing of time and disintegration of human personality.

To translate a work of art is not to invoke a substitute. Even within literature itself this has been demonstrated over and over again. The Schlegels's Shakespeare was a case in point. Gérard de Nerval translated the first part of *Faust* on very little knowledge of German and a large supply of enthusiasm; Goethe wrote to him that he had never understood himself so well until he had read Nerval's "translation." Mental states on whose depiction symbolists like Poe, Conrad, Hamsun, Proust or Alain-Fournier relied are notoriously unamenable to cinema, since the latter is an externalising art and such states are what they are thanks to physical absence. (Zola usually makes good cinema.) The failure of film to deal with Conrad is that, as our consideration of *The Secret Sharer* and *Lord Jim* will show, he has all too often been conceived of as a writer of action, when in fact he is thoroughly psychological and philosophical. As George Bluestone said: "If the film has difficulty presenting streams of consciousness, it has even more difficulty presenting states of mind precisely by the absence in them of the visible world."

Thus, the silent-film audiences did not "miss out on" sound any more than we miss out on feel, for they were thinking by what they saw, and the camera was serving conception. In fact, the reverse is said to obtain: the arrival of sound, as later of colour, retarded "visual thinking" in cinema since at first directors were swamped by the requirements of their apparatus, rather than confidently using such. In a now famous pioneer essay in 1933 Rudolf Arnheim stated:

> As regards the other senses: No one who went unprejudiced to watch a silent film missed the noises which would have been heard if the same events had been taking place in real life . . . in order to get a full impression it is not necessary for it to be

complete in the naturalistic sense. All kinds of things may be left out which would be present in real life, so long as what is shown contains the essentials. Only after one has known talkies is the lack of sound conspicuous in a silent film. But that proves nothing and is not an argument against the potentialities of silent film, even since the introduction of sound. It is much the same with the sense of smell. There may be people who if they see a Roman Catholic service on the screen imagine that they can smell incense; but no one will miss the stimulus.*

From the start, therefore, sight has to serve for our other senses in cinema. Until fairly recently few intelligent viewers chose what film to go to see on the basis of whether it was in colour or black-and-white. By now several works have been made as talkies using silent characters. This artificial mode was transcended in films like Bergman's *Persona* where the problem was one of selective mutism, or withheld speech, on the part of the principal character. This is why Conrad and Proust are very difficult to equate filmically, and why to date there has never been a satisfactory picture made from the canon of either. It is also why the teaching of literature via other media can be extremely damaging to a child's fantasy life, and result in just that misconception made by the Hollywood front office of old, namely that the written word is a mere ancillary to other forms, both more exciting and easier to assimilate. One picture is worth a thousand words, and so on.

In the strictest sense literature is the art of letters. It is a communicative act. Very few, if any, novels have been written without any communication between human beings. Illiterates cannot produce literature, and we do not normally allow that babies, the insane, or sundry simpletons are likely candidates for the Nobel Prize. Literature is channelled in language, a distinctly human ability for

---

* In fact, suggestive sound stimulus can be, and is, frequently inserted; Thorold Dickinson tells that he matched a prisoner's solitude on the screen with "the whistle of a distant train echoing over a windy landscape."

expressing thought. It is therefore a category. If film is a medium, it is a hybrid one.

In the case of pre-literate forms such as the ballad it is sometimes alleged that these must be brought out orally; it is then alleged that one automatically assists a poem by reading it aloud, or listening to it read on a podium or screen. If you declaim a poem that has been written, however, you are essentially doing no more than you would when writing down something that had previously been uttered aloud; you are altering the medium, not changing the category. The ballad was a special case and even if the original verbalisation was pre-literate—which, in the case of the Border Ballads, it certainly was not—the resultant expression was a categoric form. That is to say, it was a determinate composition with certain formal elements at work within it (the sense of narrative may or may not be one of these). Moreover, the ballad was certainly committed to the written word soon. Probably as soon as possible.

Most ballads invented today are heard either sung by rock groups or other popular combos, with the result that the philosophical gremlin of group-produced literature has made its inevitable reappearance. Once more we are encouraged to understand that the egg laid the chicken.

Writing down a Beatles' lyric does not either compromise or validate its poetic nature. The result simply becomes reading matter. In the same way, by putting a novel into cinema only the medium is altered. What happens could be better or worse. As Mailer suggested, many films have notoriously improved the fictions on which they were based: we shall return to this point below, for it suggests another norm. Everyone would have his or her own favourite list, but any of these could include William C. de Mille's feminist *Miss Lulu Bett,* from an indifferent Zona Gale novel, the 1928 *By the Law,* Kuleshov's handling of a poor Jack London story, *The Maltese Fal-*

con and *High Sierra* of 1941, *Mildred Pierce* (1945) made from a weak James M. Cain, *The Big Sleep* (1946), co-written by William Faulkner from another Chandler thriller, or, more recently, Nichols's *The Graduate* of 1967. We do not, however, normally make a film of a painting—and to argue that a film is a series of such begs its own question —nor of music. In the latter instance, Ken Russell's 1971 film biography of Tchaikovsky, *The Music Lovers,* or Bo Widerberg's 1967 *Elvira Madigan,* which relied heavily on a sound track consisting of Mozart's famous *Militärkonzert,* the C major Piano Concerto K.467, still found themselves entangled in the inevitable bugbear of exposition and narration.

Most Border ballads read as lively literary creations today; most Beatles' lyrics do not. The alteration of the medium of an artistic category is not at issue here. Writing down a heard poem does not betray its poetic nature, or what the Germans call its *Literaturschein.* Oral poetry may or may not be better than read poetry. Both depend on intrinsic norms. Reading is not an inferior substitute for hearing. We still continue to conceptualise in both. In the first films made from Shakespeare reading seemed to be treated as secondary to visualising. As early as 1915, however, in his *The Art of the Moving Picture,* Vachel Lindsay wrote: "A list of words making a poem and a set of apparently equivalent pictures forming a photoplay may have entirely different outcomes. It may be like trying to see a perfume or listen to a taste."

Willy-nilly film has to reply to norms partially applicable in painting. Yet it is not painting. Do films of Shakespeare make the originals "come alive"? Do they fulfil Pudovkin's famous criterion, that they have "not photographic but cinematographic essence"? Language as we know it is sequential and while cinema can confer a certain degree of simultaneity of time in space, the entities are not as disparate as certain theoreticians, like Bluestone, have attempted to propose ("the filmed novel, in spite of certain resemblances, will inevitably become a different artistic entity from the novel on which it is based"). This can be seen in the fact that one can virtually make the same film again, but not the same novel. It is a question of Coleridge's primary and secondary imaginations. Each age, it is said, needs its own translations: Broadway turned *All about Eve* into *Applause;* the *Mayerling* and *Mary, Queen of Scots* remakes are notoriously legion; and John Huston made *The Maltese Falcon* only after two previous failures.

Obviously, a novel is not what is not a novel. Let us assume that a fiction by Conrad is turned into a digest, with supposedly tedious *longueurs* cut out; it is illustrated; made into a play, a film, a television short; there are *Lord Jim* dolls. These must all seem progressive divorces from a healthy original, culminating in television, where the form is (as McLuhan rightly observes) least enveloping— we can eat, drink, chat and walk about while "watching" television.

It is not that the medium is not the message, so much as that the message is not the message, as far as true art is concerned. As the Jewish saying goes, to send a message you use a telegram. Eisenstein's best propaganda, *Alexander Nevsky,* was his least impressive film. Tone-deaf Yeats writes ballads and creates some of the most subtle musical effects imaginable in poetry. Blind Milton "sees."

This point can be tested in any jet plane of large proportions today. When the screen is dropped and the projection started, passengers may or may not purchase and plug in the head-phones necessary for hearing the sound. I once saw Michael Winner's lush, photographically florid and intellectually empty *The Mechanic* (1973) on a Pan-Am flight. Without the earphones it was visually generous, constantly tempting one to imagine that some rich ideation went along with it, but the story was so banal, so ripe with clichés, that it was soon found to betray the contemplative movements of the gifted cameraman. It was *like* a good film but was not a good film, in the sense that Susanne Langer used, in *Feeling and Form,* when denying George Borodin's belief that the cinema was dance ("The basic materials of both the ballet and the film are similar"). Langer also compared the common elements of a Calder mobile with dance in the same way, concluding, with considerable pertinence to our topic here, that mere likeness between various arts guarantees very little; as she put it, "a peculiar psychological effect is not the measure of an art form."

Literature is written in language which is a uniquely human method of organising knowledge and surviving an environment. In the beginning was the word. "No tribe has ever been found," declares the great ethnographer Edward Sapir, "which is without language, and all statements to the contrary may be dismissed as mere folklore." I. A. Richards's point about the organic nature of language was put in a more allusive, yet equally suggestive, way by the French surrealist Joë Bousquet who once remarked: "After having written to a woman 'I shall take you in my arms,' I have no more than her phantom to embrace." Recent anti-empiricists like Noam Chomsky are urging the idea that language is an innate principle of great generative power. "Man is that being on earth," wrote another linguist, R. N. Anshen, "who does not have language. Man *is* language."

The creative and inventive qualities inherent in language determine the nature of our experience itself, and for that reason alone lie at the heart of moral ability. Anyone who has worked with children will be aware of this. The comic-book addict is incapable of dealing with life because his literate models are false. An understanding of language helps us to understand life; it literally helps a child to form its future. In cinema the relationship to the medium is completely different. For here the medium is a multiple of techniques. Indeed, it could be argued that this absence of a truly normative relationship to reality carries certain advantages. The credentials for being a cinema critic are vague, if they exist at all. Visual reading is what is principally required and, thanks to television or not, a new generation is apt to have this ability simply for survival's sake. In the U.S. it is surprising to find how "well-read" in cinema young people are owing to the body of old films shown on television late at night, when most of the best-known horror and science-fiction films of the Thirties and Forties are broadcast; but television prints of old films are notoriously shoddy and brutally chopped about for time requirements.

In studying cinema, however, one cannot make bibliographical standards apply as they may in literature. (Cassette films may change this and add films to our libraries.) To begin with, nitrate storage problems made it difficult to maintain film archives until recently. Stable acetate stock only became a feature of the industry after 1950. When it started operations in 1967, the American Film Institute found that over half the films produced in America before 1950 had vanished or disintegrated. In film, opinions cannot be checked by provenance; a page from another source may not be consulted *en passant*. Not only does film share with drama a rate of ingestion that is out of the critic's hands, leaving little opportunity for reflection and revision, it actually demands far faster visual reflexes than does a play due to its spatial mobility, and now its width of sound affect.

For its own sake, film must be conceded as a plural *technique* for the presentation of experience. Hence its loyalty to a technology which both assists and impedes it. As many leading directors perceived when sound was perfected, the mere addition of another technical device would not guarantee improved cinematurgy. It would depend on how it was used. In an essay in *Avant Garde* Hal J. Seldes gives an all too representative sample of the reverse persuasion, namely that tendency to make cinema an ancillary of technique itself:

> *Cinéma-vérité* is, in effect, an art form based on an item of technology. The film-maker used to have a dreary choice of equipment: either a massive sound camera requiring a whole team of men to tote, or a carryable silent camera (on a tripod) whose footage would later be given a sound track of music or narration. The big sound camera became the tool of Hollywood; the silent camera plus sound gave rise to the old-style newsreels and "documentaries." Then, 10 years ago, largely through the efforts of Leacock (and, later, Pennebaker), came the invention and refinement of the "sync-sound" system—a hand-held 16mm camera used in tandem with a synchronous, but separate, tape recorder. With this system, two people— operating, as it were, independently together—constitute a complete film crew, able to follow any subject anywhere and capture its full sight-and-sound reality. Pennebaker and Leacock were among the first to realize that this technique had more to offer than merely "better documentaries." Rather, it made possible a whole new experience of art and life.

It also made possible a whole new way of boring us to death. What has to date been produced under this rubric has been rather more *vérité* than *cinéma*—and we had already seen *Man of Aran*. Viewing a box of technical tricks can never substitute for a genuine cinematic experience, let alone provide Pudovkin's "cinematographic essence." The British director Basil Wright correctly said that "the apparatus should be subservient to the idea."

The technical content in cinema is what has produced the wide range of critical response to film. This goes far further than any mere relativity of taste. No one is asking for total objectivity of judgement in cinema, but unless we can establish some norms of discourse we shall end with the appreciation of film as what it all too often is today, at best light journalism and at worst cocktail party *bons mots*. If a group of forty people have forty different opinions about what a film-maker intended, no communication of consequence has been achieved. As the Yale Professors René Wellek and Austin Warren say in their valuable book on literary theory:

> The view that the mental experience of the reader is the poem itself leads to the absurd conclusion that a poem is non-existent unless experienced and that it is re-created in every experience. There thus would not be one *Divine Comedy* but as many Divine Comedies as there are and were and will be readers. We end in complete skepticism and anarchy and arrive at the vicious maxim of *De gustibus non est disputandum*.

It would finally be impossible ever to agree why one film is better or worse than another; and such largely being the case among the less sophisticated levels of society today, the sole arbiter comes out to be content. This puts us back in Square One with a vengeance. Criticism reports nothing to the front office.

That one person likes Burgundy and another likes Bordeaux is a matter of taste. Burgundy is not necessarily "better" than Bordeaux, it is a different kind of wine; we would generally, however, allow expert opinion to grade one Burgundy higher or lower than another Burgundy. At the start of the industrial revolution Wordsworth saw that principles of art were going to come under rapid attrition, and that to equate them with matters of taste would erode them further. Gastronomical preferences are simply not the same as aesthetic operations. Art was a serious matter, intimately linked with man's moral nature. In his famous Preface to *Lyrical Ballads* Wordsworth pleaded that the principle of selection in poetry should be related to truth and deplored those "who will converse with us as gravely about a *taste* for poetry, as they express it, as if it were a thing as indifferent as a taste for rope dancing, or Frontiniac or sherry." And he added, "Poetry is the image of man and nature."

Alas, thanks to cinema's width of reference, we are

everywhere confronted with that worst sort of dilettantism in criticism of which Wordsworth warned us in poetry. "Though we may enjoy swapping preferences and prejudices among friends," writes V. F. Perkins in *Film As Film*, "a critical judgement is of value only when it can itself be criticised and tested against others' experiences and perceptions." Some like Godard, others like Bergman. The latter director would seem to fulfil every criterion of excellence required by *auteur* critics, those who ask a film to be a total expression of a director (or "author") giving us a vision of life over a body of work. Both Bergman and Kurosawa, however, are frequently brushed aside by such critics simply because, so it seems, they are not to the critics' personal tastes. Virginia Woolf did this to an extent with Conrad and Joyce, but her taste in this respect has frequently been cited as a critical deficiency, as well as plain bias. Stanley Solomon has observed how for the body of leading American *auteur* critics today the absurdity arises that "directors like Hawks will outrank Bergman." In *Last Year at Marienbad* Alain Resnais, prompted by Alain Robbe-Grillet, tried to make a film with an open end—that is, one for which A's judgement is as valid as B's or C's. We shall discuss its success below. In the event, Resnais's admirable mastery of the medium merely seemed to make our point in reverse—*Marienbad* intrigues the viewer since it demands especial efforts on his part to form a narration.

Obviously one cannot expect the rigour of judgement of a professor in every newspaper film reviewer. Yet critical anarchy such as we are all too often faced with does result, as Wellek and Warren suggest, in a crippling scepticism. Take, for instance, Jonas Mekas. He writes regularly in *Village Voice* in the guise of a film critic and had a hand, with his brother, in the making of *Hallelujah the Hills*. Somehow Mekas represented "The New American Cinema" at the Brussels Film Exposition, a self-elevation which

even the sober *New Republic* found less than funny. Needless to say, on this occasion Brussels was regaled with films
by Mekas's friends, including Jack Smith's *Flaming Creatures*. Some of the showings evidently took place in Mekas's
own hotel bedroom. The incest arrangement evidently exasperated one letter writer to *Voice*, as follows:

> This is getting fantastic.
> At each year's end Jonas Mekas asks a number of critics and
> film commentators to name best films.
> Oddly enough, these include Jonas Mekas and Andrew Sarris;
> and while one is grateful to be introduced to such great names
> in the field as Bogdanovich, Bauchau, and Franchi, one notes
> (with a yawn) that they nearly all select *Hallelujah the Hills*
> as one of their best films. Meanwhile, across the page, Andrew
> Sarris glowingly reviews *Hallelujah the Hills* for the third (or
> is fourth?) time in your columns.

Similarly, reading a far more serious film critic, David
Mowat, one comes across a sentence such as, "Bergman,
Fellini, Godard started producing trash (only partisans will
disagree)." The subjectivity is nearly total. One might retort, Only partisans will agree. Where is Bergman's trash?

Thus, for most students today the majority of film critics
are no more than people putting their minds alongside
their own. Hence little of quality is reported to the fount
of the industry. In a situation of *de gustibus* we end up
feeling that, in film, critics do not matter, and can at most
be of merely marginal assistance. It is then tempting to
think the same of all critics. The resultant attitude suddenly makes one cultured. Irving Howe has put the quandary
as follows:

> The problem is that Pauline Kael, like everyone else review-
> ing movies, does not work out of a secure critical tradition. Its
> absence allows her a pleasing freedom of improvisation, but
> makes very hard the achievement of reflective depth and deli-
> cate judgment. When a literary critic like Empson or Trilling
> or Leavis tells us that a new poem or novel is "great," we may

agree or not, but at least we know the standards by which the judgment is being offered, the traditions of both literature itself and literary criticism that are being invoked.

In a situation like this one simply gravitates out of self-protection to those who seem to share one's own views most closely. Yet even when one does this the disparities of judgement can be damagingly distractive. In *The Film Idea,* an eminently sensible book by Stanley Solomon, there is an extended critique of Visconti's *The Damned* (1969). The symbolic use of colour is seen to validate this depiction of Nazi decadence, the premise clearly being that isolation of one aesthetic component will lead us to appreciation of the whole:

> Of course, red is also commonly associated with passion; however, as the common color of lipstick, red might seem all too familiar to have much symbolic value in ordinary color films. But when the lipstick is worn by men—as female impersonators—it becomes suggestive of the perversion of passion, which is much in evidence throughout the film. At the beginning the sexually disturbed grandson, dressed as a woman, entertains the guests at the birthday party with a kind of Marlene Dietrich impersonation . . . *The Damned,* though certainly not a pretty film, creates its own kind of pictorial fascination. Its superb color does not reveal beauty but instead implies internal ugliness. Red becomes the color of evil, and Visconti understands that it is not a pleasant color to look at for a long period of time.

Despite these observations, however, *The Damned* still bored a lot of viewers. Arbitrary assignations of values to colours can be highly subjective; what if someone finds red a most pleasant colour to look at for a long period? To a Moslem red might not suggest the flames of hell at all. The innocent kidnapped child in the second version of Hitchcock's *The Man Who Knew Too Much* (1956) is throughout associated with red. In *The Red Desert* we find the same colour being used by Antonioni for a totally dif-

ferent purpose, while in *Cries and Whispers* Bergman soaks
the screen in red throughout and makes it an exceedingly
"pleasant colour to look at for a long period of time." His
symbolic intention here is radically different from that of
the use of the same colour in *The Damned*. In Coppola's
The Godfather (1972) the redness of the blood of various
killings is punned with the redness of spaghetti sauce con-
sumed by the Mafiosi involved. In *The Cinema As Art*
Ralph Stephenson and J. R. Debrix find that "Red may be
just as suitable for the gaiety of a musical, the excitement
of a battle or the violence of a murder." They go on to
show red used for a wide variety of dramatic tones, each
totally different, in such films as Hitchcock's *Marnie*, Vadim's *Les Bijoutiers du clair de lune*, Veit Harlan's *The
Golden City*, and others. On Madison Avenue red is said
to be sexy. The Chinese mourn in white. In short, the
injection of so many symbolic ingredients will not guarantee excellence in a work of art, any more than inserting
charms into a plum pudding will make it taste good. One
could have all Visconti's colour aims in a totally empty
work—such as George Lucas's *THX 1138*.* The director's
use of white as a positive colour element was here spell-
binding, notably in the first third of the film, but nothing
very much was said.

In corollary, one could point to a contemporary work
of another kind like *Cabaret*, which achieved the effect of
similar national decadence without recourse to the same
colour symbolism; or one might even look back to black-
and-white films like *M* and *The Blue Angel*, not to mention the multitude of melodramas codified by Kracauer,
which showed identical tendencies without any colour at all.
Solomon's book concludes with an encomium for *Fellini-
Satyricon*, a self-indulgent work of considerable pretension
and rather less effect. Criticism turns into a shrug when

---

* I refer to the second 1971 version of this work, an enlargement of what the
same director had done for television.

reduced to the level of coffee-shop chatter—I like one thing, you like another. Thus, Judith Crist protested too much in her adulation of the indifferent *Mickey One* simply because no one seemed to listen to her, while Pauline Kael's attack on the modest, unassuming *Butch Cassidy and the Sundance Kid* consisted of pages and pages of pointless critical vitriol. Another helpful book on cinema, *Close-Up* by Marsha Kinder and Beverle Houston, ends with a rhapsody for *Performance* (1970), one more film that is all surface and a philosophical muddle in the middle.

Yet once again, *De gustibus non est disputandum*. Peter Schjeldahl of the *New York Times* praised the "organic unity" of *Performance*. Still other critics perceive symbolic linking devices and verbo-visual puns galore in this film, none of which—for us—makes it any better. It is useless to have to be told in a book, after leaving the cinema, that the reason why the main character in Godard's *Contempt* (1963) wears a large black hat—even in the bath—is that it was actually Godard's hat. The Hungarian critic Béla Balázs told us that "Everything had first to be reality before it could become a picture." We are first of all faced with a black hat; only a tiny fraction of humanity knew that this was Godard's own head-covering. Again, in the same work, another character is seen as "explicitly linked to Levine, one of the producers with whom Godard had had so much trouble." We can accredit these touches as sly digs by a knowing director but they remain outside the film itself; the image is the thing.

Such anxious cross-pollination is, together with ant-like scholarship, the death of art. *The Last Picture Show* was laden with "in" allusions and puns, including clips from Vincente Minnelli's *Father of the Bride* and Howard Hawks's *Red River*. François Truffaut directed his pseudo-Hitchcockian *The Bride Wore Black* to a score by Bernard Herrmann, who wrote the music for Wyler's *Wuthering Heights* as well as many other suspense romances. The

French may call this *hommage,* but it does not make the film any better or worse.

There are odd dividends to be gleaned from the free-for-all that is called cinema criticism today. In an extended analysis of Chaplin's *The Great Dictator* in *New Solidarity* (September 11–15, 1972) Steven Getzov re-reads the barber's final speech to the people of Osterlich. The Jewish barber-tramp is, it will be remembered, an heroic figure. Injured in the First World War he has returned to his profession, only to be confronted by Hynkel's storm-troopers. His liberal credentials established, he makes an impassioned speech which reverses Hynkel's earlier harangue ("Democracy shtunk! Freishpechen shtunk! Liberty shtunk!"); this speech sounds like straight Popular Front endorsement of the time. Getzov, however, claims that the film itself has destroyed this point of view, and filmically mirrored Leni Riefenstahl's *Triumph of the Will* at the close—mindless crowds cheering for yet another dictator. The irony then applies that what will destroy fascism will be a form of bourgeois dictatorship, against whose ideology Chaplin had stood. "That accomplishment," Getzov writes, "is worthy of recognition by the revolutionary movement—for neither Pudovkin nor Eisenstein, let alone Stanley Kubrick, could say as much."

There is a moral sensibility at stake when Joyce transplants Homer to modern Dublin, or Picasso imitates Pompeian murals. There is even a snide comment on the lack of consideration for writers today when Joyce makes a more recondite allusion—probably missed (and no matter) by much of his readership—doffing his literary hat to his predecessor in caustic realism, Flaubert. When Bloom's name is printed in the newspaper at the end of *Ulysses* the *l* is left out. So it was with Flaubert, whose name over the initial appearance of *Madame Bovary* came out *Faubert*. This kind of irony and ambiguity can have great resonance in literature, but to have Fritz Lang playing a character called

Fritz Lang (rather badly), as does Godard in *Contempt,* or a hero's wife played by his own wife in Eric Rohmer's *Love in the Afternoon/Chloé in the Afternoon* (Rohmer reputedly took his pseudonymous first name from von Stroheim), does not accomplish much outside extending the general triviality, and thereby demeaning meaning; the seriousness of cinema is once more reduced.

We are told that in *Performance* "after Chas appears with the red paint washed out of his hair, there is a head-spinning series of plays on 'die,' 'dye,' 'died,' 'dyed,' and 'dead.' The most powerful and significant pun of the film is developed with originality around the phrase 'blow your mind.' Just before killing him, Chas tells Joey who he is. 'I am a bullet,' he announces and proves his self-knowledge as he indeed shoots Joey" (Kinder/Houston). In this way, sophistry substitutes for criticism: not one of these "head-spinning" puns makes the film the slightest part better. Finally, to tell us—as do these critics—that the film is really Herman Hesse's *Steppenwolf* is uselessly to cross the boundaries between medium and category and do no more than wear one of those supposedly authenticating lapel buttons marked Joyce, or Baudelaire, or Kafka. In one unforgettable sequence in *A Day at the Races* the Marx Brothers played the part of surgeons. They dashed around, daubed with blood, constantly washing and rewashing their hands and arms, until someone said, "You guys must be crazy." To which Groucho replied, "That's what they said about Pasteur."

Film, then, is an industrial technique for communicating experience (the word cinema is significantly picked up again in kinesics). As V. F. Perkins says in his admirable *Film As Film*:

> Film belongs in the first place to its inventors. It is appropriated by artists but at every stage in the creation and presentation of their work they are dependent upon, and often at the mercy of, the machine and its operators.

In such a plural form (Méliès was a magician) judicial appraisal is rendered almost impossible. Matters of taste seem solely at stake. Objectivity demands a comprehensive perspective and such is impeded by a form that exists by virtue of being revolutionary. We cannot discern aesthetic value in a mode in perpetual flux. Value requires some form of permanence. A constant turn-over of trends puts premium on originality as virtually the only quality of consequence. Edison's famous Black Maria studio was only established, with the British W. K. L. Dickson, as recently as 1896. In being such a rigorously technological artefact cinema has a closer analogy with science than art. The knowledge of science is cumulative and in constant progress. We cannot regress to previous scientific experiments; it is principally historians who go back to earlier films.

In cinema this sense of technological advance has normally been equated with success. From the phantasmatrope to *This Is Cinerama!* in less than seventy years. Science is essentially mercantile and middle-class and collaborates with our city culture. (Flaubert rebukes it for doing so). Originality comes to have an almost morbid importance. This was not so for Chaucer, who plagiarised Deschamps to the latter's delight, and when Goethe was accused of giving one of Shakespeare's songs to Mephistopheles, he replied, "Why should I exert myself to invent one of my own, when Shakespeare's was just right and said just what was needed?" (Eckermann, January 18, 1825) Simone Martini and Duccio strike us today as extremely similar painters.

The cardinal virtue of a technology must be the invention of the new. If next year's car is not better than this year's, the economy collapses. The promoter is thus a slave to progress. In the same way, one cannot conceive of cinema reviving Eisenstein or Griffith in the manner in which, say, T. S. Eliot "revived" Dantë, or Rouault Gothic glass.

(Bergman goes back to earlier cinematic modes but refines them, with the fixed camera and long speeches.) Yet while it is possible to evaluate some degree of newness and utility, it is not possible always to relate originality to meaning and to say that a new manner is "ahead" of its time and will endure. Shakespeare is still Shakespeare, by and large, but a film based on a play by Shakespeare which is made in 1910 is less likely to be as compelling as one made yesterday. Nearly all cinema criticism remains to a greater or lesser degree a rationalisation of prejudice in the field. The door is held open to sensationalism and just those technical tricks which Basil Wright opposes, and which strive annually to delude us into thinking something is being said.

The novel has certainly changed its form since inception, yet critics like H. J. Chaytor and Father Walter Ong show that the main changes made by print on our hierarchies of knowledge had become fully embedded by the Seventeenth century. The letter series, like Richardson's *Clarissa Harlowe,* predicated on large stocks of leisure in the readership, ceded to the imposition by publisher-printer firms of three-volume novels, frequently first serialised. We know, for instance, that Charlotte Brontë's *The Professor* was declined since it only made one volume. We also know that the long form ended quite quickly, probably owing to the space requirements of lending library and railway station stall. In 1894 there were 184 such three-volume fictions published in England; by 1897 there were only four. Kipling was able to write his nostalgic *vale* to the form "The Triple-Decker."

Yet, if it has somewhat changed its form, the novel has not obeyed teleological development. The sales of Eighteenth-century novels are far higher than most new fictions today, despite the paucity of production at that time (an average of seven titles a year between 1700 and 1740 in

England increases to a mere forty by the end of the century). Joyce's supposedly "difficult" *Ulysses* sells over forty thousand copies a year in the U.S. alone. Even the letter novel, perhaps the most divorced in form from any of our fiction today, and dependent on a different, more scriptural society than ours, still attracts. Indeed, a transposition of such a fiction to film makes pertinent points in this regard.

LES LIAISONS DANGEREUSES (1959)*

Choderlos de Laclos's sole work of fiction, *Les liaisons dangereuses* of 1782 is one of the most spectacular cases of sexual revenge by a woman in the whole of literature, including that of the Renaissance. It is significant that when Roger Vadim persuaded the Marxist novelist Roger Vailland (author of *The Law*, to be made into a vehicle for Gina Lollobrigida) to script it for a film, the result was so tame that the director had to tack on an egregious introduction, in which he himself appeared and emphasised the feminist content to come. The film was a French *cause célèbre* and the date of 1960 added to the title.

The original was perhaps the apogee of the epistolary novel. We know that Laclos admired Richardson. *Clarissa* is mentioned in his pages and Miss Howe helped him with his central megaera of the action, Madame de Merteuil (played by Jeanne Moreau *chez* Vadim). It is hard today

---

* The Vailland/Vadim/Claude Brulé screenplay, in a translation by Bernard Shir-Cliff, was published by Ballantine Books in 1962: limited to those over sixteen, the film of *Les liaisons dangereuses* broke every French attendance record to date (over a million in the capital alone). Its exhibition outside France was forbidden for a year.

83

to judge the appeal of fiction in the form of letters. They have become matters of business, annually decreasing beside telephone, tape-recorder, and the like. It is hard to find a witty letter-writer today. But in the transition of Laclos's fiction into film some basic distinctions are re-emphasised between a medium and a technique.

Even a generation ago girls (certainly in Europe) wrote long, involved and emotional letters to each other; boys at school often communicated in writing with others at the same establishment though it would have been simpler and speedier to have called on them. The number of letters passed between characters living together in *King Lear* is an unlikelihood only fairly recently, in an age of increasing verisimilitude, ridiculed. Early on in Laclos's work the young, virginal Cécile Volanges begins a letter to the experienced Madame de Merteuil as follows: "How well you understand that it would be easier for me to write to you than to speak to you!" (Letter 27). Laclos's form replied to his content. The only way the Vadim-Vailland team could duplicate or respond to this sense in their original was by means of what we shall call below an *analogy*. It did not work, for it could not work. Laclos was writing in a society that repressed women and where such outpourings were a secular confessional, a surrogate *journal intime*. In Richardson's work quite a few of Pamela's letters are penned in the knowledge that they will never reach their destination (will fall into the hands of Mrs. Jewkes, etc.) ; and after Pamela's arrival in Lincolnshire, her letters shadow into her Journal, which then becomes reciprocally rich in letters. The same "artificiality" holds true, to an extent, with Laclos's Cécile; her mother is evidently vigilant enough to spot a minute difference in a key, yet the girl goes on writing absurdly self-incriminating letters. The case is even more extreme with Madame de Tourvel, a religious and circumspect person who might be expected to know better. She falls prey, however, to "love" or unreason, and is seen in Laclos's work finally begging Valmont to return "those letters which ought never to have existed" (Letter 136). Why, one wonders, did she ever let them do so in the first place? The answer is that the principal convention of the new form was that such letters were not really letters at all. They were what Cécile says they were, dramatic soliloquies, intimate revelations of a new and nascent sexual class, which are only really recognisable when written out.

These emotional diaries thus constitute a form which must "date" a modern film, even if they do not appear within it, for they are as much content as form. In the Eighteenth century a psychological vein was being deployed on behalf of womanhood; Vadim virtually reverses this. He could still have made a work of art in so doing, but only if he had been acting consciously; and he appears, in this film at least, to have remained totally unconscious. It is interesting that the few contemporary epistolary novels which now see the light of day nearly always take recourse, at some point, to authorial narrative and reflective passages. *The Capri Letters*, Italy's Premio Strega of 1954, was a case in point, being by the then well-known film director Mario Soldati. A clever minor novel, it could have been written with equal effect in almost any other way.

This is not true of Laclos's story, and the head-on narrative Vadim made of it proves such amply. Laclos garnered many strands in his work, from the libertine letter tradition of Mlle. de Saint-Léger and Pierre Henri Treysac (or Treyssat) to the more serious handlings of the technique by Defoe, Richardson, Burney, Diderot and Restif de la Bretonne. He was able to seal the tradition, and what followed in the form—such as the experiments by Galt or Anne Brontë—seem inevitably minor. Laclos pefects the 'genre by parody. He features every form of letter transmission. Not only are there letters within letters (e.g. 141), or enclosed within them, but he also has them delivered by hand, stuffed into pockets or bodices (Letter 76), anonymous, re-signed, and so forth. One letter from Valmont to the *"intendante"* Tourvel travels back and forth, as she refuses it, like an epistolary yo-yo—"it has always been the same letter going back and forth; I only change the envelope" (Letter 110). The method was an anagram of power politics.

Vailland clearly tried to mimic it. For instance: there is the celebrated epistle written by Valmont, who must have had a steady hand, on a whore's back or belly—the slut Emilie serves as his desk in Letters 47 and 48, and is so referred to later in Letter 138. In the film we see Gérard Philippe as Valmont writing on Cécile's back in her bedroom in the ski resort. (Godard probably replied to this by having a character called Prokosch in *Contempt,* a few years later, write out a cheque on his secretary Francesca's back.) But the film presentation does not work with the delightful excess of the original here. Laclos's epistolary business gives us a sexual minuet which parodied the political forms of his decadent male society; his metaphorical vocabulary—the boudoir seen as battleground—buttresses the whole.

Vailland did his best to report a masterpiece by analogy, but what he produced turned out to be simply more comment on media. We see the young Jean-Louis Trintignant, as Cécile's devoted *"soupirant"* Danceny, using a tape-recorder of the time, and since it is such an elementary model, the film is suddenly dated, as the novel is not. Valmont then plays a tape from Danceny to Cécile while lying on her bed, thus supervising the relationship. Later, Moreau/Merteuil dictates the telegram of rupture, severing Valmont from la Tourvel, in front of the former. All these touches succeed in telling us that we are no longer a scriptural society, that our communication depends increasingly on the mechanical, on tapes, telegrams, telephones (some TV is also seen). But that is all. A far better transposition of the spirit of the original is given in the scene at the *conciergerie* of the ski resort, when Cécile receives a letter from Danceny in front of her mother; wanting to conceal it, she passes it quickly to Valmont, saying that it is his, an act of complicity which begins her undoing.

What the visualisation of Vadim-Vailland fails to give us is the mental rape of Valmont's victims before their bodies are touched. The seducer's stratagems become purely physical (Gérard Philippe turns into an expert skier). Hence the story had to be fixed to this end: Valmont is shown as married to la Merteuil—such a total contravention of Laclos's text that one wonders why it was used in the first place. The whole point about Laclos's "female Tartuffe," as Madame de Merteuil has been called, is that she is not simply a vulgar *femme fatale*. She is an immensely independent woman who has made her own character and owes nobody anything, as she herself observes in the long Delilah letter (81)—"I can say that I am my own work." Directly Valmont starts imagining he has rights over her, she takes off, seduces Danceny (accounted for in the film by an unbelievable scene round a park bench), shows him the letters indicting Valmont as his rival and thus, as it were, sets him like her hound at Valmont's throat—Laclos has Danceny kill Valmont in a duel.

To marry this woman to Valmont is unnecessarily to lessen her as a major character, and convert her into a simple shrew whose end leaves us unmoved. No wonder that Vadim, finding so little of sexual revenge left in his writer's version, had to come forward before the pretty chessboard credits to tell us there was so much. Laclos's book documents far more than a vendetta against a single, unfortunate individual, the Comte de Gercourt; it passes into an attack on the male sex itself. Vadim vulgarised this objective wherever he did not obliterate it entirely.

In the novel Gercourt exists principally as a kind of absence—he is apparently an officer campaigning in Corsica. Laclos gives us an early footnote informing us that poor Gercourt had had the temerity to abandon his beloved of the time, the Marquise de Merteuil, for a lady who had reciprocally betrayed the Vicomte de Valmont for his favours, and "that it was then that the Marquise and Vicomte became attached to each other." In the original Gercourt has been the source of sexual insult to both Madame de Merteuil and Valmont. This is what unites these anti-lovers who abolish love and use sex to subvert the family. For Gercourt is Cécile's "intended," and Laclos manages to make the arranged marriage of the time look curiously disgusting, a girl of fifteen being disposed of like cattle against the backdrop of a hyper-refined society with the most subtle scruples in other matters.

Vailland places it within a French jet-set and, worse, brings Gercourt on the stage as a whiskey-swilling American called, in an unworthy pun, Jerry Court. (Needless American references were put into the film, which had some Thelonius Monk music at the end: for some reason Madame de Merteuil is given visits to New York.) Laclos is simply far stronger in every way: in his pages Gercourt is forgotten, and the twin avengers go far beyond the literal requirements of their task, to the destruction of conventional morality itself. By the end, and before Laclos afflicts her with smallpox in a highly factitious retribution (rendered in the film as burn scars), Madame de Merteuil has manoeuvred the following: her new lover and accomplice Valmont has violently seduced Gercourt's betrothed; he has caused her to have a painful miscarriage, an "accident" that drives her sentimental admirer Danceny nearly insane, but over which the pair exult, la Merteuil herself merely remarking to Valmont, "let me offer you my condolences on the loss of your posterity." Her end is spurious. She has ripped the pretty pastoral backdrop apart like the tawdry tinsel it was, and should have been seen sitting round the first of the guillotines. In his notes on the book Baudelaire indeed observed, "The revolution was made by voluptuous men. Licentious books therefore comment on and explain the revolution."

That is why *Les liaisons dangereuses* was a novel, rather than a poem or play. It shared positively in the whole secular, cutting-down mentality which gave rise to fiction. It was a genuinely revolutionary document and its domestication into chic by Vadim attests to this. He cannot artificially reproduce the content that gave rise to the form, so avoids every issue posed by the original, including Laclos's final suggestion that, a constant sexual experimenter, Madame de Merteuil may be ready to seduce Cécile herself (a scene in the resort hotel reflects this but weakly). With Vadim male supremacy remains male supremacy and his few successes are the result of borrowings from the Don Juan legend.

Throughout the film flames are used to symbolise illicit sexual gluttony. Gérard Philippe, knocked out at a party by Danceny, dies with his head in a grate, while Jeanne Moreau all but burns herself to death by spilling a kerosene lamp. Tone contrasts are bleached out, to symbolise the consuming flames of Valmont's passion, as he looks at a female victim. His first passionate kiss of Madame de Tourvel is treated in this way. Valmont is generally given black to wear and one good shot expresses much when he is seen standing on a railway platform seeing a train off (the real-life Merteuil would have taken a plane). As the steam billows about him, his coat hangs off his shoulders in a sudden suggestion of a Mephistophelean cape, and we need no words. Less usefully, Vadim replied to this image in a scene showing la Merteuil emerging from her bathroom shrouded in steam. All symbolism, it meant little.

Finally, one wonders why the ski resort was chosen as location—even though Laclos soldiered in Grenoble; one pictures such people more easily in the south of France, sunning on the Riviera. However, the snow seems right, cold and somehow cerebral, being also rather obviously associated with purity. Annette Vadim/Madame de Tourvel reeks of the association and it is to a suggestively exaggerated hissing that Gérard Philippe cuts through this cold element the first time he comes upon her—making her laugh when he falls. All these touches are small dividends, however, to pay for such thematic loss. The effort of analogy in the transposition of fiction to film is one of the most demanding we shall pursue. Vadim fails to answer it thanks to an insensitivity to the relationship between content and form—which his original so perfectly personified. At its worst the mode of analogy prompts one to ask why the attempt was ever made. One *Crime and Punishment,* transposed to a middle-American town of the Thirties, reduced Raskolnikov to a mindless student whose murder of a loan shark turns out, in the end, to have been no more than a dream. Vadim, too, leaves us very little of Laclos but the name, and himself creates nothing in his place. Enough was left, however, for Congresswoman Kathryn O'Hay Granahan, in the chair of the committee of Post Office operations, to mount an especial attack against its showing on the basis that its "obscenity" was "part of an international Communist plot." Vadim must have smiled. His press agents had done their work well.

Two:
HISTORY

The Reproduction of Reality

It is worth while to refute thoroughly and systematically the charge that photography and film are only mechanical reproductions and that they therefore have no connection with art—for this is an excellent method of getting to understand the nature of film art.

Thus the late Rudolf Arnheim, in his pioneer essay on the relationship between film and reality. Arnheim was concerned to rebut the belief that cinema could never be art and to show that, like the novel, it was simply a new way of seeing. Griffith's alleged remark, "The task I'm trying to achieve is above all to make you see," appears to be, as already noted, a close echo of Conrad's 1897 Preface to *The Nigger of the 'Narcissus'*—Conrad's comment coming at the conclusion of a long apostrophe to the synaesthesic possibilities of language—"It must strenuously aspire to the plasticity of sculpture, to the colour of painting, and to the magic suggestiveness of music"—which amply explains his mild interest in cinema, to become a mixed marriage of the arts. "Sensing *PLUS* selecting *PLUS* perceiving *EQUALS* seeing," wrote Aldous Huxley, in *The Art of Seeing.*

The author of numerous books on film as well as the celebrated *Visual Thinking,* Arnheim represents the fount of a certain purism in cinematurgy. In the Thirties he tried—and tried perhaps too hard—to emphasise that in cinema the image is all-important. What was perceived in reality and what appeared as a screen image held a difference of distance that called up vital artistic resources. Thus, black-and-white silent films had every right to be as good as, and could frequently be seen as better than, colour talkies. This seems an extension of the Ogden/Richards position in *The Meaning of Meaning* (first published in 1923).

Let one illustration suffice. In the Dali-Buñuel *Un chien andalou* of 1928 there are a number of arresting images, based on surreal metaphors. At the start a man (Buñuel himself) sees a cloud slicing through a full moon and then slits the eyeball of a young woman with his razor. The assault on what is real thus begins; it ends in the *kitsch* of much advertising today. Revlon insist that their latest lipstick is "like a cannon." This is fetching the articles of the metaphor from afar, yet not necessarily making meaning, since nothing is added to either end of the comparison. The metaphoric activity, however, is not compromised by its misuse. In *Un chien andalou* there is a shot of a bedroom with two pianos in it, side by side. Under the lids of these grand pianos lie, respectively, a donkey and a deer. The association is far richer with meaning, and more shocking, when in the 1972 *The Godfather* a bloody horse's head was placed at the bottom of the bed of a rebel to the Mafia (as it had been in real life). The whole situation is well described by Ogden/Richards as follows: "The connotation of a word determines its denotation which in turn determines its comprehension, i.e. the properties common to the things to which it can be applied."

In a 1936 lecture given at Bryn Mawr Richards went so far as to say, "visualisation is a mere distraction and of no service."

Deprived of linguistic obligations, film could be film. That is where the road opened up by Arnheim ends. The very limitations of technique (static cameras and the like) simply provoke art out of the form. The critic Roger Manvell says as much. "All works of art," he writes, in a somewhat shaky analysis in *Film*, "are successful because of, not in spite of, the limitations their form imposes on them." Thus, the speechless image impelled aesthetic rearrangements and compensations which elevated many silent films into art. As V. F. Perkins represents it, "They achieved something like perfection within the available range."

The other angle of approach is that taken by Siegfried Kracauer and André Bazin. The former's 1960 *Theory of the Film* argues that "film is essentially an extension of photography and therefore shares with this medium a marked affinity for the visible world around us." One feels reassured. Artificially to recreate today—as do Warhol and Pennebaker—deficiences of technique as aesthetic substitutes is as fruitless as the same might be (indeed is) in contemporary painting or sculpture. For such an approach is a complete misunderstanding. The aesthetic of a photograph exists by omission. This was realized by Dr. P. M. Roget as early as 1824. Kracauer stated that a photograph "is in character only if it precludes the notion of completeness." If the thesis that "all progress in movies has been towards achieving a more effective reality" (as per Lewis Jacobs) be taken literally, we would scarcely need directors at all, merely engineers. Finally, as those customers of Hale's Tours at the start of the century found, sitting in an artificially-rocked railway carriage with simulated views of scenery passing by the windows, we would have to ask why watching reality itself might not be more rewarding. In his theatre days Eisenstein in fact staged a play about a gas factory in a gas factory, the audience having to move to another part of the plant for each act. Professor Robert Richardson has effectively argued that watching *Around the World in 80 Days* is much more rewarding than eighty actual days around the world—"You see all the sights, and from the best vantages, without the dreary hotels, endless railways, bad food, tepid beer, and tired feet." Some films of Paris, like Agnès Varda's *Cléo from 5 to 7,* are better than a tour of the city itself.

The cinematic hunt for illusion, reality, as an aesthetic dead end is put succinctly enough in the comment of Paul Rotha that "perhaps the greatest handicap imposed on aesthetic progress was the camera's misleading faculty of being able to record the actual." This is really an extreme echo of Roget and, indeed, of the French painters first confronted by the camera image. It simply wasn't true. Delacroix said as much. If the image is to be total reality, why have an image? In real life no one dies in quite as poetic positions as on the famous Odessa steps in *Battleship Potemkin;* equally, one could say that no one dies so totally and tellingly.*

The answer, the midway ground between the illusionists and the aesthetes, has to be sought in some knowledge of what photography is. On one hand, Béla Balázs finds in cinema "an independent, basically new art," while in *Film* Arnheim claims that "film art . . . follows the same age-old canons and principles as every other art." Can we have it both ways? In a sense we can, and here must, since cinema is a marriage between a number of arts, including literature. All these arts, without exception, rely on acts of omission, of selection, and rearrangement. This gap, as it were, into which art infiltrates, is perhaps least visible in cinema since the form is so enclosing. We

---

* If timed, the soldiers' descent will be found to be three or four times slower than what would have actually happened.

really feel we are seeing reality, the that's-how-it-was of
Citizen Kane, and when art fails of its office in cinema we
all too often blame it on a lack of reality. But credibility
and reality are separate entities. In *Film Technique and
Film Acting* Vsevolod Pudovkin described this meeting-
ground best, since least dogmatically: "Between the natural event and its appearance on the screen there is a marked
difference. It is exactly this difference that makes the film
an art." And it is exactly this difference which, as Mailer
observed, makes directors, hesitant to change classic fictions,
serve us up in their place so many unsatisfactory simulacra.

Writing prior to colour, and only shortly after the introduction of talkies, Arnheim was genuinely helpful in
defining much of Pudovkin's "marked difference" for us.
He was early concerned to show that film does not simply
make a mechanical reproduction of reality. The retention
on the retina of an image after it has disappeared—on
which cinema relies—was observed and exploited in the
Eighteen Twenties and Thirties, in a variety of optical
toys like the phenakistascope.* The way in which an image
is recorded, before being thrown on the eyeball, certainly
results in affect, or meaning. The latter can be conditioned
by varieties of speed, film stock, the lens used, and so on.
Sound now accompanying film images is highly selective,
not real sound at all, but image retention is a norm of
cinema. Thorold Dickinson explains it another way:

---

* In May, 1973, the New York Cultural Center mounted a useful exhibit of
the work of Eadweard Muybridge (1830–1904). This included an 1832
phenakistascope of Joseph Plateau, an 1877 praxinoscope of Emile Rey-
naud, and a well functioning copy of the Muybridge zoöpraxiscope (sometimes known as a zoetrope or Daedelum) as shown to Leland Stanford in
August, 1879, and now reposing in the Central Library at Kingston-upon-
Thames in Surrey. The Filoscope was a gadget that could fit into one hand
and flick through a sequence of photos, to give a moving image; one such
sequence of Queen Victoria's Jubilee Parade of 1887 is extant. As a schoolboy in Lyons, Baudelaire was given a phenakistascope by his stepfather and
accurately describes it in a letter to his brother of 23rd. November 1833.

I will only insist that in fact for 30% of the time during which a film is apparently on the screen, the screen is blank. . . The appearance of continuity is not achieved by the persistence of images on the retina of the eye but because of the slowness of the brain to sort out the impulses transmitted from the retina.

Much as I admire the sometime Slade Professor of Film at the University of London, I still find this explanation no more than a classic case of *post hoc* reasoning. The image rests on the retina / my brain is slow / the image rests on the retina. Whichever way you read it the norm still obtains and by now Arnheim's correction of philistine mis-judgements of the time is the accepted attitude of most people of any sophistication visiting a cinema; there are large distinctions to be noted in the way in which reality has since been rendered by expressive devices in film.

The human eye is not a mechanical process, like the camera, yet the retina does register an image much in the way in which lenses direct light rays on a sensitised sur-face where chemical changes take place. (Perhaps this is why Buñuel sliced into an eyeball at the start of his career.) Vladimir Nilsen puts these difficulties best in his *The Cinema As Graphic Art*:

> The notion of the real world and its space obtained by direct visual perception is based on binocular vision. But the con-struction of the cinematographic image on the plane of the frame is achieved through the monocular action of the photo-graphic lens. The optical system embodied in the cinemato-graph camera is an intermediary technical means of construct-ing the form and outlining the details of the image in the shot. The character of cinematographic representation depends on the specific peculiarities of this optical system. So we may regard optics in its various forms of creative exploitation as a compositional resource.

The painter's eye sends messages to his hand holding a brush in order to reflect or "redeem" that reality, as the case may be. But the camera is a constant. The human eye is not, in its direct relationship with the brain and human nervous system. In the Eighteen Fifties Jules Champfleury made a number of elaborate defences of realist painting; in one, subsequent to the 1853 *salon,* he challenged ten photographers and ten landscape painters to render an identical landscape. The photographs would, he wagered, have no variation, whereas not one of the paintings would be like another, though each artist would have faithfully copied the scene under scrutiny. "Man not being a machine," he concluded, "cannot render objects like a machine."

Arnheim clearly took this position into account, and when discussing perspective set down what every art teacher knows:

> In a photograph of someone sitting with his feet stretched out far in front of him the subject comes out with enormous feet and much too small a head. Curiously enough, however, we do not in real life get impressions to accord with the images on the retina. If a man is standing three feet away and another equally tall six feet away, the area of the image of the second does not appear to be only a quarter of that of the first. Nor if a man stretches out his hand toward one does it look disproportionately large. One sees the two men as equal in size and the hand as normal. This phenomenon is known as the constancy of size. It is impossible for most people—*excepting* those accustomed to drawing and painting, that is artificially trained—to see according to the image on the retina. (My italics)

In teaching someone to draw, it is often helpful to show an ear, say, as a mere solid, so much occupancy of space, rather than as a human ear. The work of Robbe-Grillet and the French *chosistes* has been to emphasise this reseeing in literature, while in painting the Mexican David Siqueiros has frequently recorded on walls or canvas exaggerated retinal visions of huge hands coming at the viewer. The scene in *Hunger* (mentioned below) when the protagonist confronts a dog for possession of a bone is an example of retinal reportage in film. In any mode the divorce from reality in order to render reality is, of course, an initial aesthetic act.

What Arnheim is saying is that the camera is a monocular retina, and in painting we allow the rendition or distortion of what appears on the retina to bear the name of art. Today we even allow the ignorance of any retinal image at all to be dignified by this term, though we do not usually consider the blind to be likely Michelangelos—that is, inasmuch as sculpture is kept out of the question. Why then, asks Arnheim, cannot we allow cinema to be true art?

By now we can and do. Yet there must remain considerable reservations in the comparison, for in cinema the dependency of man upon a machine, and its operators, is high. Perhaps a little mischievously, Hitchcock told Richard Schickel that he is scarcely interested in content at all—"it would be the same as a painter worrying about whether the apples he's painting are sweet or sour. Who cares? It's his style, his manner of painting them—that's where the emotion comes." The analogy is patently false, possibly borrowed from Collingwood; one might equally argue that the relevance of sweet or sour apples is equivalent to the actors being kind or unkind people. In the same interview Hitchcock echoed what Joë Bousquet said about taking a woman in his arms—that once he had written about it, there had been a completion and the actual act was unnecessary. Similarly, Hitchcock claims that once he has completed his visual "score," and learnt every shot by heart—i.e. intellectualised the whole process—the technical side of the film becomes a bore: "I wish I didn't have to go on the stage and shoot the film, because from a creative point of view one has gone through that process."

The human retina is not a discrete process like the mechanical camera, it is emotively linked with perception. The interference or "static," as it were, between reality and the eye of a film director is completely different from what it is for a painter. Here another paradox enters. During the many centuries since man has first been painting, or even scratching images on cave walls, the human retina has remained a constant. During the seventy-five years or so of motion pictures the retina equivalent in cinema has been under constant change. In the first photographs, taken with twenty-minute exposures under harsh sunlight, the sitters often appeared with their eyes closed; their eyes were then artificially opened by re-touching, the situation being remedied in 1860 by the bunsen batteries of that ardent balloonist Nadar. Retinal equivalence of the camera has clearly made heavy calls on the most artistic of film-makers.

Thus, when sound came in, complex problems common to all verbalisation arose . . . and silence became silence. It is usually assumed that the advent of sound set the artistic quotient of cinema back until the new techniques, such as those involving image-motivated music, were absorbed—as soon they were by men like Ford and von Sternberg. Stanley Solomon tells us typically enough, "Suddenly the movies found themselves right back where they were at the turn of the century."* Free camera movement had to be restricted since actors had to keep close to the microphone, thus duplicating stage movements and tempting producers to buy dramas, wherein the language had, after all, been "pre-tested." Moreover, stage language is far more stylised than daily conversation; this is its art. Indoor locations, plus those painted sets which look so artificial to us today, were initially desirable. Films stood in danger of becoming what Hitchcock derided the first talkies for being —"photographs of people talking."

Maybe by now this critical attitude has been overdone. The main point here was that directly language was heard, the category changed. Cinema became something to hear as

---

* In actual fact, a process for sound recording was brought out in Sweden in 1921, but was kept quiet.

well as to look at (and silence a positive value to listen to) . As soon as literary values obtained more directly, the screenplay acquired importance and intelligent directors had to call on expressive devices that departed from reality in order, once again, to render reality. The murderer's heavy breathing in *M* is a celebrated instance, often cited at this point—if we hear someone breathing heavily at the other end of a telephone we are put on the alert. More recently, in *Repulsion,* Polanski played the gasps of sexual ecstasy of the heroine's sister against gasps of horror, in an auditory pun on the pain-pleasure relationship that made for the central derangement shown in the film. Furthermore, it was soon found that information could be transmitted by ear in addition to that sensed by the eye; thus, one could have an explosion heard by an actor who was himself removed from the source of that sound. Silence could be used as a pre-verbal pause, and so on.

The attitude may have been overdone in that we forget that sound seems to have been present—in the wings—as an ancillary to the film from the start. By their nature pictures were always like the Wagnerian *Gesamtkunstwerk,* regardless of whether words or colour or smell accompanied their images. The phonograph was invented as long ago as 1877 and Edison's Kinetoscope—commercially unsuccessful, it seems—attempted to add visuals to it in 1894. After the First World War patents poured in, yet even before it Lee De Forest, who had invented the audion amplifier tube in 1906, had attempted some form of talking picture as early, it is said, as 1900. De Forest went corporate in 1922, with sound newsreels being introduced two years later, when the Movietone process was sold to Fox (Warner Brothers buying Vitaphone on the verge of bankruptcy) .

It is often said that *The Jazz Singer,* released in October 1927, was the first "talkie," but it contained less than three hundred spoken words and was preceded by more than a year by the Vitaphone *Don Juan,* a synchronous sound vehicle. The point is, however, that the camera retina, if we may term it such, the monocular discontinuous eye, is not related to sound origins in the way in which the eye-ear human system is. All sorts of compensatory expressive techniques have to be dreamt up and are, with extreme sophistication, as a result. Asynchronous sound, like the once popular and (for modern tastes) over-used incidental music, is scarcely sound at all, rather psychology. A man makes a threatening gesture, or approaches danger, and we "see" it in early sound films through, as it were, a heavy fog of menacing mood music. This device is now usually relegated to some realistic source—juke box or car radio.

Theoretically, there must have been the same artificiality in the silent cinema with its connotative orchestral accompaniments. Indeed, merely to have human lips moving and no sounds emerging is artificial, despite the theory that such audiences could read lips with skill. Nevertheless, Coleridge's celebrated "suspension of disbelief" is a powerful ingredient in the imaginative encounter. We readily accept actors singing all their information in opera. Part of the aesthetic operation requires, and is indeed enhanced by, this lovely "giving-up" (without which something like *Alice in Wonderland* could never exist). The men who pore over peepshow machines are not lent much if the management decides to inject some realistic sound.

When sound vibrations were first recorded on film itself and the process patented by Lauste in 1906, the cinema had still not fallen into the hands of the mass-appeal merchants. A hypnosis of illusion was not necessarily the prime ingredient. Later, film-makers were to be so busy "recording" as realistically as possible that the previous gains in cinematurgy may well have been overlooked. It was the same, however, with the camera. Delacroix, together with his consummate spokesman in the field, Baudelaire, emphasised *at once* that the camera was a technique: man might make of it an art, but its epistemological relationship with reality (for such writers, "nature") was closer to science than art proper. "The daguerreotype," Delacroix wrote, "is only a reflection of the real, only a copy, in some ways false just because it is so exact . . . The eye corrects." His 1857 *Odalisque,* now in the Niarchos collection, is a fascinating case in point since it was confessedly based on a daguerreotype in his collection which has been preserved; and not only do we see Delacroix making the photograph (if we may paraphrase it as such) far less realistic, we also watch him making it in many ways *less* pleasing—turning awkwardly in the model's exposed toe, lifting her left arm off a languorously supporting cushion, de-emphasizing her all too solid and distractingly erotic breasts. In order to be art this painting had to be much less elegant and "interested," and much more aesthetically unified. It had to happen —rather than be a happening.

We find the same operating with Courbet's use of the camera. Courbet was the Champfleury of painting: "I look at a man with the same interest as I look at a horse," he said. The Luce documentaries we have seen *Citizen Kane* pillorying said the same. What Welles showed us was Zola's greatness—that any reporter must be selective, even one who uses the allegedly objective "camera eye." (Of Courbet, Ingres evidently remarked, "Ce garçon-là, c'est un œil.") Certainly, as in early cinema, the ideal was in question in Courbet's paintings of the Eighteen Fifties. Spectacular in size and trivial in subject they seemed to the scandalised pantheon of art critics of the time, one of whom called one "a faulty daguerreotype."

Today, however, we note Courbet's *correction* of a mechanical process whenever he deliberately used a photo (as in the 1855 *L'atelier*). How mindless Gérôme, Hamon and Picou were by comparison. Courbet usually used Carjat's photographs, but it hardly matters, since even he invariably distorted the literal. His undoubted interest in massive buttocks rivalled that of Russ Meyer today; a comparison between Courbet's 1853 *Les Baigneuses* and Julien Villeneuve's nude photograph on which a detail of it was based shows Courbet capaciously enlarging and preoccupying himself with the buttock basin of one girl until both Nadar and the Empress Eugénie were independently drawn to talk of those all too abundant hemispheres in the identical image, as plump as a Percheron's rump ("une espèce Percheronne"). In passing by it Louis Napoléon thumped this daring bather's backside not because, as Aaron Scharf puts it in his historiography of art and photography (which so admirably fills the lacuna remarked by George Moore in 1898), "she was nude, nor even because her gigantic posterior and other proletarian attributes were visually distressing. She was spanked by the outraged Emperor because nude *and* proletarian, she was masquerading as a nymph." Science had aspired to art.

The Emperor may have been wrong, but many have said the same as him since. In the 1853 photograph Villeneuve's lovely backside is more erotic and less artistic than Courbet's transformation of it into an ideal. We recall that Hogarth rejected the *camera obscura* as too literal. When a painter like Vernet virtually imitated a photograph, Baudelaire scoffed, "Who knows better than he the correct number of buttons on each uniform, or the anatomy of a gaiter or a boot?" The man had "a memory like an almanac." The best film directors today would surely find themselves in sympathy with such a comment; in any case, the camera retina, as we have termed it, was far more varied then than now, Gavard's diagraph producing quite different qualities from the hyalograph, physionotrace, or even Talbot's famous calotypes, one of which was closely copied for a so-called self-portrait by William Etty. The differentiation seems to have been even greater than the loss of tonal qualities when reducing reality from colour to black-and-white.

We have mentioned that colour symbolism is culturally

coded, and can have a knee-jerk nature (black for mourning, red representing the flames of hell). Thus, the coming of colour to motion pictures does not really seem as important as some critics have made it, alleging that it set back aesthetics. James Clerk Maxwell had shown a successful colour process in 1861 and some colour photos were exhibited in Paris in 1863, if only briefly, at half-hour intervals. Films tinted by hand were seen in America in 1895. Pathé Frères applied the process mechanically as early as 1907. In fact, the so-called "subtractive" colour process in vogue in the late Twenties, whereby a third hue was produced by imposing one colour on another, achieved results that look rather charming today (as in the Carole Lombard vehicle, *Campus Vamp*).

Elaborate colour tests by Swiss analysts like Max Pfister and Max Lüscher eventually came down to cultural patterning or just plain preference; the former's Colour Pyramid Test would appear to be about as much help in psychoanalysis as in hit-or-miss advertising. "To say a word 'means' something," writes Arthur Owen Barfield, "implies that it means that same something more than once." For colour to convey "meaning" in the true sense, for it to be genuinely symbolic, it would have to cross the sense barriers in the manner forever ridiculed, albeit charmingly, in Huysmans's effete Des Esseintes who, inspired by both Baudelaire and Nerval, heard a "music of liqueurs" and accorded colours to certain tastes and sounds. In fact, Eisenstein did pursue a "synchronisation of the senses" in the cinema. He had learnt Japanese in the army and, in later discussing the Kabuki theatre, wrote:

> Not even what is eaten in this theatre is accidental! I had no opportunity to discover if it is ritual food eaten. Do they eat whatever happens to be there or is there a definite menu? If the latter, we must also include in the ensemble the sense of taste.

Proust perfected the synaesthesic erudition of this sort of

hyperaesthesia, and gave us the most confident expression of it available either in literature or, in all probability, analysis. It cannot be maintained, however, that the *"moment privilégié"* of his Marcel is widely shared: the feel of a cobble under a thin shoe-sole does not invariably transport all of us—alas—to the Duchesse de Guermantes's courtyard and a string of erotic experiences thereafter.

Most sense-crossing of this sort drives over into, at worst, insanity or, at best, inspired surrealism, as in early Buñuel. It finds an obvious use when imagery is backed by quite disparate sound (we recall that László Moholy-Nágy produced paintings by telephone). What Kubrick added to Burgess's *A Clockwork Orange* was the *guignol* of the song "Singing in the Rain" (used in the film, though not in the novel, to identify the narrator later) as accompaniment to the hoodlums' violence in the house at the start; this device had been used before, notably when Hitchcock ran the "Merry Widow" waltz behind the actions of bluebeard Joseph Cotten in *Shadow of a Doubt,* but there it merely carried affect.

The Soviet psychologist Alexandr Romanovich Luria put on record a case in which colour could acquire sheer meaning, in his work with a mnemonist at the Budenko Neurological Hospital in Moscow. This individual, whom Luria called "S.", found it hard to follow ordinary conversations since they dizzied him with so many images of colour and texture. "What a yellow voice you have," he would object, quite seriously. The condition was an affliction; "S." could barely read. "Other people *think* as they read," he told Luria, "but I *see* it all." In his universe, and Luria presents it as an appalling one, from which the subject longed to escape, there was "no dividing line between colour and sound, between sensations of taste and of touch."

For most of us there must be. The human individual needs definition and identity (hence all the well-known taboos on exusions from the body), so that the sense-crossing which recent "psychedelics" copied from the French eccentrics of the Eighteen Thirties comes over to most normal people, not addicted to a drug, as a deeply threatening state. Luria's "S." found it almost impossible to read poetry, for instance. We may use colour metaphorically and call some hues warm or cold, talk about people being green with envy, and such like; but Luria shows us that "S." 's synaesthesia (Eisenstein's "synchronisation of the senses") which led the man himself to fame on the stage, able to recall in public in a fantastic way thanks to colour significance, was a deeply disturbing affair, one that separated "S." from, rather than elevated him above, the rest of his fellow beings. To be able to think of Friday as yellow or Monday as pink is not such an advantage, as far as meaning goes. Ingmar Bergman has told us that, as a child, he used to sit under the table in his grandmother's apartment, " 'listening' to the sunshine which came in through the gigantic windows." As a *child*, yes.

Part of this can doubtless participate in art. One office of colour in film may be informative, but its service in connotation is high. An 1857 article by Elizabeth Eastlake, first published in the *Quarterly Review*, ably grappled with what was soon realised at the time—that the black-and-white photograph would so dampen tonality that form relationships, beautifully evident in nature, would be lost. In pre-colour films form had to be defined rapidly by light: hence much of the early chiaroscuro effect we find clumsily melodramatic today. The true genius of Warners's 1933 *The Mystery of the Wax Museum* was to use the limited two-colour process as an advantage rather than a limitation, thereby suggesting wax-like humans and human waxworks (Fay Wray as Marie Antoinette). Since that time there has been a myriad of processes—Magnacolor, Prizma, Gasparcolor, Eastmancolor, and so on—and only occasional attempts, generally by means of filters, to make a technical deficiency repair reality. The Judy Garland *A Star Is Born,*

Lelouch's *A Man and a Woman,* parts of Godard's *Contempt* worked in this vein, with artificial colour lack or deprivation located in advanced colour work itself and genuinely aiding emotional effect. Resnais's *Night and Fog* established changes between past and present as between black-and-white and colour.

Just as it "depends what you mean by" art, so it depends what you mean by optical truth. Everyone is probably familiar with one or another of those perception tests in which a subject is shown a picture and asked to identify what he or she sees—a bride or a mother-in-law, a vase or two faces (in the particular example with which Picasso has played). The older among us will see first the haggard mother-in-law, the young the rapturous bride. By the focussing of a spotlight on a white bristol board the colours left behind by a morsel of dark velvet, suddenly removed, will also vary according to the ages of the percipients.

The human eye is thus far more subjective—unreliable, if you will—than the mechanical camera retina. This is what makes it possible for someone like Cocteau to call the photograph inaccurate ("Photography is unreal, it alters tone and perspective . . . "). In a major sense it is. You can lose shape through loss of tone variations, and have to compensate for this loss in cinema; you must render reality and then distort it in order to suggest the *reality* of human visual perception. A group of objects in colour with no tone variation will look quite flat. This is the point at which Arnheim is somewhat less helpful than he might be, since really there is no such thing as a camera retina. The eyes see reality directly, with more or less muscular distortions and adjustments; that same reality is first chopped into an image by the rigidly monocular camera and it is this image, at second hand, which the human retina then reports.

This relationship can be seen in the attitudes of leading Nineteenth-century painters to the new invention. For these were individuals who wanted to render aesthetic reality. True, the camera threatened their livelihoods, but when that bitter pill had been swallowed, men like Monet and Degas set about utilising photographic accidents and imperfections precisely to achieve retinal reality. One of the best examples of this can surely be seen in Monet's *Boulevard des Capucins*, of 1873. Thanks to long exposures and slow emulsions the first city photographs showed people as (at most) passing blurs, vestigial shadows, mere wheels and hooves. Men with several legs appeared, and horses with as many heads. This lack of ability in the given mechanism was seized by Monet to suggest just how we do see a busy street from a distance (and, in his case, an elevation). It resulted in a prophecy of the cinema which would eventually, with faster shutters and film, play art back to itself. It was partly for this reason that, in France, photography was officially adjudged an art in 1862 (in the famous Mayer and Pierson case), with the same claim independently honoured in Britain in the International Exhibition of the same year.*

We now know that both Millais and Seurat used the (quite accidental) figure-severing devices of early photography, while it is said that even Ingres's portraits differed in colour after he had seen Nadar's work with the camera. Finally, Degas made the most daring use of the then-instantaneous photograph and, in the process, taught us many lessons about the pictorial representation of reality. Like Zola, Degas owned a camera and used it intelligently. His cut-off figures replied to photographic experiments just as art had anticipated them (Donatello's reliefs in Mantegna, early Japanese prints). It was not for nothing that Resnais's first film was on van Gogh.

---

* Perhaps the most thorough, and most comprehensively illustrated, study of this area of our inquiry to date is Van Deren Coke's *The Painter and the Photograph* (1964: revised and enlarged, 1972).

Degas prefigured the motion picture in his consecutive sketches of dancers in similar positions, as in some serial progression of "frames." In this he actually anticipated the celebrated experiments of Eadweard Muybridge (or Marey before him) in photographing animal locomotion (notably of horses) in a succession of still shots. These were first shown in Paris in 1878 and, while they convinced equestrian sceptics that a horse lifts all four legs off the ground for a moment, Rodin was still to object: "Now I believe that it is Géricault who is right, and not the camera, for his horses *appear* to run."

Appearance and reality: here lay the film's impasse. To demonstrate empirically, as did the cinema's main medium, that a horse was airborne for an instant while cantering added absolutely nothing to the common illusion of reality. It belonged more in the realm of research. Willy Busch (1832-1908) thus realised that a certain falsification was closer to human retinal reality, and so drew a pianist with extra fingers. In this Busch, in common with Degas's first kinetic compositions, gave us perceptual reality, leaving a sixth finger in our eyes that corresponded to that residual image relinquished on the retina after its first appearence—on which principle cinema established its primary norm. Marcel Duchamp founded a reputation on duplicating, in paint, the superimposed images of the chronotograph. The Italian Futurists—Boccioni, Balla, Carrà—equally tamely followed suit. By the turn of the century the camera retina had wholly insinuated itself into the general aesthetic consciousness. When this happened, when the idea of the camera as an illusionist had been partially digested, the reproduction of reality could be seen to be more of an organic matter, a task of affect. In sensing the essential of the affect in making a communication, both visual and verbal, Eisenstein was undoubtedly ahead of his time, placing primary emphasis on metaphor, imagery, connotation. This is why he studied the leading anthropologists of his day. Yet novelists—condemned to purely verbal communication—had done the same. "The direct animal intuitions," we read in Aldous Huxley's *After Many a Summer Dies the Swan,* "aren't rendered by words; the words merely remind you of your memories of similar experiences." The interior monologue of Dujardin, expanded by Joyce, returned language to its pre-verbal, sensuous origins, and we know that Joyce said that if *Ulysses* were given to a director, it should be to either Eisenstein or Ruttmann. In the event, a fairly head-on attack was made on the narrative by Joseph Strick.

In the reproduction of reality, therefore, the film director seems to have soon been confronted with the taxing task of creating a harmonious ensemble of sensory perceptions. In the early Seventeenth century Cyrano de Bergerac, in his *Histoire comique des états et empire de la lune et du soleil,* adumbrated a muscular language ("le language musculaire") in imagined extra-terrestrial races. "Certain parts of the body," he wrote, "signified entire discourses." Frowns, finger movements, and bows were all seen as primary aspects of dialogue. Flaubert was well aware, in *Madame Bovary,* that such could be sturdy vehicles in the transmission of thought. Even his placing of Emma at a window at significant moments has frequently been commented on. Since human beings are human, everything around them is going to claim some symbolic rights—an empty chair will "signify" absence, a barred window "mean" confinement. The camera has quickly emphasised our cultural coding of such signals. Bertrand Russell, referring to the Frenchman's shrug, commented: "Any kind of externally perceptible bodily movement may become a word, if social usage so ordains." In this sense, in the context of language as a total symbiotic system, the claims of Mailer or Bergman that "film has nothing to do with literature" may be properly entertained.

Nor, one might continue, does technology have "anything to do with" the rendition of reality in this sense. "To show one is weeping," writes Roland Barthes, "one must weep." Must one? Print did not really alter content, though it may have influenced the physical form of the novel. McLuhan made much mileage out of this notion, which was first lengthily advanced by H. J. Chaytor in a doctoral dissertation over forty years ago, one on which McLuhan relied heavily throughout *The Gutenberg Galaxy*. Print brought changes in the manner in which certain verbal representations could be effected in art. Video recorders with film cartridges can now be played on most TV sets; what alteration to content this new "medium" or channel may make remains to be seen.

When novel publishers began passing technical requirements back to the author, and criticising by declining then as now, they did no more than emphasise size. We have observed that Charlotte Brontë's *The Professor* was declined since it could only form one volume instead of the then-requisite three. It has even been conjectured that the elliptical style of some of the best novelists caught in the reverse squeeze—Conrad, James, the early Ford—was thus forced on them by economic requirements, as much as being chosen by themselves. They had to omit more than they wanted to, often to the bafflement of their first readers. An author cannot always predict the size of the subject matter with which he comes in contact; Thomas Mann tells us he began his immense *The Magic Mountain* imagining that he was going to write a short story.

Today we have seen the growth of the paperback reprint at first influencing an output of sex, fast narrative, and violence. Such gluttony abated with the relaxing of pornography laws. Almost no large publishing firm nowadays either side of the Atlantic is still privately owned in the way such was even a quarter of a century ago. The well-spring of the industry, in both novel and cinema, can certainly be seen influencing what reality is represented; but in the long run it is powerless to censor the representations of that reality. In fact, the invasions of the Hollywood mogul into just this latter arena are what has held cinema back, rather than the injection into the art object of a purely technical innovation. Technological change dates a film in a way no change in the format of a read novel can, but a really crass picture made in 1960, say, still looks older and more tired than a *Citizen Kane* made some twenty years before, in which form and content have met and married well.

We know that Griffith did not want the human voice at all ("I am quite positive that when a century has passed, all thought of our so-called speaking pictures will have been abandoned") ; he seems clearly to have felt that the novel, like a poem, was an ontological whole and that for a film to be such its "author" (his term) should only venture into other senses inasmuch as they reinforced the image. Music could do this, for Griffith, as for Bergman ("I would say that there is no art form that has so much in common with film as music"), but speech would dilute the author's first message, that of his icon. It would, Griffith realised, alter the category:

> To me those images on the screen must always be silent. Anything else would work at cross purposes with the real object of this new medium of expression. There will never be speaking pictures. . . .

Perhaps there should not have been. When seeing a film as purely and poetically visual as the Flaherty's *Louisiana Story* (1948) one feels a descent when dialogue is introduced, and the family scenes inside the shack are disproportionately inferior. Film is external "seeing," the novel internal. This is essentially emphasised in the frontal attacks on reality made in the form of temporal equivalence: we know that Sterne toyed with the idea of the time of a fictional happening coinciding with the time taken to

read about it (in the manner of Mathieu's battle paintings). *Ulysses* covers eighteen hours and forty-five minutes
in its "action," purportedly the time taken to read through
the book in a single session. The prime example of this
in cinema, to examine which illustrates many points we
have been making here, was Erich von Stroheim's *Greed*.
This originally enormous work confronts the problem—is
the representation of written reality by literal image,
scene for scene, a possible cultural exchange? As V. F. Perkins points out, *Greed* in fact defeats criticism; thus, in
The Art of the Film Ernest Lindgren cites the work as a
masterpiece, while its avowed situation as almost so much
book illustration makes it simultaneously nugatory by the
same critic's criteria—"if a cinematograph production is not
filmic there is no film in the proper sense to criticise."

GREED (1923)

To begin with, Stroheim's *Greed* almost never saw the light of day. Based on Frank Norris's *McTeague,* which was started in 1895 and published in 1899, *Greed* consisted in its original version of seventy reels. It ran for almost twenty hours, which is rather more than anyone's total reading time for the novel. The action takes far longer.

Almost nobody has seen this mammoth in its entirety, so it is perhaps fairly pointless writing about it. M-G-M finally made the director edit it down to ten reels (2½ hours) —the version seen today. A far shorter one was recently released on U.S. television, resulting in a mere series of images, a meaningless montage of McTeague's decline, culminating in the celebrated Death Valley murder when he finds himself handcuffed to his victim, Marcus Schouler, his wife's cousin and sometime aspirant to her hand. Apparently, taking the word of those who have seen the whole on trust, Stroheim's only liberty with the text was an insertion of a mere two and a half hours (now the showing time of the whole) to delineate rather more clearly McTeague's ancestry.

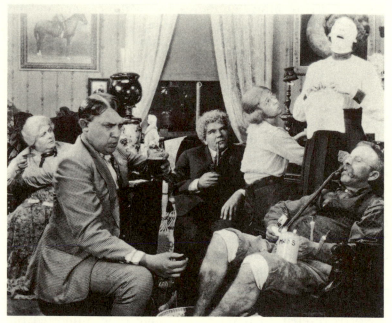

GREED (1923, von Stroheim): typical attitudinisings of the silent cinema.

So faithful did Stroheim try to be that he shot much of his film in the very house where the 1893 murder of a kindergarten's janitress, which drew Norris to his subject, took place. (A stickler for this sort of detail, he later made his *Merry Widow* extras wear genuine Prussian underwear.) *Greed* was one of the first of many major films to arise from a celebrated murder, or series of murders. More than a novel, a film requires some strong or highly interesting character at its core, and a murderer readily provides such. Novels also thrive off strong characters but Balázs did well to remind us that character is the *sine qua non* of film: "Our eyes are in the camera and become identical with the gaze of the characters. They see with our eyes . . . Nothing like this 'identification' has ever occurred as the effect of any other system of art and it is here that the film manifests its absolute artistic novelty." David Mowat agrees: "Brilliant and compelling films have been virtually plotless—*Il Posto, La Notte, L'Eclisse.* But they do—this is their triumphant quality—they do explore a character in depth and in detail."

In *M* Lang quickly responded to red-neck public opinion following the beheading of the famous Düsseldorf murderer, Peter Kurten, a psychopath like de Sade's Gernande or, in London later, John George Haigh (on whom another film has been based), driven to ejaculation by visions of his victim's gore. Even in Hitchcock's inept *Frenzy* (1972), the interest concentrates on the tie murderer rather than on the "hero" suspect, or the pusillanimous detective inspector —enough so to arouse the vociferous objections of a number of feminist critics.

Norris revered Zola, yet at the same time supported the British in the Boer War, which he reported at first hand. Unlike Crane and Zola, and in common with Jack London, Norris had little verbal facility. Whenever he could he fell into *clichés;* as a result, Stroheim frequently refined his original. His silent conclusion, of the two figures in the desert, rings with conviction, a thematic authority that the prose belies in the original—"Marcus was dead now; McTeague was locked to the body. All about him, vast, interminable, stretched the measureless leagues of Death Valley. McTeague remained stupidly looking around him, now at the distant horizon, now at the ground, now at the half-dead canary chittering feebly in its little gilt prison." Lacking words, Stroheim used the bird as a symbol far more tellingly than Norris. For the latter it was a mere element of crude characterisation, his hero's love for it serving to emphasise the *bête humaine* nature beneath;

it had been effected before by Zola to characterise his Lantier and was to be done to death later by subsequent American realists (*cp.* Steinbeck's *Of Mice and Men*). Stroheim brings the bird forward as a thematic marker, even starting McTeague's association with it earlier. The dentist presents Trina with a pair of lovebirds as a wedding present and it is soon visually suggested that there are also bars around McTeague's life. Stroheim enlists our pity for the feeble, vulnerable bird as pity for the victimised McTeague, sympathetically played by Gibson Gowland (whereas ZaSu Pitts was mis-cast as Trina).

Norris excelled at sharp, coarse brush-strokes of characterisation and a narrative pace that gave the reader little time to dwell on finesse. When he essays a retrospect he becomes cumbersome, and Stroheim's vehicle rightly eschewed such. Though he followed his original faithfully he kept his eye on symbolising the theme visually. The funeral *cortège* glimpsed during the wedding of Mac and Trina in the film is a serious addition to the original. Norris had transmuted Trina's sensuality into a greed for gold —she hoards coins, dreams of gold and is killed for it. The association is everywhere, in fact a little too heavy in some touches—"it was his great delight to call her into the 'Dental Parlors' when a patient was in the chair and, while he held the plugger, to have her rap in the gold fillings with the little box-wood mallet as he had taught her."

Stroheim concentrates on the dentistry *motif* even earlier in the film and features it, perhaps having read *Buddenbrooks,* as a perfect capitalist anagram, sturdy commercialism thriving off decay. The sign of the gold tooth is much less leaden in the filmed than in the written version. Further, Stroheim intensifies Trina's obsession as can still be seen in his handling of the sequence when McTeague sells his gold tooth to a rival and sends Trina out to buy some meat. Here the director employs words, for as Trina scans the meat in the dingy store she turns to a cheaper barrel at one side, intending to save money from the sale—and we read, "THIS MEAT AIN'T FIT FOR A DOG."

Several of the titles defeat, rather than underline, Stroheim's skill with his theme. When *Greed* was chopped up, many sub-titles were tossed out; at the last minute new ones had to be hastily thought up to account for the lacunae. One of these slices causes the film to render Trina's greed as stemming from an unruly wedding night, whereas Norris has them at first in sexual harmony.

Later, Trina becomes as much a "human beast" in her way as was McTeague in his. Above all, Stroheim's film indicts society far more directly. There is no easy deterministic let-out for the audience, as to an extent there was for Norris's readers. McTeague's characterisation is a Zolaesque *tempérament,* as Zola defined such in the Preface to the Second Edition of *Thérèse Raquin.* Like Etienne in *Germinal,* he is the son of an alcoholic father, with more than a suggestion that he too is inevitably destined ("determined") to repeat, helplessly, the pattern; similarly, Trina's frugality is an echo of her Swiss-German parentage.

By externalising the human brute so vividly, by confronting his theme without any such let-outs, Stroheim was able to give us almost everything that Norris tried to in a silent form, without words at all. We shall see that this object lesson in cinematurgy recurs even today, in some of the best of Bergman or a film like *Hunger,* treated below, in which there is little verbalisation and what there is in Swedish, ununderstandable to the majority of English viewers. In the latter case, too, the director used such harsh black-and-white photography as to make the bulk of what subtitles were appended unreadable. It did not matter. The imagery said it all.

THE BLUE ANGEL (1929)

Germany was approaching a political crisis when sound first made itself felt in cinema. Prior to sound film German expressionism, developed in the theatre, had genuinely advanced silent cinematurgy, through men like Wiene, Pabst, Lang, Murnau, as well as others working in Germany alongside them, such as Dupont. In his justly celebrated book Siegfried Kracauer sees much of this cinema as unconscious revelations of a national mood. Robert Wiene's 1919 *The Cabinet of Dr. Caligari,* co-written by Carl Mayer and perhaps a trifle overestimated today, set a pattern in boldly subjective settings, crazy architecture and spatial distortions to characterise the mind of the central character Francis (provided you accept, of the two endings, the one that has Francis mad, i.e. a paranoiac pre-Hitler). Murnau's *The Last Laugh* (1924), also written by Mayer, suggests the same latent sadism in the national *Geist*. Even though von Sternberg took Marlene Dietrich back with him to Hollywood, *The Blue Angel* was ineluctably German in its prophetic symbolism. Not far off his screen we seem to read the small ads in the underground press—"Dominant Female demands Docile. . . ."

Isaac Asimov has written: "It is easy to predict an automobile in 1880; it is very hard to predict a traffic problem." Kracauer did a valuable service in showing how the disintegrating, self-pitying postwar years in Germany threw up a sometimes brilliant cinema predictive of the Nazi era. In *Parade of Pleasure* I tried to show the same prediction of the McCarthy period in America in brutal "B" films before it.

If sadism and hysteria lie just beneath the surface, the psychology of cinema is such that these trends will be rapidly revealed to us on celluloid. It is easy to be wise after the event—as in *The Damned* or *Cabaret*. If language can be said in any sense to influence thought, if certain linguistic structures facilitate the passage of some ideas rather than others, then let us urge iconography on to dramatise these for us. There is a convincing theory first expounded by Dolf Sternberger in his *Aus dem Wörterbuch des Unmenschen* of 1945 and expanded by Cornelia Berning's 1965 *Von ,Abstammungsnachweis' zum ,Zuchtwart',* namely that German grammar was such at the time that Nazi policies lodged easily within the language. Neologisms like *Judenfrage* and *Entjudung* became current in the 1880s; habits of inflected epithets, of highly abstract suffixes and generally tormented syntax are said to have been ready to house the "thought" of Hitler, Goebbels, and even Streicher. If so, the hypotheses of the late Benjamin Lee Whorf find some sort of shocking corroboration.

The interesting point about *The Blue Angel* is that it is a literal transposition of Heinrich Mann's *Professor Unrath* of 1905. Yet the political background has completely changed and Mann's sexual decadence, a Jungian *anima* legend, is staged by von Sternberg as a social sickness. No wonder that when his protest seemed to have failed, when Nazism seemed triumphant, he relapsed into a certain anomy, weaving empty patterns around the lovely *protégée* he had discovered in Germany.

THE BLUE ANGEL (1929, von Sternberg): gargoyles and grotesques surround the provocative sex of Marlene Dietrich as Lola Lola (compare the night-club world of *Cabaret* forty-three years later).

By 1929 von Sternberg (a man with a curious facial resemblance to Hitler in his youth) had already made seven silent films in Hollywood, including *The Salvation Hunters* and *Underworld*. All were notable for care in composition and texture, and when he went to Berlin for *The Blue Angel* he shot an English as well as a German version. First shown in both England and America, the former has now perished, but in neither did he follow the then popular technique of photographing theatre, clinging instead to the few traditions established by silent cinema. That is why the film can be seen again today with enjoyment. Its scant dialogue is almost wholly narrative, at times a series of directions; the impact is pictorial, which was probably what made the French ban the German version (though a Blue Angel nightclub opened in the capital shortly after a first showing of the film). Exhibition in both America and England was held back until *Morocco* (1930) had created the Anglo-Saxon stereotype of Dietrich that has persisted to the present day, and to which, were it not for a comic gift as well as a remarkable personality, she would have early succumbed. Films like *A Foreign Affair* and *Stage Fright* show how her theatrical presence, her celluloid charisma, resists the patina of *femme fatale* which directors liked to cast over it. Yet more than one generation reverberated to this aspect of the Dionysiac *femme fatale,* top-hatted, silky-limbed, speaking in an accent that seems absurd by modern standards (and is mocked in *Blazing Saddles* of 1974) but with which she could still, in her sixties, make staid *Burghers* weep to her rendition of "Lili Marlene."

In *The Blue Angel,* set in the Berlin of the late Twenties, von Sternberg created Dietrich's first and last real role, one that Kracauer has described as follows:

> Her Lola Lola was a new incarnation of sex. This pretty bourgeois tart, with her provocative legs and easy manners, showed an impassivity which incited one to grope behind her callous egoism and cool insolence. That such a secret existed was also intimated by her veiled voice, which, when she sang about her interest in love-making and nothing else, vibrated with nostalgic reminiscences and smoldering hopes.*

This, then, was Dietrich's one character study before her glamorisation into the vacuous siren of England and America, one that looks so depressing re-seen today, a stylised

---

* The extract is taken from Siegfried Kracauer, *From Caligari to Hitler,* New York: Noonday, 1959. The English needs refining, however: a *petit-bourgeois* tart is not a pretty bourgeois tart. Far from it.

sphinx who, presented with idiot regularity in film after film, would have annihilated a lesser being. There is no nonentity in the Lola Lola of *The Blue Angel*. Von Sternberg organises in her person a penetrating critique of existent social conditions, moving Mann's novel into a genuinely new dimension. German *bourgeois* society is examined in the spirit of his brother Thomas. With the acquisition of knowledge guilt results, and decadence—it is a little Garden of Eden in embryo. "If we had looked harder at *The Blue Angel* in 1931," Richard Griffith has written, "we might have had some glimpse of Berlin's future." To convey this decay, this sense of warning, von Sternberg fully exploits all he can find in his medium. As the same critic puts it,

> In this portrait of a middle-aged professor led to his downfall by a café entertainer, objects, buildings, and landscapes take on a life of their own; everything visible and audible accentuates the theme of the helpless and fatal pursuit of pleasure, the draining away of all social values.

The anticipation of *chosisme* is there (although I cannot recall a single landscape in the picture). Mass sadism, mass hysteria, were about to break out in Germany and through the Mann original von Sternberg gives us a study of the spiritual torture by humiliation and degradation of a small-town official with whom everyone can readily identify. In an Introduction to an unacknowledged English translation of the novel (London: Jarrolds), J. Leslie Mitchell, who wrote in Lallans under the pseudonym Lewis Grassic Gibbon, calls the tragically strayed professor "an incarnation of the multitudes that time and circumstance have shaped to dull and foolish lives in civilisation's back reaches." In Mann's original Rosa Fröhlich (of the symbolic name, the Lola Lola of the cabaret) is suggestively domineering. Von Sternberg perceptively intensified this. As Kracauer says:

He deepened this sadistic tendency by making Lola Lola destroy not only Jannings himself but his entire environment. A running *motif* in the film is the old church clock which chimes a popular German tune devoted to the praise of loyalty and honesty. . . —a tune expressive of Janning's inherited beliefs. In the concluding passage, immediately after Lola Lola's song has faded away, this tune is heard for the last time as the camera shows the dead Jannings. Lola Lola has killed him, and in addition her song has defeated the chimes.

Moreover, one might add, the bells are first heard by Lola Lola when the professor tells her he is unmarried; they sound again when, in the empty classroom, he puts down the books on his desk, renounces his old life, and takes up the carnation she had given him. This kind of leitmotif, on which film can play (and almost pun), was prevalent in European literature at this time. Heinrich's brother Thomas had already emphasized these moments of involuntary memory; in *Tonio Kröger* he had given us the symbolic linking devices of this nature in walnut-tree, rusty gate, fountain, and the like. Once again, therefore, it is fiction that anticipates film. Despite Ibsen drama does not offer us, at this time, these epiphanic *moments privilégiés.*

The degradation that follows in von Sternberg's film is filled with pathos for a modern audience, since it is precisely that humiliation which came to the Jews (Heinrich Mann was to write a moving obituary over the village of Lidice). Professor Rath, the Apollonian intellectual, over whose bed hangs the sign *Tue Recht und scheue niemand,* is reduced at last to the *Zauberlehrling* of the conjurer, ordered to kneel at Lola Lola's feet to pull on her stockings, condemned to stand on the stage before an audience of Aryans to have eggs broken over his pate and to cry like a cock.

Even at the beginning of the film the professor was, in several shots, haunted by the figure of a clown in the background: the one man of ideals, he himself is but a clown when he enters the world of "The Blue Angel." (Angels should not be blue, in any case.) At the start, therefore, the cabaret he enters looks disorderly, chaotic, like that in *Cabaret;* almost surrealist with its whirling clouds, miasmic veils and shifting backdrops it is strongly indebted to Wiene's *Caligari.* Birds fly through the air, dwarves loll around,* at one point Eisenstein's peacock seems to be there. At the end, when the professor is part of this world, it is steady and brutal in its clarity. Everything connected with the professor sharpens this interpretation—his favourite pupil being called Angst, the mitigation of his masculine nose-blowing (to become cock-crowing) after meeting Lola Lola, the very nickname Unrath (excrement) which was later conferred on the Jews in official publications, as well as on the streets. Jannings brought to this role experience in similar character decline, having brilliantly portrayed, as a man of only twenty-nine, the ageing doorman of Murnau's 1924 *The Last Laugh.* In this film, too, demoted by the manager and finally stripped of all rank as a lavatory attendant in the bowels of an hotel, Jannings showed his immense ability to universalise the human condition.

In *The Blue Angel,* however, the main themes are sex and sadism, individual and social. Closer to Nazism Josef von Sternberg could here tighten the focus of his fictional original. The imagery of Günther Rittau's camera reflects these themes with care. The dead bird—which the professor is told, in the first scene, will never sing again—is singing again in Lola Lola's boudoir, and sings in the last shot of all in the person of Lola Lola herself, the *Ewig-Weibliche.* Then, for an instant, the twelve apostles in agonised poses of broken stone file slowly round the great Hamburg church clock, and finally Marlene sings the lines which

---

* Their presence is suggestive, since for the sake of perspective early German expressionist cinema sometimes used dwarves or small children as distant adults.

sum up the film—when a man burns in lust, who can find him salvation? We remember that the very days of this ignoble adventure had been ripped off the calendar by the professor with Lola Lola's hair-curlers, the burning tongs of lust.

The sexual tension carries its own corollary of nostalgia and despair. Ecstasy, by its nature, cannot endure. In contrast to the frenetic cabaret scenes, the camera tracks slowly back down the empty classroom as Jannings is about to leave it for good, and in this last lingering embrace tenderly dramatises the protagonist's loneliness and inner longing for his past profession. Banal as it was, it had a strong persona with which he might confront life, as well as the irrecoverable gift of innocence. Nor, in the final analysis, is Lola Lola herself wholly evil. As the maddened professor grips her by the throat, she asks him what he wants of her, and the pathos of her predicament is glimpsed—what more, one feels, is such a woman able to give?

Photographic compositions here perfectly personify the dramatic construction and centre on the sex of Lola Lola herself. Their force and logic make the presentation infinitely more gripping than the somewhat hypocritical eroticism of the same director's later Hollywood productions. Von Sternberg was not to know the same independence again, as here under Erich Pommer's friendly hand; of *Macao* he was actually to fume, "Instead of fingers in that pie, half a dozen clowns immersed various parts of their anatomy in it."

Siegfried Kracauer tells us that "*M* confirms the moral of *The Blue Angel*: that in the wake of retrogression terrible outbursts of sadism are inevitable." It is hard to feel today, however, that Lang's first talkie is as much an anagram of the social condition as was von Sternberg's. For a start, the child murderer Becker, so brilliantly played by Peter Lorre, is barely seen until two-thirds of the way through—he is glimpsed by shadows, or through foliage, heard by his whistle. We lack a strong character at the centre of this film. Yet doubtless Lang was right not to show Lorre too much, since he was playing the role with such pathos, and the director did not want to evoke any more sympathy for the Düsseldorf killer than he allowed to be shown in the kangaroo court at the end, clearly borrowed from Brecht's *Dreigroschenoper*, of which Pabst made a film in the same year as *M*.

Lang's film has memorable images. One usually cited is of Lorre looking into a cutlery shop photographed so that his face is framed by knives while a girl victim is reflected walking past behind him.* There is, however, the equally telling shot of the girl seen against another shop window, one with a revolving target and a descending arrow; this shot tells us just as much with the same economy. Sound too was most imaginatively used and that some of Lang's effects have become platitudes today does not detract from the vividness of their inception. Not only are there the fine exaggerations of the cornered Lorre's breathing in the lumber room; as of his whistling of Grieg before a killing, there are sharp defining notes such as the harshly predatory snap made by his switchblade knife as he opens it . . . to peel an orange. Yet, all in all, *M* is a talky talkie; it happened to become, however, the prototype for hundreds of detection films. How many times since have we been given that picture of a child innocently bouncing a ball before some horror is committed?

Von Sternberg went further into sexual pathology simply because he was able to; he could keep his protagonist monumentally before us throughout. Further, he served his atmosphere with an almost suffocating eroticism of costume. For, contrary to popular opinion, the milieu of a cabaret

---

* In Robbe-Grillet's *The Voyeur* the watch-salesman protagonist, who rapes and murders thirteen-year-old girls, provides an echo of this moment as he peers in a shop-window: "A dozen identical little knives—mounted on a cardboard strip, like watches—formed a circle, all pointing toward a tiny design at the centre. . . . "

can prove highly anti-erotic on the screen. Mere sexiness wages its war against true eroticism and caused otherwise intelligent critics like Maurice Bardèche and Robert Brasillach to fulminate against this film as "a coarse melodrama . . . in bad taste."

It was in beautifully bad taste. The costuming of *The Blue Angel* was consummate. A fur fetishist, von Sternberg was to cover his heroines in feathers, plumes, and ostrich boas. Evelyn Brent's nickname in *Underworld* was in fact "Feathers" and in this film, as in others from von Sternberg, the set would be inundated with oceans of swansdown. Resnais put a brief parody of this Thirties bird-woman heroine into *Marienbad;* the trend was in large part due to Travis Banton, who had joined Paramount in 1924 and put Louise Brooks in *The Canary Murder Case* (1929) in almost exactly the same cap of feathers as Evelyn Brent. Von Sternberg saw to it that in nearly every Dietrich film—*Morocco, Shanghai Express, Desire*—the star of *The Blue Angel* should at some moment arise under a toque of feathers. We live far closer to these pelts and feathers in film than ever we may on the stage.

In *The Blue Angel* Marlene is literally described by her costume. Lola Lola's blowzy cabaret clothes are a positive attribute of her character, the rustly silk stockings of the era tethered spinnaker-taut by black suspenders crossing her thighs to vanish under the snowy frills of her pantalette. André Maugé has described von Sternberg's flair for costumes as follows:

> il connaît la valeur d'une robe et ce qu'elle peut apporter à une femme de troublant et de désirable. Il aime la douceur des plumes autour du cou, les dessous de dentelle, les pieds cambrés sur les hauts talons absurdes, les longs bas transparents, les jarretières et les jarretelles, tout un érotisme un peu suranné de corsets et de chevilles fines. . . .

In *The Blue Angel*, therefore, we have a meeting-point of many elements, relatively successfully blended: not only fiction and film, with the latter here strengthening the former, but the sound film with the silent, for Jannings's gestures had been trained for the latter cinema. Of Mann's book a historian of modern German literature, Jethro Bithell, has said that its theme works itself out (through the professor) by Balzacian exaggeration; the method was certainly in the air in German fiction of the first decade of this century—as witness Wedekind's grotesque sexual distortions and monomanias—and it is on such exaggeration that cinema thrives. Emil Jannings acted splendidly in this his first talking film, but throughout it, even without him, von Sternberg's whole style had the fluidity of confidence—"a smooth and easy blending of sequences through dissolves, and music and song which moved with the images," as Lewis Jacobs describes it in *The Rise of the American Film,* justly adding, "This technically superb picture had all the qualities Sternberg was to overemphasise in his later efforts."

Indeed, this gifted director was to travesty both himself and Dietrich. After responding so intensely to a social situation, that of pre-Nazi Germany, he returned to America to compose films in an elegant vacuum. Instead of characterising socio-political implications, his star became a puppet whose sins were romantic, upper-class and superficial, a doll whose world-weariness passed for wisdom and who could accordingly, in real life, call Erich Maria Remarque a great writer. In *The Blue Angel* we find a fine transition of fiction into film and a Dietrich whose place in life was classically tragic, a vision of the Dionysiac tendencies about to overthrow Germany, a true image of flesh and blood.

Psychology of Cinema

In watching a film the curtain between fact and fantasy is torn brusquely aside. We are engrossed as "spectators" more than in any other art form. An attempt is made at immediate involvement in material that disturbs and envelops us, perhaps more completely—certainly more swiftly —than anywhere else.

Radio early shattered that detachment with which the psyche asks to handle an illusion. The bells of England may have tolled when Clarissa Harlowe "died"—a fanciful notion, in my opinion, and in how many villages?—but an entire township ran out into the streets in New Jersey upon Orson Welles' 1938 dramatisation of H. G. Wells's *War of the Worlds* (the panic was more excusable than some suppose, since the country had just been officially alerted to the broadcasting of an important radio message; Welles cleverly exploited this moment). Eleven years later a similar radio dramatisation created havoc in Quito, Equador, where, when the fraud was discovered, the infuriated citizenry turned on their radio station, with bloody results. There were also riots in American cities when *The Birth of a Nation* was first shown.

132

Parallel passions, identifying this assumption of the symbolic for the real in new media, still come through in the floods of letters on film, and now TV, characters. In the Thirties Fredric March played so many drunks on screen that his wife (Florence Eldridge) was inundated with letters of sympathy from wives married to alcoholics: Edward G. Robinson was once given an especial reception by gangsters in Chicago. When Clark Gable showed in *It Happened One Night* that he scorned to wear an undershirt the men's underwear industry declined 50%. George Sanders's *Memoirs of a Professional Cad* relates many instances of this sort of misevaluation, more seriously studied in Henry James's story "The Real Thing." It occurs with the stage, too, and of course with TV. "Grandpa Hughes" received two tons of mail in the care of CBS on his seventieth "birthday," though the actor portraying him on the television show, Santos Ortega, was in his fifties at the time. Film will, however, always be notably pretentious in this regard, its claim on so many senses threatening to engulf that psychical distance which has nearly always been applied to written work and that is essential to an understanding of it. When, at the end of her moving concentration-camp memories, the British spy "Odette" Churchill was taken out to be, as she thought, shot in a field, she could not help seeing the scene in terms of cinema:

> The whole *mise-en-scène*—the wood, the bonfire, the napkin, the cherries and the guardian carloads of SS waiting in the crumbling Reich on their master's pleasure—belonged to the realms of Dr. Caligari.

The English critic Dilys Powell has written glowingly, throughout her long and distinguished career, on John Wayne as an actor while obviously, herself a Bloomsbury liberal, detesting him as a politician. Similarly, in *Movies in America*, William Kuhns tells us: "One night recently I watched as a friend, a staunch pacifist, cheered John

Wayne on as the Duke slaughtered platoons of Japanese in *Sands of Iwo Jima.*" The dissociation or, indeed, disruption of sensibility here undoubtedly attains the proportions of serious psychological distortion. Vichy-French propaganda films, such as *The Stranger in the House* (1942) made from a Simenon story, were watched contentedly in England after the second World War despite the fact that they issued from Goebbels's Continentale company and were made by directors in prison for collaboration. They actively justified Nazism.

Cinema's contribution to such misevaluations has surely been considerable. In *New Writing in Europe* (1940) John Lehmann made the following astonishing confession regarding the efficacy of his generation as political barometer:

> I think it is hardly an exaggeration to say that the arrival of the great Soviet films of the "epic" period in London, films such as *Mother, The General Line, Storm over Asia, Earth,* was an event which had a decisive formative influence on the minds of the most alert of the new generation.

Were they alert? For Stephen Spender's essay in *The God That Failed* reiterates precisely this romantic excitement, his list being *"Earth, Potemkin, Mother, Turksib, Ten Days That Shook the World, The Way into Life."* Before entirely ridiculing this thirtyish infatuation, however, it should be remembered that many of these films were not, at the time, licensed for public showing by the British Board of Film Censors. That they had the attraction of taboo and were sneaked into cinemas like the London Rialto under sundry certificates was certainly the case. I first saw *Mother* in London in company with a school friend on the understanding of its publicity—that since it was in some way forbidden it had to be sexy (and how supremely boring, and probably bad, was *Ecstasy* in return for about twenty seconds of Hedy Lamarr's backside). To see *Mother* my friend and I slunk past the cashier trying to look like adults, dozed throughout, and walked away with pounding pulses past any policemen in the streets around. *Eheu fugaces.* . . .

So part of the power of this "presence" of cinema is clearly psychological. The novel was written in a room alone by one who addressed another reading the result in a room alone. The Victorian family evening reading hour was exceptional and, indeed, an attempt by the paterfamilias to keep some control over the crescent fantasy life of his offspring, as Mrs. Western had tried over Sophia. Dickens's public readings were equally exceptional, pure theatre when they were not, apparently, circus.

In the cinema the viewer came to sit isolated, comfortable, warm, *in the dark,* far more on his own than in the theatre (bursting into light and conviviality at intermissions) or, needless to say, TV today. Thus, the film is psychologically far closer to a dream than almost any other art form. Its handling of time alone evinces this. Inaction is much less tolerated than on the stage or, for that matter, in real life. Film's liberty with time is total and can be both pleasing (as a source of relief from an element that constricts us) and frightening (as chaos when divorced from its usual unity). Cinema makes an all-out assault on the way in which we structure ourselves temporally. And it was guided into this by fiction, rather than drama.

If cinema is a waking dream, it evokes identifications with an immediacy and intensity that threaten us very deeply. The form of a novel is internal, inside its own content as it were, and thereby throws up a defence against the fears and anxieties its subject matter arouses. For Robert Gorham Davis fictional form achieves this most clearly by "the way it returns upon itself instead of merging with the world outside." In cinema the line between our own psychic life and that of the characters on the screen is less clearly drawn, and in poor hands it breaks down altogether—resulting in those bombings or nijackings that annually take place after some individual has seen a film about bombing or hijacking. The spirit of play has not been understood, and like furious children such viewers could not subconsciously brook the symbolic in such representations. They had to take their revenge on life. Some even shoot their TV sets.

It is perhaps for this very reason—film's hold on several of our senses simultaneously—that cinema has been able to afford a plethora of conventions, and probably will continue to be able to. In this it rivals a scene in opera, watched through an inexistent fourth wall with stylised motions and everyone singing. All art is naturally seen through its conventions—those of ballet, with its rhetoric of dance notation, being particularly stylised—but we never "see" anyone as closely as we do in cinema.

In seeing cinema we allow, or certainly used to allow, an invisible orchestra behind a park bench or a six-gun to fire twenty rounds without reloading (one convention explicitly corrected in *High Noon*), not to mention characters packing cases in seconds and drinking so much scotch that in real life they would be unable to stand—to say nothing, also, of hitting other characters with objects that would hospitalise any normal human being for life. We allow this because of our five senses two, the visual and auditory, are so assaulted that the others are deadened, "auto-amputated" in the phraseology of Jonas and Selye who observed that the nervous system protects itself, in this way, from "superstimulation." Edgar had said the same in *King Lear*,

Why then, your other senses grow imperfect
By your eyes' anguish. . . .

Under the superstimulation of cinema we pardon the grossest of deceptions. Even the initial unit of perception in film, the notorious "frame,"* is a fraud. Ernst Gombrich,

---

* The term is, equally notoriously, elastic. It is here used as the image on a rectangular strip of celluloid, the equivalent, in fact, of a still photograph. Under projection the strip of celluloid yields a moving image on a screen which is also sometimes referred to as a "frame."

Rudolf Arnheim and dozens of other aestheticians have informed us of this photographic artificiality, one intensified with the wide screen which for a while threatened to present life seen through the shutter of a tank or the periscope of a submarine. The frame is simply not the way we pass information from eye to brain. Furthermore, we are not limited in life to a *sequence* of frames. The human body is gifted with a degree of what is called "continuous vision" (a horse has much more). As Arnheim says:

> It is utterly false for certain theorists, and some practitioners, of the motion picture to assert that the circumscribed picture on the screen is an image of our circumscribed view in real life. That is poor psychology. The limitations of a film picture and the limitations of sight cannot be compared because in the actual range of human vision the limitation simply does not exist. The field of vision is in practice unlimited and infinite. A whole room may be taken as a continuous field of vision, although our eyes cannot survey this room from a single position, for when we are looking at anything our gaze is not fixed but moving. Because our head and eyes move we visualize the entire room as an unbroken whole.

The only way we could "see" as a film camera sees would be, in the ingenious suggestion of Stanley Solomon, to "close our eyes, turn our head, open our eyes, close them, turn our head, etc." We do not do this, however, unless we are mad.

As instanced above, art has occasionally toyed with such distortions, physiological in origin: Degas's steep perspectives and cut-off figures have now been shown to be indebted as much to the *ukiyo-e* prints of Hokusai as to the camera, for all such tricks are at base artificial concentrations of attention. Since our eyes do not behave in the manner of a camera shutter, the film's frame is axiomatically a selection. Every monocular camera must select more than does the human eye and in this respect it has been instructive to watch the decline and ultimate demise of *Life* magazine in front of American television; the latter simply selected, or cut up, life before *Life* did, whereupon the latter came to seem a somewhat tame duplication, which it certainly was not in, say, the Forties.

Thus, in every way the very artificiality of film tends to make it psychologically irresistible, calling on the deepest resources of form on the part of directors and considerable maturity on the part of viewers watching repressed emotions let loose, if not actually running amok. It is perfectly possible to discuss and examine a film afterwards (if without it in front of one), but the superstimulation of the mode brushes aside at the time that reflection and criticism which were, from the first, a *sine qua non* of the novel.

It is not only that film hits so many senses at once and can move spatially and temporally so fast. The theatre can participate in part of this, and in *Film As Art* Arnheim was rightly at pains to refute as valid cinematurgy "effects that are also possible on the stage." It is that, in a great film, the director is making a personal impact. Kubrick's worst film to date was *Lolita* in which, with an even greater artist, in the form of the book's author, looking over one shoulder, he failed to transmit this contact; the point of view of his Humbert Humbert was far more diffused in the film than it was in the novel, though in his early *The Killing* Kubrick had shown his gift for powerful personal impact. In *A Clockwork Orange* he was even more intense. The good director must give you the feeling that he is speaking to you directly, not showing you images or tricks and, above all, not looking at you as a crowd. The psychology of cinema lies in this, as it lay at the core of Franklin Roosevelt's appeal. To look at the viewer as a crowd has been the bane of cinema, and, roughly translated, comes out as the old front-office *cliché*, "No one ever lost any money underestimating the taste of the American public." At worst, the attitude leads to that literalism with which the word Hollywood has so long been associated, and reminds us, at best, that von Sternberg wrote, "verisimilitude, whatever its virtue, is in opposition to every approach to art."

It is when we push film into fact that we can see how it affects us with fiction. It is clear that vicarious participation in any art form relieves our tensions: we understand a situation presented to us, live through it, and liquidate our anxieties by the end. Hence that sense of sober exhilaration with which one emerges from the bloodiest of Shakespearean tragedies. On the most obvious level this Aristotelian catharsis is expressed in the western or detective film; problems are reduced to the simplicity of a child's colouring-book and are resolved by a good right hook, or bullet in the belly. We are calmed. We have watched from a comfortable distance, munching chocolate and holding hands, and we are reassured that the villain, whatever else he may be, is not us.

In what I have elsewhere called "thesis cinema," however, this self-forgiveness is no longer, or less, possible. We have to accept the responsibility of the fictive act in a far deeper way. As a matter of fact, *Hamlet* is so disturbing, and great, because it unleashes so many forbidden impulses and aggressions that we customarily shunt from sight, and still manages to confront and recognise and finally unify them. It is said that a jealous husband finds it too painful altogether to see a good *Othello;* certainly I would wager that anyone who has been in prison incommunicado for any length of time would find Nanni Loy's *Why* a harrowing experience. Here, in cases like these brought almost unbearably close to us, the commission of the crime is too much ours. Dilys Powell observed at the time that we have a right to know if the conditions of capital punishment in France are really such as Spaak depicts in *Nous sommes tous des Assassins,* with officials tip-toeing down prison corridors to pounce on unsuspecting death-cell victims and drag them screaming to the guillotine. *Why* has a similar Zolaesque *j'accuse* in its ending—can men really be held for months and years without seeing a lawyer or hearing the charge against them in an Italy of 1972?

It was Lucretius who first noticeably observed that watching others knocked around, seeing a shipwreck from safe land, confers on the viewer a spurious sense of escape, and thus superiority. The child watches TV mayhem from a comfortable armchair with a cup in one hand. If the ego establishes control too easily (as in pollyanna fiction and film alike), reality is lost, it just does not happen that simply in our lives. Hence the "escape" syndrome (generally postulated about mystery stories) and hence David Riesman's point that an easy safety-valve effect of this sort makes us more willing to accept the going harness of a given culture.

The semi-factual film does not falsify issues, indeed it harshens them; the happy ending sidesteps reality and while some stage drama has also told us we are guilty rather than innocent (notably Ibsen, Antoine's *théâtre libre,* of a century ago), the film has had particular power to persuade us that we are, indeed, all assassins—another way of putting Otto Fenichel's comment on great tragedy, that "actor and audience feel, 'We do it together.'" In *The Philosophy of Literary Form* Kenneth Burke put this "law" of covert participation, under which we escape the laws of the real world (sex, time, age), and so acquire exceptional understanding, as follows:

> A tragedy is not profound unless the poet *imagines* the crime—and in thus imagining it, he symbolically commits it. Similarly, in so far as the audience participates in the imaginings, it also participates in the offense.

The thesis film, situated somewhere between documentaries like *The Sorrow and the Pity, Millhouse,* the pop rock rubbish already mentioned, and sophisticated cinema, disallows catharsis. Empathy, identification with the central character, here causes the reverse effect, intensifies anxiety rather than relief, since the hero or heroine is usually an agent of chaos (in common, of course, with Hamlet, Lear, Anna Karenina, Raskolnikov and other intellectual outcasts). Moreover, the filmic form does not so apparently wind back on itself. There is a pattern in such films, but they do not visibly hold disorder at bay.

These generalisations are exemplified in the Spaak/Clouzot/Cayatte films of the Fifties, ignored and probably little-known today. Born in 1903, the son of a theatrical producer and brother of a celebrated Belgian statesman-to-be, Charles Spaak wrote a number of films in this mode after the war, co-directing most of them with either Henri-Georges Clouzot or André Cayatte. At least four of these were exceptional: *Retour à la vie* (where the brief episode dealing with Girard, played by Louis Jouvet, was written by Clouzot), *Justice est faite, Nous sommes tous des Assassins,* and *Avant le Déluge.* All received "X" certificates in England at the time, and were mutilated—lacerated—before showing in America. The main problems dealt with were capital punishment, chauvinism, anti-Semitism, juvenile delinquency. The films were so prescient that it is small surprise to find no one running them again today, when Spaak's mantle in this respect has fallen on Costa-Gavras; the latter has made even more black-and-white thesis films, though leavening them with occasional comic elements (the *opéra-bouffe* exits and entrances of the generals in *Z* or the loud-speaker section in the—extremely grim—university raid in *State of Siege*). The tradition of such films is here strongly continued, however, notably the convention of nearly all the young revolutionaries, especially the girls, looking extremely attractive, and intelligent, and being atypically efficient.

Presumably, the nadir of such cinema is to be found in the Russia of Zhdanov's cultural commissarship. To produce, often literally at pistol-point, a monthly series of morale films entitled *Victory Will Be Ours* could be calculated to turn even the most optimistic person into an "agent of the opposition." Though Eisenstein's *Ivan the Terrible* rode roughshod over historical fact, showing autocratic Ivan as a genially progressive ruler, it was visually interesting; but Eisenstein's subsequent attempt to rid himself of the Party man-on-his-back in a sequel is pathetic. It was banned and, despite a cringing confession of "ideological errors," Eisenstein never lived to complete it. Nor did Mayakovski ever produce a memorable script, falling back for one of his best on an American fiction, Jack London's simplistic "Martin Eden."

Here the inefficiency was all. The famous ice battle in *Alexander Nevsky* had to be shot on artificial ice (in Russia of all places) in July, simply because the Kremlin suddenly decided that this "movie factory" had to show a triumphant defeat of its schedule date. A notebook kept at the Lenfilm studio in 1936 reads like a skit by Waugh: "Filming of the picture *Peter the Great* was stopped because of the cold in the studio. Actor Cherkasov refused to be filmed wearing only a shirt . . . Sound recording for *The Youth of the Poet* was delayed four hours because the roof leaked . . . It is discovered that an actor is holding a different script today. A search begins for yesterday's script . . . At the booth there are always dramatic scenes, for there is only one booth, while there are many directors."

What Lenin once called "the most important of all the arts for us" turns into a travesty when statistical charts of ethnic nationality of villains are consulted and the images implanted on unsuspecting minds are seen for the fraudulence they are, Sovkino for long serving up a monotonous diet of British characters in the guise of drunken savages torturing children with regularity, to the tune of many Stalin Prizes.

Even grossly loaded, however, the thesis cinema teaches one a lesson in how indexical or phenomenological realism can swamp the viewer. Psychologically, it could be said that in a novel you control the medium; but film controls you. When, at the start of *Avant le Déluge* (written and co-directed by Spaak), the camera pans from the *tricolore* waving bravely over the Palais de Justice in Paris to a harshly modern enamel plate below it marked "Place d'Arrêt," the whole thesis of this film and many others from the Clouzot-Cayatte stable has been presented, namely that we are all assassins and justice is never done. The contrast between the happy, patriotic engineer Di Noi, in *Why,* chanting poetry as he re-enters Italy, and the same character squatting on the privy of a brutally dismal prison cell some minutes later is extreme, and extremely slanted; on the stage (as even in good Gorki) it would look absurd. But cinema can get away with it since it appears generally, in its better forms, to take man seriously and engrosses us quickly in his actions. Also, it is far less artificial than a play; the viewer starts by assuming that the images he sees are so many facts.

What we learn from this cinema is the power of visual affect in principally ideological subject-matter. Each of Spaak's films made at this time contend, point by point, the arguments against their own ' thesis. In *Retour à la vie,* lineally linked with *La grande Illusion,* Franco-German relations are studied through five individuals making a post-war return to "life" in France, among them the principal Louis (well acted by Serge Reggiani) coming back with his German Elsa. In *Justice est faite* we identify with seven jurors, involved in deciding the guilt of Elsa Lundenstein (Claude Nollier) who has killed her cancer-ridden lover-employer out of mercy. In *Nous sommes tous des Assassins* we identify in turn with five potential victims of the guillotine; in *Avant le Déluge* with the parents of five guilty adolescents.

In work like this we find that though form is there, and shows human happenings as consequences, it simply does not control content for us enough, nor try to. The accusation is everywhere in the air, as it was in the open end of *Bovary* or much Zola. At the same time, a film director can employ a sensory language of objects that enormously advantages him as polemicist. We do not normally look at objects as indexical and we cannot really do so when seeing a stage drama. Roland Barthes has written about "a kind of natural *being-there* of the object" in film, and we shall examine how objects are very much "there" in *Marienbad*. Flaherty, Murnau, von Stroheim, certainly the Welles of *Kane,* had all astutely realised the connotative power of concentration. Objects could become so many little Schopenhauerian emblems, as idiosyncratic and sometimes malicious as in a true dream. As Erwin Panofsky put it, "A checkered table-cloth meant, once for all, a 'poor but honest' milieu." Robbe-Grillet may have now revolted against such inherited acceptances, but Italian neo-realism after the war strongly supported them. André Bazin, one of the highly esteemed founders of *Cahiers du Cinéma,* saw this imagery as film's essence, much admiring *Bicycle Thieves*—"Things are there," said Rossellini, "why manipulate them?" Alberto Moravia has, in long fiction, moved away from psychological inspection of character states to the indexical aspects of the world as it is at certain moments, in certain places, and his *Two Women* was able to be translated fairly directly into film as a consequence, while his earlier *The Conformist* required considerable restructuring to be viable. A secondary world had to be constructed by the director.

There are even those who feel that this ability to invest the icon with expressive power links Godard (presumably the Godard of *La Chinoise*) with Lumière and Méliès in some form of more or less direct ancestry. Surely an arty claim. For all objects are signs. They tell us, as Gaston Bachelard has noted, more about ourselves than we about them. Wall Street is a sign hung over a certain defined expanse of asphalt; it is either Wall Street or Stone Street or Broad Street. But if a society chooses to symbolise something called "Wall Street" as an aspect of its financial activities, which another society likes to collect under the term "running dogs of the imperialists" and "wicked hyenas" and suchlike, we are into the realm of culturally-coded symbols. The Christian cross is presumably meaningless in most of China. Still and all, the film director can be seen to be working in what Peter Wollen calls "the most semiologically complex of all media," one that is therefore the most immediately overpowering. A true sign must both reveal and conceal, as Carlyle said. Cinema's does this.

The *roman-à-thèse* must be ready—and the reader knows it must be ready—to meet specific factual criticism on paper. Zola met it on paper, frequently, but the screen is different. It is in a sense a bigger and, for a while, a more hypnotic mesmerist—or liar. "André Cayatte is not fair," David Fisher wrote in *Sight and Sound,* adding, "And for that reason I personally welcome him as a new and interesting personality in the cinema." The lesson of the importance of affective iconic accompaniment to a verbal thesis may be learnt by seeing not merely the Spaak/Cayatte canon but thesis films which are deficient in visual support of often burning critiques, e.g. *Gentlemen's Agreement* or the far better, if equally slackly thought-through, *The Best Years of Our Lives.* Buñuel's chief thesis film was *Los Olvidados,* a highly sentimental piece more concerned with cinematic mannerisms than with people, bolstered by much fashionable nastiness comparable, in painting, to the (fast-vanishing) work of Soutine. Unfortunately this sort of film is just what a philistine TV audience is looking for as an excuse for not taking cinema seriously. Spaak carefully avoided the pitfalls of glib surrealism, which might let his viewers off the hook. This is defined by imitations of him of the era, like *L'Âge de l'amour* (written by Carlo Rim and co-directed with Lionello de Felice). The faceted cubism of Spaak's writing in *Avant le Déluge* depends, in any case, strongly on fiction, yet its achieved intention is really non-fiction; whereas a film like Kazan's *On the Waterfront*, though ostensibly concerned with social reform, is equally concerned to entertain and therefore pacify more—we take less of it out into the world with us than from *Why*.

In *Avant le Déluge* the corruption of a homosexual relationship by social norms is more than reminiscent of the first two seminal volumes of Roger Martin du Gard's *Les Thibault*. Spaak transposes the problem to a society on the verge of a Third World War, with a World Citizen Professor perpetually engaged in barren argument with his Communist son. Here a mutinously calm Marina Vlady plays the part of a sensual, unquestioning adolescent, a Moravian innocent who gives a ring to swell the funds for escape to a desert island (when in reality she has to give herself), who confuses the daily papers she must bring with the breakfast bread (*Figaro* in front of her World Citizen father, *Humanité* before her Communist brother), and who eventually muddles up the final political intrigue while being quite sure of herself in love. There is one delightful scene in which, lacking cash to buy herself new clothes, she appears in a dress cut entirely from copies of *Humanité*, to the fury of her brother who needed the newspaper for more of his fanatical political research. It should be said that Spaak's effects are probably augmented by the small band of players he employed; in common with Bergman he used again and again the same excellent team, including Noël Roquevert, Jean Brochart, and Bernard Blier.

In short, film gives dream a factitious coherence. In a sense it is unfair: it thrives off illicit arousals and taxes us with imagistic disjunctions of them. For instance, we believe more deeply in the shower-murder of Janet Leigh in *Psycho* in the way Hitchcock presented it (as a jangled, jumbled montage) than if it had been presented straight, through the eye of a fixed camera in the roof, for instance. We are hypnotised, mesmerised in a narcissistic way—in fact, in the manner of McLuhan's "narcissus-narcosis." The images are us. This is the contemporary group hypnosis criticised in Thomas Mann's *Mario and the Magician.*

Fiction is a secondary world which helps us to enjoy what Freud called "substitute gratification" and so satisfy desires and reduce tensions. Great films also absorb tensions but they do not require the same kind of participation. In reading a novel we must translate a symbol on a printed page; in a film people and things pass before our gaze as literally as they do in the primary world. Hence, fiction can allay anxieties and desires because it requires an active mental effort of engagement. Simon Lesser, in his *Fiction and the Unconscious,* hypothesises that no one in a strong state of sexual desire feels like settling down to an evening with a book. Much depends on the character of the work, but in general Lesser's observations hold:

> Even when one is somewhat disturbed, one may be able to become absorbed in a movie or a fast-moving thriller but not, let us say, in a typical nineteenth-century English novel. When anxiety or instinctual pressure becomes too urgent, however, no form of fiction is likely to engage or hold one's interest. *A certain degree of freedom from anxiety and instinctual pressure is necessary before one is likely to want to read or can enjoy reading.* (Original italics)

Film's illusion does not always make this competition with another area of discourse; that is to say, its images are not asking to be translated into words. In this respect it is a "hot" medium, in McLuhanese, whereas language is cool and one can walk around in it. Language nearly always takes one beyond language—pornography, which creates a physical crescendo (as Nabokov realised in his Epilogue to *Lolita*), is about the nearest to a point where it does not— but film requires no "translation," at least not in the sense of into some discretely discernible significance. This is no mere House-of-Lords way of saying that literature requires the imagination to work, whereas film does the imagining for the spectator; it is not quite as simple as that. In the cinema the participation in the offence that Burke mentions is obviously far more immediately intense; we are genuine accomplices, and often want someone to succeed with a theft. Hitchcock's *Marnie* traded on this, as did the fine Joseph Cotten vehicle *The Steel Trap* where the bank robbery made tremendous illicit appeals, insupportable in real life. The point of pursuing thesis cinema here has been to show that in this kind of non-fictive imagery the spectator truly suffers. I left *Why* seriously wondering how wise it would be to drive into Italy again, as I so often have, through the Aosta border station indicted on the screen.

A daily newspaper would have to defend the authenticity of loaded criticism like this in print. We are given much less shield in cinema. Like Nagisa Oshima's *Death by Hanging*, Spaak's *Nous sommes tous des Assassins* dramatises execution techniques without pity, and makes us closely wonder, as we leave the cinema, whether it is worse to know the date of one's execution rather than to be kept in ignorance of it. Hollywood may be what Hortense Powdermaker called "the dream-factory," but in the cinema of social reform no strong *id* is established to allay our fears, and the form which should hold at bay the content, inform it with a pattern, is found to be that of real life. The Spaak-Cayatte canon is peppered with specific newspaper headlines, which we can all recognise as "true." The Korean war wends its well-known way. The Communist *Humanité* is directly challenged. At one point, in *Avant le Déluge*, Spaak has a worried father pick up two violent murder-mystery novels, in which life is taken cheaply, in his daughter's bedroom; with their slick identifications with sheer power the two are precisely calculated to corrupt youth—Mickey Spillane's *I, the Jury* and Boris Vian's American fabrication *J'irais cracher sur vos Tombes*.

Yet this "faction," if we may purloin a term coined by

Dr. Desmond Flower, is offered as cognate with grossly loaded imagery: judges delivering death sentences with coarsely concealed relish, caricatural Nazi officers—though it must be admitted that real Nazi officers appear to have acted as cinema caricatures at times, and the shot of Le Guen, in *Assassins,* disposing of a Nazi's body in a barrel-organ leaking blood, loving splash by splash, is both desperately thrilling and persuasively Germanophobic. We do not have to have weak egos to fear such fantasy. Spaak so passionately nails his intellectual points into reality that we may not awaken from this dream as we leave the cinema. At the end of *Avant le Déluge* the mother of one of the victims is seen walking away forlornly in search of a taxi, the camera shooting her through the prison-like railings around the Palais de Justice. We know that the Korean peace has been signed, yet the newspaper-sellers are plucking copies of *France-Soir* off their stands to the cries of "GUERRE DE PETROLE!" War is everywhere. We are in a sense all in prison.

Here we reach, therefore, a borderline between fiction and fact in both forms; films like *The French Connection, To Die of Love,* and *State of Siege* were based on real incidents, the first on the smuggling of heroin into the United States and the second on the case of a French *lycée* teacher, Gabrielle Russier, who fell in love with one of her students and later killed herself after contemptible official persecution. These films visually simplified their original stories so much that the viewer was allowed to slip off the hook. It was impossible to have a car chase under an elevated subway in New York with such impunity as depicted in the conveniently empty streets of *The French Connection*—ergo, belief in the whole matter was eroded. Of *To Die of Love* Robert Brown wrote: "The printed word had led me much more deeply into all this, told me more about the passions and the laws involved than the images on the screen." True thesis cinema must be an illumination, not simply an illustration; its lessons must arise from its images, it is at its best a form of inspired sociology.

By looking into the unsparing mirror that thesis cinema holds up we can come full circle to the realisation that usually cinema *does* let us off the hook. The dreams that it manufactures relax the ego, invite us to let go, concertina time, present easy vicarious participations, and then send us into the street with some form of control, often extremely spurious, and therefore fragile, established over our dammed-up instinctual demands. It has frequently been pointed out that the Nineteenth-century reading hour was the evening, in a darkened drawing room, near a fire; under such comfortable conditions children could attend closely and enjoy imaginatively. This drowsy period before bedtime, on a full stomach, was ideal for story-telling, Padraic Colum reminds us, adding: "A rhythm that was compulsive, fitted to daily tasks, waned, and a rhythm that was acquiescent, fitted to wishes, took its place." Similar fantasy formation is duplicated today by television, in front of which sit pyjamaed tots sipping cocoa and munching biscuits. Still greater privacy and quicker dream-manufacture are encouraged, with even less effort, in the cinema where, in Ivor Montagu's words, the viewer "has only to sit back, relax, revel in the warmth, the music, the upholstery, the focus of attention out of dimness into a wavering bright light in the centre—all particularly conducive to submission to Svengali. . . ." At Oxford Gerard Manley Hopkins recorded in one of his Notebooks, "Not to sit in armchair except can work no other way."

It is surely a platitude by now to point out that if you arouse subconscious mayhem and impose no pattern on it at all, let alone some sort of ego control, you will give a very false dream indeed. The imaginary world must be more real than the real world for it to be credited. Even children, Simon Lesser tells us, disavow or grow tired of sheer stretches of uncontrolled gratification of pleasure and "are dissatisfied when these effects are attained at the expense of the reality principle" (it has even been suggested that the regularity of the commercial-break on American TV helps to form some of the formlessness for them). The laborious studies conducted by Dr. Martha Wolfenstein show that as people achieve sophistication and maturity, so they eschew the conventional "happy ending" of pollyanna films and fiction alike, which sidestep reality and try to assure us of our innocence. It is instructive to watch audiences emerging from cinema auditoria: if the film has been some slick, sunny fable their faces have simply been washed over with images and adjust fairly easily to street life—no real psychic transformation has been effected; those coming from deeply-engrossing, artistic works, on the other hand, appear more like somnambulists—at such moments the outside world seems unusually dreary and some minutes of adjustment to it may be necessary.

It is in this sense that Norman Mailer has called the cinema a religious experience: "When the religious enter a church, they feel a sense of relaxation and of death which is equivalent to the way movie-lovers feel when they enter a movie house. There's that same sense of relaxation and of death as the deeper parts of their psyches are engaged." Mailer's comparison is suggestive; who, in those seconds before an impending car-crash, has not inwardly felt, *But this is like a bad film?* "Film," Mailer added, "may be a natural psychic state comparable to memory, to sex, to dream, or to death."

Realism is supposed to be the restraining rein on fantasy —in daily life we do not satisfy our desires—yet when reality has run amok, as on the streets of a city like New York today, we are compelled to try to contain these elements within us, to be both victim and executioner, as in Baudelaire's terms of the event. Society does not help; so the best cinema makes us work. To form coherence from rapid disunity involves us in a patterning activity, makes us make ourselves see that happenings are consequences. Laughter is a short-cut response to containing unbearable anxieties, and the great film comedians like Chaplin, Keaton, and the Marx Brothers have used humour in this way. Nervous titters at moments of incest, or even vampirism, represent this form of attempted inoculation on the part of an unsophisticated audience. Teenagers roared with laughter through *The Exorcist*. Yet even among the sophisticated it takes place. My wife worked on the translation of Sheridan Le Fanu's *Uncle Silas* (1864) into film, Jean Simmons's first starring picture; at the première there was laughter at the wrong moments though a large number of those watching had seen and participated in some way in the construction of the individual units of which the total was made. Canned laughter is sometimes used this way in TV, to syphon off psychic danger. All the same, we surely play in such cases a fairly spurious id; the sense of control over the so direct imagistic experience vanishes more rapidly than is the case when reading a novel over a stretch of two weeks or more. Accordingly, the identifications we make may be significantly shallow.

Empathy is simply not an aesthetic norm. I do not empathise—experience "self-recognition"—when reading *The Brothers Karamazov*, or *Lear* or *Hamlet* for that matter. Yet my satisfaction is at the titanic release of life at full flood depicted. Vast emotions, excessive situations, gigantic characters are here spilt out before us in such works and for a while make us feel fearful, certainly puny. But the understanding of them, their very portrayal, the awareness of their implications, is a formal resource. We have faced ourselves—been made to do so—and thus for a second have become slightly less vulnerable, slightly less frail. The other end, indeed the reverse, of this spectrum is to show Sainte Bernadette as the girl-next-door on screen; this was the form in Hollywood historicals for a long time. Self-recogni-

tion is an easy enough device, but when the girl-next-door
is in every way implementing the directives of something
like *Screw* magazine all you have done is to intensify the
going anxieties, in the manner of much advertising which
also pretends to allay them. Furthermore, it is the contention of Pauline Kael, in *I Lost It at the Movies,* that the
wish-fulfillment of the old mass audience shares many prop-
ties with the attitude of the liberal intelligentsia before so-
called sophisticated cinema today: "The 'mass' audience
looks up at the 'stars'; the educated audience looks down
sympathetically, as if reading a case history. They all stew
in their own narcissism." Viewing *Hiroshima mon amour* in
New York Miss Kael seemed surprised: "Here was the audience soaking it up—audiences of social workers, scientists,
doctors, architects, professors—living and loving and suffering just like the stenographer watching Susan Hayward."

It is certainly true that the great studies of Gothic romance show such fiction paying court to its public in the
manner of today's TV. Adulterers (even blasphemers) were
punished then as now, while a continual erithistic titillation
proceeded apace in the background, and not always only
there. Escapist fantasy that is a sop of this sort, as was the
worst of Gothic fiction and as is the worst of "Hollywood,"
still cannot help but be a corroboration of the ruling ethic,
a form of assent. Here like elderly infants we turn to such
fantasy for "escape"—which is no escape. President Kennedy created the James Bond boom in the U.S. because
(he confessed) there were such easy and apparent resolu-
tions within Fleming's fiction, and he was himself a man
perplexed by multi-valued problems, many apparently in-
soluble. Let one at least be solved by a left hook.

So we see our enemies punished and the world re-
ordered, in both fiction and film. We confirm hardened attitudes, we secure impossible, illicit, or frankly inhibited desires. We dissolve, as Aristotle proposed, unbearable and
unpleasant emotions. We daydream, we are forgiven—so

goes the argument. The most perverse form of longings (including a woman copulating artistically with a dog, in one celebrated and little-seen Swedish film) are permitted to be explored and, by extension, to be anaesthetised, to be deemed innocent. "The cinema," said Jung, "makes it possible to experience without danger all the excitement, passion and desirousness which must be repressed in a humanitarian ordering of life." Of what life? Much of contemporary America is running make-believe. Mere identifications cannot cope with it. Its life is so intense that something like cinema has to swell its play of fantasy inordinately. Reciprocally, the policeman of the intellect, the straitjacket of Apollo, requires great energy for resurrection, under the grave of taboo. The objects of aversion (to reverse Freud) become objects of veneration. A pursuit-of-pleasure capitalism can legitimatise nearly all illicit impulses. The cosmetics industry stirs up as many desires as *Screw* (which is, by comparison, often closer to a gynaecological text). The American stage of late has celebrated the indictment of an incumbent President for political assassination, openly advocated homosexuality, lesbianism, nudism, necrophilia, and bestiality. In one famous, and remarkably realistic, instance a boy had his entrails pulled out by courtesy of the Ford-funded American Place Theatre. *Animal Lover,* a film showing a girl coupling with a pig, among other animals, ran for months in New York in 1974 and was even brought back to the theatre "by popular demand." What would de Sade have thought of the Formentor Award being given to a novel replete with pony-girl fantasies, a Guggenheim to one whose latest play contained "sodomy performed on stage," or to the exhibition, at about the same time, of "sculptured" excrement on display in a plush Manhattan art gallery, to be greeted by mere yawns from the *New York Times* ("These aggregations of colonic calligraphy contain many formal excellences . . . ")? In 1965 Supreme Court Justice Douglas decided, "I would put an end to all forms and types of censorship and give full literal meaning to the command of the First Amendment."

In cinema the ordering of these demons of our psyche requires an especial degree of psychic energy since the "shield" is so thin. Not only is the communicative act highly direct, unlike its impingement in, say, a lengthy Proustian novel, but the suggestivity of the medium lets loose all sorts of unsuspected devils. In film anything can happen, and probably will. Its limits are more the possible than the probable, and in daily life we act by the latter, or else go insane. By superstimulation, by immediacy and instant acceptability, film undoes our repressions. For a moment we surmount the limitations of life: we live as a woman, a Black, a child, a crone, even as a dog (Jules Romains and Rudyard Kipling among others anticipating). For a while we forget our local determinations, to races, sexes, ages, jobs, towns, countries. We even forget that we all have to die and must all at some time, like Tolstoy's Ivan Ilych, become involved with the anguish of this knowledge.

In cinema a pitched battle of the human consciousness is played out. So it is on the stage. But there the sentinel of conscience (which is in Russian contained in the word *consciousness*) is clearly advanced by language, and its human compact. With the film we are all voyeurs. We see *images*. We can stare at every pimple and sore on a face exposed before us, and this spurious or pseudo-"identification" (we all have faces, after all) reassures us, increases our Lucretian sense of safety. "Seeing safely is, in part, seeing without being seen," writes V. F. Perkins. "We attain faceless anonymity, a sort of public privacy."

THE HOUSE OF USHER (1960)

Film has been notoriously unsuccessful in dealing with fictions of inner states. Writers like Poe and Conrad are essentially internal; yet both have drawn directors like magnets since there is usually, in each, a tempting degree of external action. Or so it seems.

Seven versions of various Conrad fictions had reached the screen by the start of talkies; and, despite a bold attempt at restructuring *The Secret Agent** by Hitchcock, the only considerable film made of the whole Conrad *oeuvre* up to the Second World War, and perhaps even to our own day, was Marc Allegret's 1936 *Razumov* (from *Under Western Eyes*), in which André Gide had a hand. Griffith made a film called *Edgar Allan Poe* in 1909 and in his *The Avenging Conscience,* later, incorporated material from several Poe stories, including *William Wilson. The Fall of the House of Usher* has been attempted, to my knowledge, four times. Perhaps more. Rather than considering the expressionist versions of silent days, Roger Corman's characteris-

---

* Not to be confused with the 1936 British film of this name, also directed by Hitchcock but based on Maugham's *Ashenden.*

156

tic Vincent Price vehicle of 1960, a perennial on late-night
TV, will be examined here since it points up essential difficulties in the psychology of cinema. Furthermore, it usefully adheres to the story. This is more than can be said
for much Corman Poe: *The Haunted Palace,* starring Lon
Chaney Jr., takes its title from the poem in *Usher,* yet has
but tangential reference to Poe.

The Fall of the House of Usher was first published in
Burton's Gentleman's Magazine for September 1839. *William Wilson* appeared there the next month, *The Man of
the Crowd* coming out in the same journal in December
1840. The Dupin stories appeared the next year. Poe's tales
"of conscience" were turning into tales "of ratiocination."
He himself was living in some poverty at this time, as an
underpaid assistant editor to the Philadelphia magazine
publishing him, his main emotional support coming from
his celebrated "child bride" cousin, Virginia Clemm. Why
among all these productions of a tormented time in Poe's
life has *Usher* lured director after director?

The story is a strange and exceedingly rich work in the
Gothic vein. To enter into it, however, one has to shear
aside the usual underbrush of verbal clichés, not to say
plain hokum, that makes some of Baudelaire's translations
read rather better than their originals. Aldous Huxley had
his day with the Poe cliché in a memorable article on the
poem "Ulalume." In Poe's *Ligeia* of 1838, for instance, light
falls with "a ghastly lustre," a "deadly pallor" overspreads
faces when a "livid hue" does not; Allen Tate was right to
wonder why we persist in reading Poe at all, the language
being so trite. Poe, however, is with us and in us, and films
made from his compelling little legends of the soul under
stress are favourites on the "B" circuits.

From a first glance the cinema would seem to be at an
advantage in this respect. The lush verbal style can be
avoided, the over-musical language—which Baudelaire so
admired—be rendered by . . . music. The heavy décor that

THE HOUSE OF USHER (1960, Corman): the restless Lady Madeline about to be entombed, with Vincent Price as Roderick Usher looking on at right.

seems so overdone at first reading can be duplicated to effect by a clever set decorator. Having said as much, one realises that one is left with a plot of pure *kitsch*, impossible to visualise at all realistically. An inefficiently immured lady called "the lady Madeline (for so she was called)" bursts out of her tomb (few Poe corpses being buried under the earth), breaks into her twin brother's room bleeding freely, and "with a low moaning cry" collapses on him and kills him. After which the house collapses. Having said that much, one suddenly realises that very few of these elements really engage Poe's mind at all—he could have

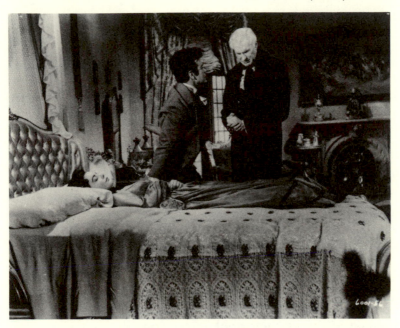

THE HOUSE OF USHER (1960, Corman): Lady Madeline on her deathbed—with Poe she had been emaciated and menacing; as Myrna Fahey plays her she is all too solid flesh.

made the plot more realistic had he wanted to—but are there to serve what he is concentrating on, namely some sort of strange symptomatology. In short, and this is why a great poet like Baudelaire could spend so much of his life translating him, the real is only there in that it is symbolic, and helps Poe to show a certain state of mind. Almost any film made from Poe's canon is going to start the other way around: the closest to the spirit of Poe's intentions I have myself seen in the cinema would be something like *Marienbad,* or perhaps *Caligari.* States of schizophrenia, like those depicted in *Images,* are obviously going to be more successful in cinema.

Poe's stories of this time are true prose poems and the Corman-Price films made from them show clearly that a prose paraphrase omits the essentials of a poem. These films were direct, "realistic" translations and sometimes unintentionally funny when the claims on our suspension of disbelief became outrageous. The only way to handle Poe literally on the screen is to make an analogy, in the manner of Malle's version, with Brigitte Bardot, of *William Wilson* (inserted into a triad of films called *Histoires extraordinaires,* the final element of which is Fellini's modern analogy to Poe's life). One way of contemporising Poe is to read these short stories as addict agonies—and the vampire was an addict, one of the undead requiring his or her "fix" of blood. The eschatology of vampirism has tempted notable addicts, such as Coleridge, Baudelaire, and Poe. An intelligent director, provided he did not spell out too much, could make a filmic analogy about drug addiction today, rooted in the psychology of vampirism.

To do this would immediately require a degree of seriousness. Bram Stoker's *Dracula* is one of the most preposterous of all vampire stories, but Murnau's 1922 adaptation, *Nosferatu,* was successful not simply for its expressionist photography but because the script writer, Henrik Galeen, created an analogous story in which he wanted to show the great power of love. Similarly, *Caligari*'s pressure derives from a story that is essentially serious—not in the sense of solemn, but artistically deep, demanding. By the end of *Caligari* a virtually balletic rhythm has been set up and when the puppet is hauled from the coffin at the end, one has become so imbued with expressionist fantasy that for a second one wonders whether Francis is meant to see it as real. Lang's *Dr. Mabuse,* which followed hard on the heels of *Caligari,* is in parts equally anarchic visually but again owes its power to a basic seriousness of intention; outside the film Lang said that he wanted to create a social document, of a world rushing to its doom.

Poe certainly gave hints of the vampire as addict, together with that infection spread from both; and it is interesting that both he and Baudelaire dramatised the vampira, or succubus, who does not make an appearance until the turn of the Nineteenth century, Southey's being one of the earliest in England, and who is quite ignored as a menace by Holy Church (as in the encyclopaedic Seventeenth-century work by Dom Calmet) until that date. *The Man of the Crowd* shows an alcohol mania, but *Usher* has to do with drugs. The Venus is, with Poe, very sick. In the Tod Browning *Dracula* of 1931 there is a scene where the infected fiancée refuses to kiss her betrothed, John, and dismisses him from her favours in a manner that summons up thoughts of that venereal infection Baudelaire apostrophised. Poe thoroughly invites the reading of such stories as case-histories of some semi-neurotic addiction. The first description of Ligeia, in the story of that name, emphasises her blood-deprived emaciation and pallor, her beauty being attributed to "the radiance of an opium-dream." The narrator is later described as "wild with the excitement of an immoderate dose of opium." *Usher* teems with such references. As the protagonist comes to the house, he feels the typical "down" of the Poe addict, that note on which *The Man of the Crowd* also specifically begins; he is possessed by "an utter depression of soul which I can compare to no earthly sensation more properly than to the after-dream of the reveller upon opium—the bitter lapse into everyday life—the hideous dropping off of the veil" (*viz.* withdrawal symptoms). On meeting his old friend Roderick again, with his customary "ghastly pallor," he is reminded of "the lost drunkard, or the irreclaimable eater of opium." A physician is encountered on the stairs—and sedulously excluded from the film. Fungi are twice mentioned as overspreading the stones of which the house is made.

The narrator, however, is not really entering a house. With its "eye-like windows" the house is Poe's mind; he is entering himself and realising that he is freaking out. The parallel is clear in "The Haunted Palace" poem inserted into the story, just after Usher seems to become conscious of "the tottering of his lofty reason." Richard Wilbur is therefore right: the story is a study of artistic consciousness (or undoing of such), Maurice Beebe adding that it derives from Poe's cosmology, as expressed in *Eureka,* one founded on alternating attractions and repulsions, so that in a sense Roderick is struggling against insanity, the total breakdown of mind. Hypnagogic states of this nature should always be avoided as the *source* of cinema; images give them too high definition. Poe's story here is constantly equivocal and keeps us off-balance since we are never certain of any reality in it; we see through the eyes of a narrator who is distinctly peculiar himself, who feels "a sensation of stupor" at his first sight of Madeline (while Roderick simply buries his head in his hands as she passes by) and who certainly hears her heartbeats as she bursts through the house at the end. Corman, for some reason, makes the narrator into the suitor for Madeline's hand, and Roderick his chief opponent to the match. This effectively kills off most of Poe at the start, since the important element of twins has to go; busty Myrna Fahey cannot possibly be presented as Vincent Price's twin sister, since she looks more like his daughter. Weak hints of incest thrown into the film merely make the confusion worse confounded. In Poe Madeline is an off-stage figure of enormous sexual potency. She fills the narrator with unaccountable "dread" when he sees her, and when he hears her coming for Roderick at the end "there sat upon my very heart an incubus of utterly causeless alarm." He is then "overpowered by an intense sentiment of horror, unaccountable yet unendurable." Mark Damon plays Philip Winthrop, Corman's narrator, like a village-idiot football player denied his girl for a Saturday date, while anyone less "emaciated" and less threatening than Myrna Fahey would be hard to imagine.

In fact, Richard Matheson's screenplay hurts its original far more than it need. The fissure in the house (which Marie Bonaparte, needless to say, saw as menacing female genitalia) led the writer to animate the whole building in a crazy revenge against Winthrop which destroys all our credulity at the start. The hyper-aesthesia Poe so knowingly delineates in Usher, his "morbid acuteness of the senses" which makes it possible for him only to wear light clothing, eat insipid foods—this is all told verbally by the suffering character (Vincent Price) in the film. The latter makes certain attempts to reproduce its original by auditory effects (the exaggeration of Madeline's scream at the end being how the hypersensitive Roderick would hear it), but the result is simply to make us more and more detached and disbelieving as the convention is infringed—Winthrop, for instance, yells at Roderick nearby without noticeable adverse affect. The screenwriter makes Madeline tell her betrothed of her brother, "He has to take drugs to sleep," but once more this spelling-out achieves nothing. Finally, the absurd butler, in a sop to a scientific culture, tells us that Usher's illness has a name, catalepsy.

To engage a mind in a fantasy something has to be left to the imagination, for the imagination is an operative factor in meaning. The intensity of Poe's stories comes from just this—*he believes in them.* Why are these distortions valid for him? We obviously cannot have character identifications in tales of this nature, but we can respond to their sense of extremity—here one of strung-out hypocondria and aestheticism. In Poe's *Usher* we never quite know: the narrator is told that "the lady Madeline was no more," assists "the *temporary* entombment" (my italic) and we are then left to speculate on much. We become Dupin, the detective. In the film Corman laboriously establishes in front of our eyes the fact that Madeline is alive in her coffin. She twitches her fingers, which Usher notices but Winthrop (unbelievably enough) does not.

We shall return to point of view in narration below, but if you tell a story through the eyes of a possibly untrustworthy narrator you start off with a great advantage. In filming *Usher* Corman found he could not do this (though Wiene had with *Caligari*) ; hence he constantly established elements as real, outside the narrator's vision. In Poe's story we always see Usher through his visitor's eyes; in the film we frequently see him outside Winthrop's. Hence, Usher exists. Thus, the ridiculous (yet psychologically compelling) conclusion of the original has to be literally accounted for: Corman stages a fire, from which Winthrop escapes just in time. The only interesting part of the film is the one passage that has absolutely nothing whatsoever to do with the story, a sequence of Winthrop's sensory hallucinations at the end.

As a founder-member of Hollywood's Count Dracula Film Club, I yield to no one in my enjoyment of good horror cinema. Yet as we ran programme after programme of these, I began to realise that the best examples depended on states of reality extrapolated into dreams of terror, rather than the other way around. Nearly always Poe starts off with an irreality and tells you so; he is dramatising his dreams, or nightmares. Thereby he ties your hands behind your back. The narrator may be untrustworthy. The camera is not. Only in extremely clever films like Robert Mulligan's *The Other* or Jack Clayton's *The Innocents* (from *The Turn of the Screw*) do we find the camera pushed into a lie, which we must later visually correct. Accordingly, films like *Willard*, *The Incredible Shrinking Man*, even *Invasion of the Body Snatchers,* are successful because the base is, in each case, rooted in some form of reality. I have always found remarkable the audience participation in *The Incredible Shrinking Man,* especially considering its material. The allusion to bodily processes is more real than is the case with less effective horror films, e.g. *The Day of the Triffids, 1 Was a Teenage Werewolf,* and the *Dracula* rubbish where the suspension of disbelief has to be high.

In the first person narrative of Conrad and Poe no reality has been established. We simply listen to a narrator. The reality may be erased at any moment. *The Other* was one film that eradicated reality in this way: the camera pretended to see the two young boys as existing together, as real. Only later did we learn (and it was much later for the non-visual readers amongst us) that one of the boys was a corpse, a figment of the other's imagination. *"We have put her living in the tomb!"* shrieks Roderick at the end of *Usher,* just before he calls the mild-mannered narrator a "madman." By implication, society seems pretty close to an insane asylum in the work of Edgar Allan Poe.

Four of his major narrators (if you include the original version of *Berenice*) are opium addicts, and at least two others (also allowing the original versions of *The Oval Portrait* and *Loss of Breath*) are close to such. Their evidence is therefore strongly suspect. You could almost say that in the first-person narrations of both Conrad and Poe no reality is present at all. Perhaps Marlow is simply lying, the Captain in *The Secret Sharer* having a bad dream. Camera must, however, record these dreams as true, in a sense. The erasure of reality in *The Other* was daringly unconventional. The novel on which this film was based tipped its readers off far earlier.

In the depiction of mental states it is essential to let the imagination complete the image, as did Poe. Some gap is necessary. Such can be seen when comparing, even within cinema itself, important murder sequences. In *Psycho* Hitchcock was not *primarily* interested in entering the mind of a psychopath. Hence, his visualisation of Janet Leigh's murder could be relatively direct—he was to establish the psychopathological "motive" by showing Anthony Perkins laconically chewing gum while her car sank in the pond later. Mental pain of the Poe kind requires imaginative co-operation for its comprehension, as any analyst knows. Physical pain does not. We enter a pornographic movie for direct physical stimulation, for sex at full *chiaroscuro*. Tod Browning's *Freaks* hurts us immediately; Ken Russell's *The Devils* shows changes to the body of the burnt recusant that are almost intolerable. The blisters bloat, we feel physically damaged; mere grimaces of pain would not be enough. In *1984,* as given by Edmund O'Brien, they were not enough to suggest the intensity of Winston Smith's subhuman torture in the book. The dominant response in a film about a damaged mind must be one that invades and involves the viewer's mind. Literalism is less important. Commenting to Peter Bogdanovich about his own making of *M,* Fritz Lang was quite explicit on this score:

> If I could show what is most horrible for *me,* it may not be horrible for somebody else. *Everybody* in the audience—even the one who doesn't *dare* allow himself to understand what really happened to that poor child—has a horrible feeling that runs cold over his back. But everybody has a *different* feeling, because everybody *imagines* the most horrible thing that could happen to her. And that is something I could not have achieved by showing only one possibility—say, that he tears open the child, cuts her open. Now, in this way, I force the audience to become a collaborator of mine; by suggesting something I achieve a greater impression, a greater involvement than by showing it.

Lang claimed that his *The Big Heat* (starring Glenn Ford) also achieved this similar cinematic reticence. Precisely the opposite was effected, it seems to me, by the 1972 Hitchcock *Frenzy,* in which everything was spelt out and algolagnia so glibly credited as the source of rape that the latter became exceptional, unbelievable. The imagery followed suit. Who could ever credit that a tough London lorry-driver would behave as carelessly as he did in the Hitchcock presentation here? The material has just not been approached "seriously." Hitchcock has absolutely nothing to say in this film, and takes a long time saying it.

In "New Maps of Hell" Kingsley Amis made a useful distinction between science fiction and fantasy. For him the former is utopic, anti-utopic, or frankly extrapolatory. It would include most of Wells, Verne, More, Bacon, Voltaire and Kepler, but also Poe's two balloon stories. Something like *Frankenstein* is hard to classify since it is outrageously romantic, yet men have now produced robots and computers. "Science fiction presents with verisimilitude the human effects of spectacular changes in our environment." Fantasy is the frankly impossible or incredible, including Kafka's *Metamorphosis,* stories of mutants and monsters and messes, however compellingly recounted. "The real importance of these stories is that they liberated the medium from dependence on extrapolation," Amis concludes.

To make horror real, however, cinema has to take it seriously *at some point.* Hence, it cannot ordinarily deal with Amis's second category, that of fantasy, unless exceptional skill is used, as was the case with Jacques Tourneur's *The Night of the Demon,* which made far more credible than the M. R. James original, *The Casting of the Runes,* the idea of a scientist under the spell of black magic. *Rosemary's Baby* succeeded as far as it did by leaving much to the imagination. At one point Amis pleads for a vampire story to be allowed as science fiction, Richard Matheson's *I Am Legend,* thanks to the author's convincing, pseudo-"scientific" use of specific detail. The same sort of fidelity to conventional lore in the mode can also be seen at the start of Don Sharp's film *Kiss of the Vampire.* We cannot, however, visualize a vampire in the same way that we can —or are made to by special effects—a man growing small, or gradually invisible. Bergman's *The Face* (also known as

The Magician) was possible. The way in which an artist here terrorises the minions of a bourgeois society—a doctor, a police chief—is extremely gripping, since obviously believed by the director and more or less possible. On the other hand, when watching *Count Yorga, Vampire,* or *I Was a Teenage Werewolf,* or almost any Jekyll and Hyde films, something is lacking as it is not when watching Wells's *The Invisible Man.* We are asked to suspend too much disbelief. Horror cinema based on impossibilities, like *The House That Dripped Blood, The Blob, The Day of the Triffids,* even the interesting *The Dunwich Horror,* is never going to engage us as fully as that which takes seriously a literal possibility, some invasion of birds or rats, or just plain body-snatchers, for instance. If there is somewhere a sense of belief to which to hook the film, then internal states will be given cogent context. One of the easiest ways of doing this, as the early German cinema showed, was via madness or pathology, but there have been some extremely successful horror films of late without such resort.

It was said above that the only way to screen Poe is by analogy; in the case of *Usher* this was well effected in 1973 by John Hough's *The Legend of Hell House,* scripted and from the novel by none other than Richard Matheson. In Corman's film there had been some attempt to transpose the Poe fantasy by accounting for it rationally. Matheson's novel *I Am Legend* then went further, turning vampirism into science-fiction by ascribing the malady to an aerophobic microbe.

The Legend of Hell House owes its success to its direction, trick "psychic" effects (duplicated in *The Exorcist* later), and acting—the language is nothing. The direction is one that takes the story at face value. The collapsing and murderous house of Poe's imagination (there are even steals from the Corman *Usher* here, in the form of homicidal chandeliers) is now suffering from an excess of residual human energy, left over, as it were, from its vital and vicious human habitants; at the end it is effectively drained of this by a technological machine. Or is it? A final shot shows us the cat which had died bloodily in a shower bath (a parody of *Psycho*) still alive and menacing. Roderick Usher has turned into a sadistic dwarf who has his legs amputated in order to wear long artificial ones.

The story is corn itself; and *Hell House* could have been just as preposterous a piece of hokum as Corman's *Usher* Yet it took itself seriously (there have been mediums who have exuded ectoplasm in spectacular fashion); it does not stand aside at one remove from the events. The scene in which the ectoplasm emerges from a medium's fingernails is, in fact, a case in point, and is thoroughly spine-chilling. Polanski's *Rosemary's Baby* or Shirley Jackson's *The Haunting of Hill House* (called simply *The Haunting* as a film) come to mind in reinforcement of this point, but in *Hell House* Hough was able to go one step further. Whole passages are seen through the eyes of a young girl, a medium called Miss Tanner, who not only acknowledges poltergeist activities but even, at the start, treats them with the nonchalant contempt of a "familiar." Thus, when she is terrified by them at the end, we are also. Brilliantly played by Pamela Franklin (Flora in Clayton's *The Innocents* and the schoolgirl of *Jean Brodie*), this "mental" medium is most physically gored by a possessed cat and then raped, and evidently flogged (with parallel weal marks), by the invisible evil spirit of the house, an on-screen nonvisible seduction that Baird Searles, in *Fantasy and Science Fiction,* aptly called "a first in several ways." *Hell House* is far from a perfect horror film but it makes many of my points here with impressive vigour. The British believe in ghosts.

Finally, to clinch the point, it might be said that William Friedkin's *The Exorcist* (1973) performs the same task even better, and for the same reasons. The film does not start very promisingly, being over-faithful to the book in the cautiously-narrated archaeological scenes; but it ends strongly. The book was clearly written by an author who believed in his theme; the film manages to make this larger than merely Catholic, and to stand movingly on the side of human faith itself.

The Norms of Narration

In cinema, it is said, the narrative unit is the shot. The shot is not the still, for it can be composed of as many frames as the director wants the camera to record of the image. Since 1927 projection has been standardised to replace the frame twenty-four times a second in front of the viewer's eye. Short-duration shots are much commoner now than once they were. Directors like Bergman and Rohmer have clearly swum against this tide, declining to bombard our eyes with fast images and thereby seeming to ask our conscious intellect to operate maximally.

It was apparently Pudovkin who first suggested that the single shot was equivalent to the word, and editing the grammar of film ("To the film director each shot of the finished film subserves the same purpose as the word to the poet"). On this basis Eisenstein even went so far as to reduce (or expand) a passage of Milton to a shooting script, each "shot" plodding after each image on the printed page. By now much ink has been spilt pursuing this analogy* or

---

* "Syntax" in cinema is, for instance, quite differently yet equally loosely ascribed to film techniques by both Eisenstein and Vladimir Nilsen.

heresy which, with the best will in the world, can only be seen creating more hurdles than it endeavours to eliminate.

The most elaborate exposition of it lately has been William Jinks's *The Celluloid Literature* (1971) in America (Christian Metz's *Film Language* in France was an earlier pioneering work in this field) ; Jinks, a Miami-Dade Junior College English teacher, gives a course in the comparison. Apparently taking his point of departure from Susan Sontag's suggestion, in "Against Interpretation," that the history of cinema is a capsule version of that of the novel, Jinks compares all elements of language with those of film. The word is the frame, the paragraph a five-shot scene, the chapter a unit of filmic division (particularly visible in Lindsay Anderson's 1969 *If . . .*), while Costa-Gavras's *Z* is an "allegory." It is when he runs his theory into figures of speech that this critic becomes bogged down. "A figurative image," he writes, with numbing caution, "may be said to occur whenever a film-maker, for the sake of emphasis or freshness, departs from the conventional way of filming a subject." Metaphors and hyperboles and other print terms create such obstacles that Jinks virtually gives up—"it is much more difficult to distinguish the film metaphor from the film simile for, in film, there is no real equivalent for a connective word." One feels like asking: Why pursue the comparison in the first place? It is an exercise in futility and when it is backed up, as here, by Ezra Pound on the Chinese ideogram, in *ABC of Reading,* one realises that a serious error of evaluation is being made. "The word and the image," we are gravely informed, "are similar in that they are both visual phenomena—they must both be perceived by the eyes." The fallacy is too flagrant for the statement to make any sense at all; yet despite the fact that the one thing about "visual thinking" Arnheim was at pains to stress was that it was *not* the same as conceptual thinking, a theory has been erected on this fallacy. In *A Discovery of Cinema* Thorold Dickinson tracks down the source of the error as follows:

> It was the French who first described cinema as a *langage* The heresy arose out of the mistranslation of the word as "language." The French word for language is *langue. Langage* means speech, a way of speaking. *Le langage du cinema* means a visual way of telling a story or making a statement: the phrase was never intended to lead to a study of grammar and syntax.

Yet the error persists. And there are people who will continue to talk about the "grammar" of cinema. Grammar is a form of structure. In its linguistic sense no meaning can inhere in structure. The word *Du* in German is structurally a second person singular which requires to be followed by a verb in the same case; its accusative is *Dich* and dative *Dir*. To use this case when speaking to someone to express familiarity, or inferiority, or insult, is so much cultural patterning (it does not carry the same meaning in modern English, for instance). Not long ago I saw over a bar the sign "WE DONT SELL MINORS." If I had answered, "I wouldn't buy them if you did," I should have been replying to the structure of the sentence, taking the word "MINORS" as the grammatical object of the transitive verb "SELL." The grammatical infringement had here altered structure (omitting a dative) but, without too much hairsplitting, most of us would take the meaning, changing the verb back into an intransitive. Film editing, however, is an intensely creative task; far from syntactical, it is what repeatedly gives meaning to some fluid sequence of shots.

Nor can the single shot be considered a word. What sort of a word? A noun? We pattern *house,* however, as a noun just as we do *fire,* and anyone who has brought up a child knows what initial difficulties this causes. Chinese, Navaho, Eskimo pattern experiences completely differently. *No* has been considered to be an English sentence. *John broke his chair* follows the same structure in English as *John broke his arm*, though the experience represented differs widely. In *Bob kissed Janet* we might normally expect a certain amount of return kissing on the part of the object of the sentence (though what if Janet were dead?). In film the lexical unit—the shot—would be bound to give us what the director wanted of the nature of the experience. A shot cannot be likened to a word, nor film editing to grammar.

What can be said, however, is what Eisenstein observed of Griffith, namely that the technique of literary narrative, chiefly in the novel, is a *sine qua non* of cinema. He pointed out that Dickens's *The Cricket on the Hearth* starts out from a typical film close-up, "The kettle began it. . . ." What Eisenstein is seeing here is that film shares in the narrative *symbolism* of fiction. Coming last in the literary arts, the novel was able to pursue the characterising and affective power of close focus, which, as Eisenstein noted, it then bequeathed to cinema. European symbolism took some time gaining a hold in Britain, but the sophistication with which it was early deployed by Flaubert is at the very genesis of camera work. It could be said that Ibsen used the same to an extent on the stage, but on Flaubert's printed page there is far longer to linger on it while in poetry, in the Baudelaire of the Fifties, say, it is closer to a theory than a narrative mode.

Take the moment when Emma Bovary arrives in Yonville. The most natural thing in the world for a woman, the wife of the local *officier de santé,* who has just been posted to the inn of a new town where her husband will take up his duties, would be to go to the fire and warm her limbs after the chilly drive. Can we not leave it at that? I am afraid not. Flaubert's "lens" insists, his literal descriptions are nearly always shadowed with figurative overtones, and so we read:

> When Madame Bovary entered the kitchen she went up to the fireplace. With two fingertips she caught her dress at the knee, and having thus pulled it up to her ankle, held out her black-booted foot to the fire above the revolving leg of mutton. The

flame lit the whole of her, casting its harsh light over the pattern of her gown, the fine pores of her fair skin, and even her eyelids, when she blinked from time to time. A great red glow passed over her with the wind, blowing through the half-open door.

Surely any reader starts to be alerted by this degree of focus: Emma is to raise her skirts with a vengeance in Yonville l'Abbaye. Fires haunt her, as they did her soul. We realise that her wedding bouquet, which had pricked her finger, had just been put on the flames in her old house, with her old dreams. In her first intensity of *ennui* she feels herself "fainting with the heat of the hearth." And so on. Dickens's kettle is not used to identify in nearly the same way.

Flaubert seriously and painstakingly states woman's position in such a society by symbolic markers of this sort. Inventories have been made of these; one more instance will suffice. Throughout the first two Parts of *Bovary* there is a constant kinship made between Emma and whips, harness, bridles, curbs. These are logical enough in their settings but, focussed beside Emma, they speak to us of her and for her. As Charles first arrives at the Bertaux he stables his horse. Natural enough. But then he notices the whips around. Why? Nothing unusual there, surely? He next forgets his own. This has fallen between some sacks and the wall. Emma bends over the sacks for it. Out of politeness Charles makes to recover it also, "and as he stretched out his arms, at the same moment felt his breast brush against the back of the young girl bending beneath him. She drew herself up, scarlet, and looked at him over her shoulder as she handed him his riding crop." The pose is no accident. It recurs in the blood-letting scene, as Emma stoops to put a basin of blood under the table, her dress pulling taut across her body as Rodolphe watches. Reproduced in the Vincente Minnelli film (examined below) the moment was deprived of all significance—Jennifer Jones merely looked a flirt.

With Flaubert the integrity of focus is truly symbolic, as

indeed is human life. Everything is perfectly natural, yet everything shows Emma's state under the male whip. The guests arrive for her marriage to the cracking of whips; harness breaks as they leave. Once again, perfectly likely, yet brought to our attention. And the first thing Flaubert focuses on in the first house Emma inhabits as a wife is the door, and "behind the door hung a cloak with a small collar, a bridle. . . ." When Emma goes to the Vaubyessard estate for the ball, the Marquis does not let her leave without showing her his stables. One wonders why this should amuse Emma. In the harness-room she sees hung up "the bits, the whips, the spurs, the curbs." On the way back Charles's own traces break. After her seduction by Rodolphe while out riding, Emma looks up and sees him mending "one of the two broken bridles." Later still, she herself gives him a riding crop with a silver-gilt top, an instrument he explicitly fondles after she lies back in bed, quivering from his love-making.

Film is deeply indebted to this form of narration and characterisation since it is so firmly external. Developing something like Goethe's Sorge in *Faust II*, Flaubert even begins the tradition, exploited in expressionism, of depicting a character's inner state by an "objective correlative," e.g. the syphilitic beggar for Emma, much as the demons of Joyce's "Circe" section advance the subconscious of Bloom.* Cocteau and Fellini have attempted something of the same. Careful selection of detail is essential to filmic characterisation, and that is why the star system, with its typed or "flat" characters, did such damage to early sound cinema. It is remarkable how far a Bergman has gone in the ability to develop the interior world of characters by a strong and clearly objective visual emphasis.

---

* I purloin the suggestive Faustian parallel from: Walter H. Sokel, *The Writer in Extremis*, Stanford University Press, 1959, pp. 31–33. Here Sokel pushes it into Strindberg's *To Damascus* of 1898 which he calls "the first fully Expressionist drama ever written," and where a beggar also appears.

Proust's work questions the validity of any reality except inasmuch as it has subjective value for Marcel alone. Combray, which must always remain so much brick and stone on the screen, is only there in the novel as Marcel confers reality upon it, and is far from an enchanted Eden when he becomes older and more weary. Since art alone can unify and preserve his reality, Marcel's concepts turn into so many aesthetic criteria. He finds that he organises his inner life as he organises art; the laws of love are, for him, so much transvalued aesthetic. Time does not exist and in a sense death is defeated. This is most uncinematic. Visually all that could be done with Proust would be to concentrate on certain moments of sensory passion—the sight of three trees, a starched napkin, the ping of a spoon against a plate—and try to suggest how they may liberate the narrator's being. But even such externalisation might prove unsatisfactory, and falsify the original.

At first glance, indeed, literature would seem actually to impede the cinema. Such is cult cant at the moment. Vachel Lindsay thought that since the Anglo-Saxon is a scriptural culture, and our prime 'aesthetic response literary rather than visual, we would be reluctant to accept film as art. One wonders if, in fact, the reverse is not true, and that, as Eisenstein thought, verbal narrative literacy was an essential precursor of imagistic sensitivity in the cinema. Rudolf Arnheim's *Visual Thinking* is in parts a ponderously elaborate exposition of what seems at first glance a desolatingly obvious thesis, namely that human beings can "think" visually, unlike animals. In *Film Form* Eisenstein saw the organic nature of such perception:

> Let this past be a reproach to those thoughtless people who have displayed arrogance in reference to literature, which has contributed so much to this apparently unprecedented art and is, in the first and most important place, the art of viewing.

Britain and France were, in fact, the two countries most

hospitable to cinema from the first (if America is for the moment accepted as originally a literary ancillary of the former) ; both nations had strong prior traditions in the novel. Germany of the early Twenties set up a superb cinema since at that moment producers realised the only way open to them to conquer foreign markets was by art (*cp.* Britain after the Second World War). Furthermore, in both Britain and France, a strong dramatic tradition had poured into the novel; this is very clear in someone like Dickens who visualises his narrative in short scenes, typical of cinema. So much so, indeed, that Allardyce Nicoll was able to present his opinion, in *Film and Theatre* of 1936, that the roots of film lie rather in drama. One wants to answer, with Pound, that a good play is not a novel and that, in any case, the novel subsumed much of the dramatic quotient available before it.

The first norm of filmic narrative, therefore, appears to be its great ease of spatial movement. It is not simply that one can move around the world in minutes but rather that one does so, compellingly enough, always in the present tense. We are convinced by what is happening *now*. Since we are, time can be truncated in most arbitrary fashions; the elimination of the inaction in our daily lives is readily accepted and compensatory techniques are evolved (speed-up, slow-motion) to represent psychological time. The bodily death of Bonnie and Clyde must have been a messy and chaotic affair, but as given in the famous sequence by Arthur Penn an appanage of nostalgia is cast over all, and we live the psychology of the victims, as interpreted or "abstracted" by the director. In Carl Dreyer's words, "We must use the camera to drive away the camera."

The novel must unfold in time. Experiments in temporal *stasis* in fiction often seem like so many contradictions in term. As E. M. Forster put it, in *Aspects of the Novel*: "The time-sequence cannot be destroyed without carrying in its

ruin all that should have taken its place." Writing in *The
Sewanee Review* for Spring 1945, Joseph Frank grappled
ably with this problem and inadvertently clarified a lot of
cinema. Starting with Lessing's *Laokoön,* which saw form
in the plastic arts as necessarily spatial, Frank here argued
that a number of outstanding contemporary writers like
Eliot, Proust, Joyce, and Pound have actually refuted Lessing's definitions and produced a sort of "spatial form" in
their work. As he said, "The reader is intended to appre-
hend their work spatially, in a moment of time, rather than
as a sequence." This is exemplified for Frank in the concat-
enation or vortex of periods, cultures, and ideas latent in
what Pound proposed as his "image." It is also to be found
in Proust's highly charged *"moment privilégié."* Since the
date of Frank's article many other examples of similar literary compressions have come about, particularly in poetry. In brief, Frank feels that a spatialisation of the contemporary novel has been achieved by writers like Joyce,
Proust, and Djuna Barnes, by disrupting and/or extending
the ordinary chronological time-flow—as at the end of *Bonnie and Clyde.*

Joyce's *Finnegans Wake* is certainly a cyclical work that
can be dipped into and read forwards and backwards—or
even sideways. Marc Saporta's *Composition une* (1962)
is a novel in the form of a deck of cards which can be shuffled at will or whim, to make various stories. In the cinema
this freedom with our usual straitjacket of temporality has
been explored in Resnais's *Marienbad,* examined below.
Hugh Kenner has been at pains to claim the same kind of
"consistency of cross-reference" for *Ulysses* into which, he
asserts, we can enter and move around at will: "Consider
the pains he takes to impede the motions of linear narrative; *Ulysses* is as discontinuous a work as its author can
manage; we read it page by page, and once we have got-
ten the hang of it we can profitably read pages in isolation
. . . whatever line we follow into the past of this book, it

will meet some other line equally traceable, and return upon itself." This is all very well up to a point. Yet it can hardly be pushed too far. We know that Joyce intensely disliked Jung's comment that he could read *Ulysses* backwards, but film is able to make around a character or event rapid figures of speech which yield immediate messages, in the present, in the manner Kenner is hinting at. If it is raining, it is raining and we do not have to be reminded of it by damp umbrellas or dripping clothing or the like. In cinema it is simply there. Similarly, as I have suggested in my analysis of *The Blue Angel,* a character can be quickly described by clothing and adjacent objects.

In his Introduction to the text of *Last Year at Marienbad* Robbe-Grillet emphasised what is perhaps fairly obvious, that the cinema exists in the irresistible present:

> The essential characteristic of the image is its presentness. Whereas literature has a whole gamut of grammatical tenses which makes it possible to narrate events in relation to each other, one might say that on the screen verbs are always in the present tense (which is what is so strange, so artificial about the "novelised films" which have been restored to the past tense so dear to the traditional novel) : by its nature, what we see on the screen *is in the act of happening,* we are given the gesture itself, not an account of it.

And he added:

> In reality, our mind goes faster—or sometimes slower. Its style is more varied, richer and less reassuring: it skips certain passages, it preserves an exact record of certain "unimportant" details, it repeats and doubles back on itself. And this *mental time,* with its peculiarities, its gaps, its obsessions, its obscure areas, is the one that interests us since it is the tempo of our emotions, of our *life.*

This is simply a restatement of Bergson on behalf of film. All the recent European neo-classicists (Pound, Lewis, Benda, Seillière, Massis, Keyserling) accused Bergson of allowing time—"durée"—to play havoc with space. It is precisely what Robbe-Grillet organises in *Marienbad*. In *L'Evolution créatrice*, the substance of Bergson's Collège de France lectures in the first years of this century, the great philosopher in fact used many pre-cinematic metaphors to express his theories. Matter, Bergson proposed, presents itself to us in a constant becoming, and can only be trapped by intellect in a series of immobile, instantaneous "shots" or "frames":

> La méthode cinématographique est donc la seule pratique, puisqu'elle consiste à régler l'allure générale de la connaissance sur celle de l'action, en attendant que le détail de chaque acte se règle à son tour sur celui de la connaissance.

No doubt a literature has been erected on Bergsonism, and *Marienbad* owes to it. Pound called Bergson "crap" in *The Townsman*, but if Bergson put an unqualified emphasis on intuition in its ability to attain metaphysical reality (as in his cinematically cogent *Introduction à la métaphysique*, brought to England by Hulme), it is also true that this intuition was an effort of imaginative identification of a kind typically found in fiction and, later, in the best of film. Such intuition is an act of sympathy with and merging in the constant flow of "durée." In *L'Evolution créatrice* Bergson defines "durée" as follows: "La durée est le progrès continu du passé qui ronge l'avenir et qui gonfle en avancant." We note that in his *Marienbad* Introduction Robbe-Grillet allows himself to say of his three main characters that they "had no past," adding of X:

> And for the past the hero introduces by force into this sealed, empty world, we sense he is making it up as he goes along. There is no last year, and Marienbad is no longer to be found on any map. This past, too, has no reality beyond the moment it is evoked with sufficient force; and when it finally triumphs, it has merely become the present, as if it had never ceased to be so.

We can therefore say this: that film is presented in the present, yet this may be a dishonest or deceptive spatialising of form. Bergson's "le présent pur" is an insatiable gnawing of the past into the future. It never exists in itself. His present is a condensation of semantic events and thus intuition must plunge into memory as a vehicle for perception.

Much has been written about qualitative as against quantitative time. "To be susceptible of being measured," Thomas Mann told us, "time must flow evenly, but who ever said it did that? As far as our consciousness is concerned, it doesn't, we only assume it does for the sake of convenience; and our units of measurement are purely arbitrary, sheer conventions." Unfortunately a film does to an extent "flow evenly." There is a clock in most cinemas. Television is even more remorselessly chronological, or chronometric—it fits all film into slots. When I watched one of my own novels being hewn into shape for a one-hour thriller programme, I realised it was being restructured or re-climaxed to meet the advertising breaks each quarter of an hour. So Bergson proposed that the quality of continuous flow or "durée," which is how we experience time, does not find, in the words of Hans Meyerhoff's *Time in Literature*, "an adequate correlate in the physical concept of time." Meyerhoff adds:

> Physics, according to this view, translates time into the dimension of space; the intellect "spatializes" time, as Bergson said, by which he meant that the quality of continuous flow, duration, and "unity within multiplicity," characteristic of the experience of time, is converted, by the physical theory, into separate, distinct, measurable quantities which always remain separate, disparate, and unrelated, like points in space or marks on a chronometer.

While Bergson was assaulting physical time as a distortion of experiential time, Russell and others were reversing him in fact, by finding mathematical properties empirically verifiable in duration and flow. As far as film is concerned, these battles come down to the fact that convention must exist in any artistic form. It is singularly unhelpful to assert that by "spatializing" time film reinforces narrative identity. It may in fact falsify it thereby. It is time to give an example. I well remember the rigorous observation of blackout at night in Southern Italian towns and villages at the period of the Anzio landing. Innumerable films of this war (passages at the end of *Catch-22*, or *The Conformist*) have to show a certain amount of night-lighting in the streets of Rome, and other towns, simply in order to identify what the actors are doing. In the reality, the Italians were at that time burning an intense sort of incinerator at street corners every time a siren was heard, producing an impenetrable and lung-rasping smoke that effectively grounded any motion within hundreds of yards of it. Here Bergson again becomes cinema's acceptable convention. A fixity in space (he was careful to remind us in *Matière et mémoire*) did not necessarily confer any ultimate truth *over* time; the affective value of objects in space must yield to their identity in memory.

Spatial relationships can doubtless be clarified by a moving camera, but to build up a jigsaw puzzle of sequences of space could be meaningless on the screen. A series of Bergsonian "shots" or "frames" seems to describe Godard at his worst. On the other hand, as an explosive shorthand method of transmitting meaning immediately such juxtapositions can be an admirable synthetic, borrowed from pictorial art: much has been written about montage in the cinema, as established as a criterion in Eisenstein's *Potemkin*. George Bluestone acutely noted: "The novel renders the illusion of space by going from point to point in time; the film renders time by going from point to point in space." The rendering of psychological or mental time, however, is simply limited in cinema by the laws of optics. We cannot see what we cannot see; in fiction we can.

The image on the screen may thus fail the function accorded it in the screenplay and, when the latter is based on a prior work of art, such as a novel or a play, it may do so repeatedly. In his pioneer survey of the use of camera in film-making, *The Cinema As a Graphic Art,* Vladimir Nilsen was at pains to emphasise that the shot must contain "all the elements in the expressive construction of cinematic representation." It is little use "spatialising" time if you detract from, rather than add to, the spectator's concentration on essential elements of meaning: "Thus we are confronted with the necessity so to organise the expressive elements in the space and time of the shot that the idea at the basis of the directorial treatment will be clearly manifested."

It will not be so manifested if we are given a mere bundle of tricks. Any precedence of fiction over film obtains principally in the fact that a genuine totality of meaning exists in the greatest novels. In the best of Zola, Flaubert, Tolstoy, Dostoyevski (who goes back in time in *Notes from Underground*), form so perfectly responds to content that style itself must be vision. If the novel is a completion like this, there is, in truth, little room for a film from it. As Alain Resnais has nicely phrased it:

> I would not want to shoot the adaptation of a novel because I think that the writer has completely expressed himself in the novel and that wanting to make a film of it is a little like reheating a meal.

Yet great cinema can also be a completion. In the best of Bergman the expressive devices serve the vision of the whole with perfect style. Since film is such a hybrid, thought is here given both verbally and in externalisations that lead us to infer feelings. Cinema's ability to create spatial referents has, however, led to the belief that *thereby* some sort of extra significance is created in tricks like montage, cross-cutting, flashbacks and other spatial transitions.

All these can soon be found to be prior literary conventions, if we define a convention in the terms of Harry Levin as "a necessary difference between art and life." It is true that the effect of split-screen cannot be given on the printed page (though who is using split-screen extensively in cinema today?) ; cross-cutting, however, is completely anticipated in the agricultural fair at which the seducer Rodolphe makes his first advances to Emma Bovary. Montage, super-imposition, and flashbacks all exist in fiction of the Eighteenth century.

By the Nineteenth the novel seems virtually to be calling for cinema. The turn in point of view in *Bovary* has been frequently instanced, and seems quite similar to a film director's instruction to a cameraman. As Levin has observed, the scene involving Emma and her lover Léon making an erotic itinerary of Rouen in a curtained cab is completely cinematic. Similarly, the contrapuntal narrations of Gide, Joyce, and the early Huxley are fully filmic, while experiments in flashbacks which do not return to their original states, or else could never have been witnessed, are available in the Faulkner of the turn of the Thirties. As a matter of fact, the novel pushes ever further ahead, first: in *Les faux monnayeurs* Gide aimed at doing what Bach had done with the fugue, while Proust had already attempted a new plasticity of character. Pound saw film ever-destined to feed off established narrative technique in his *ABC of Reading*. Conrad, Ford, Joyce, Woolf, James, such authors had investigated the norms of narration to such a sophisticated degree that one seemed only able, as Griffith felt, to follow after. Wyndham Lewis alleged that Joyce had in the main merely copied Dickens's method of presenting the thought-stream of Alfred Jingle in *Pickwick Papers* for his vast unpunctuated soliloquy at the end of *Ulysses*. Obviously an unfair charge, made in both *The Art of Being Ruled* and *Time and Western Man*, it nevertheless reminds one of the "spatial" ease with which Dickens moves around in the mind of this particular character.

In his greatest films Bergman may be said, with some justice, to have achieved the totality of meaning subsumed here as true language, and alluded to as the prerogative of the great novelist; thus, Vincent Canby of the *New York Times* has written of him that "Bergman dramatises states of mind that have seldom been attempted, much less achieved, outside of written fiction." Yet Bergman, properly enough, treats cinema as, what Cocteau called it, "a form of graphic art," which is to say one founded on reality. In his *Journals* Cocteau added:

> The cinema can bear a relation to the fantastic, as I under-stand it, if it is satisfied with being a vehicle and if it does not try to produce it . . . it is imperative not to look upon it as a magician. That belongs to the habit of speaking of a worker so as to avoid analysing his real work. The cinema's privilege is not card tricks. It goes beyond juggling, which is only its syntax. The domain of the fantastic is elsewhere. *The Blood of a Poet* has no magic, nor has *Beauty and the Beast*.

Thus, Bergman can move in and out of fantasy with con-siderable authenticity since he is always essentially real; behind him stands a novelist like James, with the assurance and poise, the same formal yet basically humdrum social minuet involving a few people into which any small dis-turbance comes pat like a catastrophe.

Such a hybrid is cinema, it has even been claimed that the availability of the document to film is preceded in liter-ature: Professor Robert Richardson shows how *The Waste Land* (admittedly a poem) depends heavily on non-poetic or extra-literary documents thrust into the text. One thinks of Dos Passos and André Bazin's contention that *Citizen Kane* "would never have existed" without that author.

So plural a form as film has to attain a particularly in-tense stylisation of its content in order to be convincing. When Virginia Woolf wrote her now famous article "The Movies and Reality" in the mid-Twenties she realised how tone, style, setting had to be conveyed by images first and foremost (she was writing before talkies); the visual had to take precedence over verbal narration—

> Even the simplest image: "my love's like a red, red rose, that's newly sprung in June," presents us with impressions of moisture and warmth and the flow of crimson and the softness of petals inextricably mixed and strung upon the lift of a rhythm which is itself the voice of the passion and the hesitation of the love. All this, which is accessible to words, and to words alone, the cinema must avoid.

Yet this is not to say, as does Bluestone developing A. A. Mendilow, that the novel is "a medium antithetical to film,"* that the translation of verbal symbols into images is always destined to be disappointing; the novel is a medium, the film is many.

We have already touched on the narrative and affective use of colour. Eisenstein liked to talk of the *"meaning* of colour." Early tinting seems to have accorded certain colours emotional values, rather as on the Greek stage. Blue was idyllic, and so on. Colour can be used in the cinema to express mood and create atmosphere but it is always going to be what colour is in a painting—*there. The Leopard, The Red Desert* and a number of similar films depend very heavily on colour to convey and move along the meaning. The insertion of passages of colour into a black-and-white picture, as in the second part of Eisenstein's *Ivan the Terrible* and many films thereafter, has been another expressive device unavailable to fiction, for fiction is not painting. When reading a novel, however, a colour remains purely imaginative; it is never there on the page and so can be imbued with and carry a rich cargo of symbolism. Huysmans's Des Esseintes comes to mind. Novelists did

---

* Robert Richardson is equally categoric, claiming that "what makes a good novel rarely makes a good film." This is all very well so long as it does not insinuate, to an increasingly unlettered youth, that what is a good film, like *Tom Jones,* axiomatically derives from an indifferent novel.

not describe colours in order to have them carried out by attendant painters. No colour can be said to be "missing" from the printed page. "Literature on the other hand," argues Mendilow, "is dependent entirely on a symbolic medium that stands between the perceiver and the symbolised percepta. . . ." To follow the Bluestone-Mendilow position to its logical conclusion would be to ask for feelies, tasties, smellies all pouring "real" messages upon us at once. To take literature and eliminate it.*

Language does not stand between colour and our perception of it; it performs its own office. The whiteness of snow in Joyce's story "The Dead" has a resonance which only language can give it, like his choice of a symbolic colour for dreary Dublin, brown. Joyce's words do not ask to be completed by images; indeed, it would take an exceedingly long stretch of film to accomplish this, as is evinced by a passage of criticism of this text, from Professor W. Y. Tindall:

> By its whiteness snow is connected with Lily, the caretaker's daughter, whose name is the first word in the story. That this is not accidental is shown by the flower's traditional connections. Not only for funerals, the lily is for Easter as well. When Lily brings Gabriel three potatoes (roots, seeds, and images of Ireland), she offers life to his deadness. By its whiteness snow offers contrast to Mr. Browne, who, as he says, is "all brown," and who, as Aunt Kate observes, seems "everywhere." Since Joyce has associated brown with decay and death throughout the book, Mr. Browne, issuing out into the cold to fetch a cab, lends snow a kind of vitality. As it lies fresh, white, and cold in Phoenix Park and by the river, obvious signs of resurrection and life, Gabriel carves a "fat brown goose" indoors.

It is difficult to see how we are impeded from "symbolised

---

* Cp. "Rank inquired curiously if anyone had heard how *Hamlet* was getting on. One executive spoke up with justifiable pride. 'Yes, Mr. Rank. Larry let me see half an hour's rushes the other night.' 'And what's it like?' 'Mr. Rank, it's wonderful. You wouldn't even know it was Shakespeare.'" (Alan Wood, *Mr. Rank*.)

percepta" by the language that clothes these colours; their depiction on the screen would add absolutely nothing to what Joyce does with them.

And so it is with all forms of narration in the cinema. Directly sound arrives, all the properties of pitch patterns in rendering a verbal message aloud, the business which keeps Speech Departments in business, suddenly obtain: an actor at Stanislavski's Moscow Theatre told Roman Jakobson that he was once called on "to make forty different messages from the phrase *sevodnya vyecherom* [Tonight] by diversifying its expressive tint." Anyone who has heard a German saying *so* over and over again, at one end of a telephone conversation, knows that even more messages may be made out of this simple syllable.

Once again the cinema has to stylise. The artificial registration of sound has by now reached a high degree of sophistication, so that today we scarcely notice asynchronous sound or voice-over narration. Sound montage was early charted by Eisenstein, Pudovkin, and—in particular—Alexandrov, in a remarkably prescient manifesto of 1930 ("Experiment with sound should be concentrated on using asynchronism between sound and visuals"). Something like the electronic distortion of the ghost's voice in Olivier's *Hamlet* is often held up as a telling vocal experiment for its time, again one we would scarcely hear as unusual today. *Kane* also pioneered in the use of vocal treatments, or mistreatments, via echo chambers and the like. It is even said that when Sacha Guitry found himself in a spot, when making *Les perles de la couronne,* and wanted to give the impression of Arletty speaking Abyssinian, he simply ran the sound track of her normal French backwards! There was a celebrated Marx Brothers set-up during which one of the four would bow and smile sanctimoniously to some Mittel-European dignitary who had no English, the while saying, "You bastard . . . you sweet little sonofabitch," and so on. The other would grin and bow back, delighted. This was a perfectly proper use of commentative sound, good "body language." President Roosevelt is said to have found a reception line he once had to greet so appallingly long that, as he shook hands with each new guest, he smiled and murmured, "I just murdered my grandmother."

Non-synchronism of sound and image in the cinema (the shooting-gallery scene in *Marienbad,* for example) is the logical exploiting of something that is happening in language daily. When we say that someone has a good accent in one tongue, a poor one in another, what is going on is that a foreign speaker is failing to use the same allophones as the native speaker (it is easier to understand your wife speaking German than a German). The majority of voice-over and asynchronous tricks with sound are an artificial scrambling of meaning by making allophones impede each other. Russian tends to sound angry to the average English user. A model summary of this language situation, which has now been bizarrely imported into cinema, is provided in a passage from Micheline Maurel's *An Ordinary Camp,* a moving account of concentration-camp life in the last war:

> Often. there were fights merely because people did not speak the same language. Words that were not understood were taken as insults and were answered with blows. When a French-woman spoke to a Russian, the latter would almost invariably reply, "Nye ponimayu" ("I do not understand"). Once I saw a little Frenchwoman throw herself against a Russian with fists doubled, furiously shouting, *"Ni-pou-ni maille* yourself, you brute." Fortunately I knew Polish and enough of the other Slavic languages to be able sometimes to prevent trouble. But the fact remains that the natural intonation of some Russians and Ukrainians has a harsh and unpleasant ring to French ears.

We are today living in a noisy civilisation in which what a Spanish countryman calls silence is something many of us have never heard, or ever know. The incessant alarms and sirens in our cities, each year made more frightening, misalert our biochemical body timings until, in self-protection, the nervous system neutralises as much random, unstructured sound as possible. Modern cinema's use of sound, and silence, is ineluctably in this context and its stylisation of sound has to be quite different now from what it was in, say, 1930. The instinct on the part of the brain—to be technical, the basilar membrane in the cochlea—to make the ear reject, rather than accept, random noise is an important handling of uncertainty. Scientists have put an earphone on a subject's left ear giving him one message, and another earphone on his right ear giving him another; it is made next to impossible for the subject to acquire both messages at the same time. Nonetheless, it is theorised from such tests that he will tend to pick up most of a message he requires or needs to hear. One that touches on his survival. *The Candidate* was an interesting case in point. It tried honestly to reflect the virtual insane asylum of sounds during political interviews and addresses and conventions in America, but the report itself came out so strangulated as to defeat its own purpose. Indeed, we scarcely need recourse to the laboratory for these "scientific" assurances. Common sense daily shows us the same. Experiments with airport announcements, the "sharpening" of loudspeaker sounds and suchlike, merely demonstrate what most of us have experienced, namely that you are more likely to hear what you have to hear than what you do not have to hear. Unless housewives, for instance, "shut off" commercial radio directives to rush out and buy this or that product immediately, they would go crazy. The start of Jacques Tati's delightful *Monsieur Hulot's Holiday* played around in this spirit with unintelligible announcements on a French railway platform.

Made over by cinema into artificial listeners of sound in its widest sense (drama was generally vocal), we have lost the ability to understand silence. "The coming of the sound film," write Ralph Stephenson and J. R. Debrix, "also enabled the artist to use silence in a film with a positive dramatic effect." In a sound film, that is, silence can be especially intense, virtually a narration in itself, since it is such an infringement. Béla Balázs has insisted on this. In the cinema silence is particularly discursive. Is it not so on the stage? Certainly less so. The classic text on the use of the stage pause is perhaps Michael Chekhov's *To the Actor: On the Technique of Acting*. Here we are reminded that a stage pause prepares an audience for action, and ensuing verbalisation—"For each correct pause has in it the power to stimulate the spectator's attention and compel him to be more alert than he already is." On the stage silence is used as a space between speech units; more or less of it can mean more or less emphasis. It is pre-speech or post-speech. Scholars have shown that the pregnant pauses often allotted in a Shakespearean production today were probably inexistent at the time.

In something like Bergman's *The Silence,* involving two sisters and a boy staying in an hotel, the mutism is pregnant with meaning, since it is, once more, an intense stylisation within its field. There had been a Ray Milland film (*The Thief*) with no speech permitted at all, but it came out as artificial and empty. More often silent scenes had been inserted into the overall pattern of a talkie, as in Gabin's murder of Simone Simone in Renoir's *La Bête humaine,* on which Ernest Lindgren has percipiently commented. Bergman, however, reminds us of the truly spiritual nature of silence, of how attitudes to silence are patterned by divergent societies. Ours seems determined to eliminate it; Trappist monks, on the other hand, have developed it into a life-style. Silence has always been a normative element of Zen. Dantë's words fail him as he approaches the bliss of total harmony at the end of the *Paradiso*. In *The Silence* and *Persona,* as in the best plays by Pinter and Beckett, silence is treated not simply as a revolt against our "magpie" culture, but as a real communicative act. "What's this sudden silence," asks a character in an early novel by Robert

Musil, "that's like a language we can't hear?" The tongue is one of the most strongly muscled organs in the body and demands employment.

The development of the novel was predicated on the possession of large stocks of silence, in upper-middle-class homes, involving a deepening of privacy and an elimination of others that is suspect today. For silence is our enemy. We withold it in punishment, we mock it in "silent prayer" in schools, we "fill" it on TV where "dead air" causes terror among commercial organisations. Books on how to keep talking are perennial bestsellers in the U.S. (*cp. Speech Cosmetics*). We pattern silence as dissent; "taking the Fifth" is a notorious case in point. Every now and then someone paints a painting with nothing on it, or stages an exhibition with no pictures in it (Yves Klein), or sits at a piano and substitutes silence for a sonata (John Cage), or hands out a book of blank pages as the latest experiment in poetry. Paul Taylor once put on a "dance" in which he simply stood still on stage; his "review" in *Dance Observer* was a blank column. Like a stage pause these bizarre cultural manifestations are forcing our attention—more, they are asking us to listen again. Great artists of the cinema like Rohmer and Bergman seem to want to recover some semantic balance so that what words they do use will be listened to, and a deeper understanding effected. However, what they are reminding us of, as observers of the cinema, is that almost all sonic effects have to be stylised, and natural sounds sensitised, even down to that of a man being socked on the jaw or hit on the head.*

When sound includes music, it involves another art, and

---

* "A sock on the jaw sounds unreal when inserted on a soundtrack . . . Once, Hansen [sometime Controller of the Sound Department at 20th Century-Fox] needed the sound of a man being struck over the head with a lead pipe. To obtain it, he tried striking every kind of object, among others a cantaloupe. The cantaloupe effect was nearly right, but nearly right was not good enough. In desperation, someone suggested falling back on belaboring a real head. The result was perfection itself." (Pete Martin, *Hollywood without Make-Up*.)

cinema is made more synthetic than ever. Long discussions
of the rhetorical role of music in the cinema merely serve
to point up what an impure medium the latter is. High poetry can be called "musical," yet still not music despite the
avowedly emulative pretensions of poets like Lanier and
Poe. Film simply usurps music for affect. The borrowing is
so brazen that only the more refined musical ears among
us pause to protest the damage done on sound tracks to Mozart, Chopin, Tchaikovsky, and Beethoven. In painting the
equivalent might be to show a Rembrandt or Degas slightly touched up at a director's whim, and attributed to a character in the film. How music affects us is by now the subject of libraries of studies, and must obviously remain outside this one, which tries to relate fiction to film. Since in
film music is principally affective and metaphoric, then it
must be principally narrative in the best sense. Originally,
music was used specifically in this way to colour action with affect—menace, suspense, joy. Today it is employed with more reserve and more realism; music is usually accounted for, as arising out of elements of the setting.
Yet film music is still stylised or "canned" and, although
fans buy recorded soundtracks, very few go to a film
to hear the music first and foremost. To listen to Beethoven
one reports to the concert hall, rather than to *A Clockwork Orange.*

The best film music, therefore, is used narratively, to
ironise or in some way shape the action. Bach may be
played behind a picture of Nazis deporting Jews to concentration camps (as in the Bossak/Kazmiercak *Requiem for
500,000*). Donizetti is heard as Yossarian walks through a
Fellini-like wartime Rome at night (*Catch-22*). A church
organ intones as Michael Corleone (Al Pacino) presides
over his nephew's baptism while outside his henchmen are
wiping out a rival gang, the child's godfather becoming,
therefore, self-baptised as his father's assassin (Coppola's
The Godfather). These touches are much in vogue at present writing, perhaps a needed correction of the trite and

banal "incidental" music of another era. The new irony of
this type is certainly not intended to increase reality; it is,
rather, in the service of the general message, as Peter Brook
used Diabelli to intensify what he had to say in *Moderato
Cantabile*. Hitchcock, however, had very soon started to experiment with a musical soundtrack that mocked the images—the fairground music behind the murder in *Strangers
on a Train*, for instance. Carol Reed and others followed
suit.

By this point there remains the question whether such
application of music has not become something of a cliché
in itself. Quite often, light music, or the flippant use of serious music, works *against* rather than *for* the obtaining narrative theme. As the world is destroyed at the end
of *Dr. Strangelove* Kubrick lets us hear a popular wartime
song, a "Forces' Favourite" in Britain as sung by Vera
Lynn, "We'll meet again, don't know where, don't know
when. . . ." The question arises as to whether this ironises
the unspeakable, or simply trivialises it. At a very serious
moment in *Catch-22*, in the first close-up of Luciana's body,
the orchestra streams into the Richard Strauss music used
in Kubrick's *2001*. One of Kubrick's few changes from the
original of *A Clockwork Orange* was to have the initial
violence and invasion of the writer F. Alexander's home accompanied on the soundtrack by the casually-sung "Singin'
in the Rain" (an "opposite" of the adulated Beethoven) .

Burgess himself has said he felt this music alarmingly
trivialised the violence he had identified and pilloried and,
indeed, by the virtually balletic treatment of the whole
scene, made it innocuous and somehow even amusing. Kubrick proceeded to use the song as the method by which
the writer later recognises the young hoodlum Alex. Yet the
whole relation between sound and reality in cinema is an
immensely complex one. As with everything extra-verbal,
including colour, music must be modified by spatial demands and generally emerges as the narrative medium it is
not, but which Griffith enjoyed it for. Directors with the

best intentions come notable croppers in the handling of these forms. It is interesting that to date Bergman has been extremely conservative in his use of music, though he has also written, "I would say that there is no art form that has so much in common with film as music." Here he is saying something rather different from Griffith about music, namely that as an art form film shares with music in being "mainly rhythm; it is inhalation and exhalation in continuous sequence."

"One may sum up," write the persuasive critics, Ralph Stephenson and J. R. Debrix, "by saying that, while the spatialisation of time and the temporalisation of space are useful concepts, the two are finally inseparable. One of the achievements of the cinema is that it can effect an ideal synthesis . . . It is this which makes the cinema truly an art and one of the richest and most developed of them all." It is precisely this for which film is most indebted to narrative fiction, since the means of effecting this "ideal synthesis," of investing space-time with meaning, is achieved in the novel by point of view.

A novel is narrated by an omniscient author, a third person, or an internal character. All have only limited knowledge, or focus on events; even the omniscient author, as in the case of François Mauriac, can explain certain events as acts of God, out of his control. The camera is a point of view. For this reason alone film is frequently at its best when dealing with strong characters. "Realism," wrote Albert Camus, "is indefinite enumeration." The camera simply cannot stake out a universe in the Balzacian manner; and it was on account of this intensive objectification that Thibaudet described Balzac as one of the first novelists to compete with God—"The *Comédie humaine* is the *imitation* of God the Father." In film the universe is never as closed as is that of Balzac or Flaubert, simply since the camera has to be a single (or monocular) point of view. Balzac only proceeds when you have given in to him, and he feels sure that the world in which his characters move is completely circumscribed. Camera vision is not so circumscribed. It is astonishing the degree of consensus given to Balzac when you start setting out his lack of verisimilitude, on the "realistic" plane, and sometimes quite preposterous melodrama.

Originally, the novel was news; and so long as it presented the new its form could fluctuate. Formal conventions were small, and an author like Defoe or Stendhal could walk in and out of his fictions in a manner we have generally outlawed today, when creative writing schools are teaching the composition of the novel in a series of pigeon-holes—setting, characters, plot, mood, point of view. None of these norms seems to have been at all rigorous until around the middle of the last century. At this point we have some longish letters by George Eliot on how to compose a fiction from a point of view, and her famous Chapter XVII ("In Which the Story Pauses a Little") of *Adam Bede* where she regards the novelist's duty as "to give a faithful account of men and things as they have mirrored themselves in my mind." There are the letters exchanged between Flaubert and Sand during 1875 and 1876 on the shape of the novel. We have some parenthetical comment by G. H. Lewes, some equally parenthetical but infinitely more perceptive comment by the Goncourts between 1851 and 1870, two disappointing books on the novel by Zola, the Prefaces of Conrad and James and others, but no single body of normative discussion of novel composition until very late in its career—until, in fact, film has mimicked it. In Britain fiction only begins a serious aesthetic in the Twenties when Percy Lubbock systematised James in his *The Craft of Fiction,* to which Forster responded with his suggestive *Aspects of the Novel* (1927), with Edwin Muir and others following up apace. Today the shelves of many university libraries groan under tracts on how to write a fiction.

The long lack of legislative criticism probably worked for the best. Novels could soon feel around corners, experiment with methods of narration, without their authors always being rapped over the knuckles; it has been the bane of cinema to grow up beside its criticism. Above all was it James who saw that a narrative depends, for all its values, on the "centre of vision" or point of view whence it springs and unfolds—which is to say that it is pre-filmic. In *The Turn of the Screw* James organised a five-finger exercise in point-of-view narration; within an important frame we are told what happens by a governess and, on reflection, have to concede that she may be an unreliable, perhaps even violently irresponsible, witness. The Clayton film made from this enticing tale, *The Innocents,* in common with the Marlon Brando vehicle later (*The Nightcomers*), found it virtually impossible to achieve such ambiguity of point of view. *Caligari*'s greatness was to approach this integrity of vision, seeing all through the eyes of Francis, until he is wrapped in a straitjacket at the end. But Joyce, Conrad, James, and Ford Madox Ford (notably in *The Good Soldier*) subtly mixed points of view, and thus reality, before our mesmerised eyes. We have seen some of this duplicity in Poe, but at one point in Conrad's *Lord Jim* we find ourselves reading:

"Ah! it's you. Lend a hand quick."

If you work out the Chinese boxes of these quotation marks (what Huxley, in *Point Counter Point,* called a sort of Quaker Oats theme*), you find that a sailor is speaking

---

* "Put a novelist into the novel. He justifies aesthetic generalizations, which may be interesting—at least to me. He also justifies experiment. Specimens of his work may illustrate other possible or impossible ways of telling a story. And if you have him telling parts of the same story as you are, you can make a variation on the theme. But why draw the line at one novelist inside your novel? Why not a second inside his? And a third inside the novel of the second? And so on to infinity, like those advertisements of Quaker Oats where there's a Quaker holding a box of oats, on which etc., etc." (From Philip Quarles's Notebook, inside the novel.)

to Jim, Jim is speaking to Marlow, Marlow to his listeners, and in a sense his listeners to the author who is reporting to us. Not one of these witnesses is necessarily reliable; on the other hand, all may be.

Being a selective presence itself, inevitably a point of view, the camera simply cannot combine several, often conflicting, centres of consciousness like this. It would be too self-defeating to do so. *Rashomon* tried, but could not possibly reproduce the simultaneity available to such cross-functioning in fiction. In a film the director cannot fuse the temporal elements properly. The rendition of stream-of-consciousness in cinema, as the strict film of *Ulysses* showed, is bound to extend images in time simply in order to make them intelligible. So Kurosawa had to continue with each story in *Rashomon* until it was exhausted. But the human self is interpenetrated with a whole variety of perplexing and disparate elements that have to be handled at once; the self unifies all these experiences under the *I*. To translate the *I* into a continuity of images is to say that the subconscious is merely functional. Thus Hans Meyer-hoff:

> For what binds the chaotic pieces floating through the day-dreams and fantasies of an individual into some kind of unity is that they make "sense"—sense defined in terms of significant, associative images—only if they are referred to or seen within the perspective of the *same* self. It is this "symbolic reference" within the same self which makes them significant. Otherwise, they would indeed be nonsense. They make sense precisely because the author has constructed the individual character in such a way that the apparently chaotic pieces are all inter-related by virtue of the underlying associations and because the reader is expected to reconstruct, at least to a certain extent, this network of significant relations.

In other words, we cannot in cinema play with too many points of view; the imagistic associations aroused would begin to be meaningless, would cease to contribute to structural unity and general sense. The centre of consciousness has been so pre-eminent in the novel simply because fiction does *not* have to depend on images, which often tend to dissipate identity, rather than build it up.

As Gerald R. Barrett and Thomas L. Erskine put it: "Film does not have the luxury of succeeding with as many points of view. It follows, then, that the quality of some literary works is not accessible to film. With care, an acceptable third-person-limited film can be made, but film customarily is narrated from a third-person-ominiscient point of view . . . Thus, first-person narrations can be achieved, but the outcome is seldom cinematically satisfactory in the fiction film." It is seldom so since this is what fiction is. In Joseph Losey's version of L. P. Hartley's *The Go-Between* the all-important point of view, the first-person narration, was attempted by intercalating sequences showing the old man into whom the young boy is destined to grow. In *A Separate Peace* great fidelity to point of view was attempted (with the novel's dialogue used verbatim for stretches of the screenplay). This story of a school called Devon (Exeter in actuality) is seen through the eyes of the grown-up Gene; in the film the camera shoots him only from the rear. We hear his voice, but never see his face. In *Deliverance,* made at the same time, the director wisely decided to abandon the book's direct narration. Scores of illustrations could be given of this supreme stumbling-block of cinema, for only when a film-maker realises that point-of-view *is* itself narration can he begin to encompass the meaning of a literary original.

On the "David Frost Show" of June 1970, Orson Welles explained the genesis of *Kane* as follows: "I'll tell you how it started—an idea that was used years later in a Japanese film called *Rashomon,* which is several people telling a story. You see the same story again from each point of view, and each time it's different. . . ." It is astonishing that Welles saw anything at all original in the multiple points of view of this fine film; the technique of mirroring an event in the relativity of various minds had surely been done to death in fiction by the time this film appeared. Gide exhausted it in the Eighteen-Nineties. The magnificent shot of Kane reduced in a series of mirrors outside Susan's bedroom, which he has just destroyed, is as fine a visualisation of points of view that I know. For Kane has just shattered himself. Almost blubbering, he has pleaded with her, "You —you can't do this to me, Susan." The visual image here perfectly marries with Kane's devastated self-image, and in Welles's later *Lady from Shanghai* an almost identical hall-of-mirrors shot is somehow empty, a mere trick. One wonders, furthermore, whether Welles was aware when he saw *Rashomon* that Kurosawa took it from a fiction of the same name by Ryunosuke Akutagawa, but borrowed his whole structure of conflicting points of view from another story by the same author called *In a Grove*. Since novelistic point-of-view is the key to how cinema communicates artistic experience, we will look at its handling in a typical Conrad transposition below.

At the risk of being repetitious, therefore, it must be re-emphasised that a film is going to live or die by the solidity and universality of its norms of narration. That visuality, action, cannot eventually overtake some sort of intellection is evinced by the death, today, of the hundreds of mindless rock documentaries made in the Sixties and early Seventies. Indeed, if norms were purely visual a *genre* in cinema, such as the western or detective thriller, could be set up and its examples evaluated by arbitrary standards of the *genre*. However, generic criticism has not survived in this field.

Throughout the Twenties, via extended attacks on Bergson, Joyce, Gertrude Stein and others, Wyndham Lewis tried to stimulate "a philosophy that will be as much a *spatial-philosophy* as Bergson's is a *time-philosophy*." Yet Bergson remained durable, essentially ahead of his detractors like Lewis and, in France, Julien Benda; he observed that the intellect distorts reality if it unfolds everything in space (*Essai sur les données immédiates de la conscience*). In the critical mind intellect has to operate willy-nilly and Kant properly reminded us how deeply our sense of human identity is rooted in time.

Cinema's temporal artificialities have led some recent critics to proclaim that there is an autonomous world of film, with its own sanctities of space and time. "Though language is the most efficient and valuable medium for sharing ideas and experiences," write Marsha Kinder and Beverle Houston in *Close-Up,* "its linear nature limits its ability to describe certain phenomena. Cinema can offer a great number of visual events simultaneously, linking them in unpredictable ways." Without entering into the tautology of just how "linear" language is (Chinese? Arabic?), or directing these critics to Eisenstein on the ideogram (in a 1929 epilogue to N. Kaufman's Moscow publication on *Japanese Cinema*), one must soon concede, after seeing a number of recent films, that if the ability of language to "describe" is limited, its ability to analyse is not. How many of us have come away from some film, bombarded by the superstimulation of technique, only to begin to think through the philosophy behind the images and find it insultingly empty? The process of meaning can be wholly demeaned by the "spatialising" of cinema. Writing in *Lifestyle,* Robert Brown asks much the same question:

> With movies worth talking about at all a critic must juggle the appreciation of craft and the analysis of meaning in ways that are, as yet, much vaguer than anyone would like or, alas, than most critics seem to realize. The glee with which the word "masterpiece" was hurled at *The Last Picture Show* merely shows how mindless enthusiasm, stimulated by a movie self-evidently superior to, say, the average western, can substitute for analysis. It must, to some extent, be a matter of emphasis. Does *Carnal Knowledge,* inspired by a rootless cynicism that misrepresents reality and debases humanity, condemn at least three fine performances to futility? For the film junkie, perhaps not; for the critic, probably yes.

The area of film discussed in this book intensifies, rather than relieves, this problem. When the source of a film is a prior work of art, perhaps a well-known novel, there is an extra-curricular meaning to start with. The "linear" printed word has already sunk its jaws, as it were, into meaning and simply will not let go. It is for this reason that the *auteur* school of criticism tried, as intransigently as possible, to sever all connections with literature, to shout in our ears that literary training is irrelevant and, thereby, to reverse what Eisenstein had more quietly told us. For these new polemicists literary critics cannot *per se* see the significance of films; only the visually-educated can read composition and direction (one wonders why there are so few painters among them).

There is a moment in *Easy Rider* when the protagonists stumble on a hippie commune in the midst of nowhere. One of the long-haired youths, so dedicated to Truth and Freedom, breathes out, "D. H. Lawrence, man," to which Peter Fonda breathes back an awed, "Wow!" Not only would D. H. Lawrence have loathed the drug-induced euphoria presented as the ultimate Nirvana here, but he was also a man who ardently, all too ardently, analysed his society intellectually and formed some constructive ideas about it; these he worked hard to phrase in the only manner available to him. *Easy Rider* was a classic case of how character cannot be action alone; the direction, so sympathetic to the heroes with its colour and movement (and lovely views of America), constantly contradicted what narrative was left over from the images. The two motorcyclist drug-pushers, Dennis Hopper and Peter Fonda, are never associated with the effects of their trade; the casual double-murder of the pair at the end is shown with spiralling smoke, and rising credits, as a summation of the horror of America, entirely omitting the fact that pushers are murderers themselves in the first place. At another point the two interfere in a parade and are put in prison. The director expresses the action in the belief that such will again arouse liberal indignation in his audience but, if thought through, this restraint of two anti-social hooligans is rather less than repressive.* Hirsute and bearded, the couple show hostility to any mild-mannered ordinary citizen, while during their visit to a whorehouse Hopper, at least, acts just like any lecherous travelling salesman. In a particularly brilliant and (for the time) contra-cultural review of this film Rhoda Koenig said:

> The cheap and slick quality of this movie, however, is nowhere near as disheartening as the fact of thousands of kids lined up three deep in front of movie theatres all over the country who don't want convincing. Rather, they are perfectly willing to have confirmed their belief that they've put on a new set of values along with their purposely old and carefully dirtied clothes. Dennis Hopper and Peter Fonda, the easy riders of the title, are attired in hippie regalia, straddle huge, gorgeous motorcycles, use drugs, and apparently have no parents or permanent homes. From this we are invited to infer that they are idealistic, sensitive, individualistic, peace-loving free spirits.

In fiction you could never escape with such amputation of intellect as in *Easy Rider;* a novel with such ideological holes would soon be slipped into the rubbish bin. This is because a novel is written in language in the fullest sense and, to cite once more R. N. Anshen's premise, "man is that being on earth who does not have language. Man *is* language."

The best cinema uses language in this whole sense. Seeing is not treated as daily sight at all, but rather as a kind of style. This style is high when formal control abounds.

---

* I confess to the same reaction when revisiting Truffaut's sentimental *400 Blows*. The central character is a young boy who is stood in the corner for defacing a picture during a lesson. There he scrawls on the wall, later lies, but is evidently supposed to be sympathised with. He is, of course, shouted at by his teacher and slapped by his father, but there are those of us who suffered rather more in our schooldays without turning into lovable typewriter-thieves. Ironically, in real life, Truffaut's testy *lycée* teacher would almost certainly have been a member of the Communist party.

At that point we achieve great cinematic art. This squeeze-out theory is precisely that which Noam Chomsky has applied to language:

> I know it sounds contradictory, but if you think about it, it's very natural. Quartets and sonnets are interesting because they operate within certain restraints. If you drop the whole system of constraints, you can't produce anything of value. The same is true here. It is precisely because of the very narrow restrictive initial system that you can develop a fantastically rich competence of a very explicit sort without too much data, and then use it freely for expressing and thinking. And that, I guess, is the basic use of language.

It is this "basic use of language" in its fullest sense that gives Bergman, at his best, his grip on audiences of sophistication. In *Cries and Whispers,* where the Chopin music and simplicity of photography yield just that feeling of formality and constraint Chomsky mentions, Bergman lays his hand on you and possesses you from the start. There are no unusual tricks. You cannot escape him because you cannot escape yourself. His cinema is that real. With minimal economy Bergman's camera stares at faces which stare back at it, talk directly to you for minutes on end—without interruption from other characters in the immediate vicinity —and continually inform the screen with meaning. Here everything is stylised, including the dialogue, since everything is art. In Bergman as in Flaubert (and *Cries and Whispers* parenthetically echoes *Un Coeur simple*) everything is fraught with significance, yet everything is perfectly natural. The most exact nuances of character are caught, so that what few moments of violence do arise (as on Agnes's heart-rending death-bed with the awful rasping of her breath, or Karen's stabbing of her genitals with a slice of broken glass) are made shatteringly real. We are simply there. And this claim over us can only, like that of all true art, come from total mastery of material.

FACE TO FACE (1953)

"The artist," Carl Dreyer wrote in *Dreyer in Double Reflection*, "must describe inner not outer life." In the cinema he hoped this would be done by "abstraction," by "replacing objective reality with his own subjective interpretation." John Brahm's *Face to Face*, produced by Huntington Hartford (in one of his few forays into cinema), follows Joseph Conrad's *The Secret Sharer*, an extremely "inward" tale, almost slavishly. Of all the transpositions of fiction into film considered here, it must surely rank as one of the most painstakingly faithful.

Talking to Mr. Hartford himself about it in his Antibes villa some years ago, I found that what he was chiefly proud of was this fidelity; at least neither his director nor scenarist, Aeneas MacKenzie, had massacred a masterpiece. *Face to Face*, he felt, was as close to its original text as was James Agee's screenplay for Stephen Crane's *The Bride Comes to Yellow Sky*, with which it was released by RKO and with which it was rather spuriously connected at the start. Reviewing the Conrad adaptation in the February 1953 issue of *Films in Review* Robert Cass paid tribute to the honesty of directorial intentions in this case:

> In his adaptation of "The Secret Sharer," Aeneas MacKenzie
> has adhered to Conrad's meaning and spirit. Most of the dia-
> logue is lifted directly from the text. No extraneous characters,
> no additional scenes, have been written in. As a result, "The
> Secret Sharer" is the first pure Conrad to get to the screen.

There is certainly an absence of impurity in this attempt: such could not be said for either Carol Reed's *An
Outcast of the Islands* (1952), shot in Ceylon and subsequently on two Shepperton stages largely as a vehicle for
the half-Arab starlet Kerima, or Richard Brooks's *Lord
Jim* (1965), considered below. In both these films one
feels that the director saw more action in the narrative
than actually pertained in either: long location sequences,
while the camera bathed in tropical exoticism, induced a
hypnotic monotony not at all suitable to ninety minutes
in a cinema, and when the rushes were seen, action was
peremptorily called for. Charging natives and exploding
jungle had to compensate (as rampaging elephants were
forced to in that transposition of Romain Gary's neo-Con-
radian *The Roots of Heaven*) ; in. *Lord Jim* nothing could
be more absurd, and visually destructive of all that had
been painstakingly built up, than the vision of Dahlia Lavi, looking as immaculate as if she had just stepped out of
an Elizabeth Arden salon, tripping towards a jungle compound with a spear precariously balanced in her hand.

Fortunately, *The Secret Sharer* is short; *Face to Face* replies in kind, running for less than an hour. The story is
a simple one which shares with a number of allegories Conrad wrote about a ship's command, and its necessary solitude as a "condition of existence" (as he says, in another
context, in *Lord Jim*) . The rule over a sailing ship during the end of the last century seemed to him curiously
akin, when such took place on the lonely seas of an un-
charted Orient, to the rule a man must effect over his own

soul. He pushed this comparison forward in works like *Youth, Typhoon,* and *The End of the Tether;* in the last of these insecurity at the helm may have been imagined, and blown up, by Conrad from fear for his own eyes, but in any case, as the biographies now tell us, he must also have feared, as a young French-speaking Pole, any certainty of communication at all when he first gained his British master's certificate. In *The Secret Sharer* the anonymous captain literally thinks he may be going mad. Is the intruder he has secreted on his ship real or not? Towards the end he reflects:

> An irresistible doubt of his bodily existence flitted through my mind. Can it be, I asked myself, that he is not visible to other eyes than mine? It was like being haunted. Motionless, with a grave face, he raised his hands slightly at me in a gesture which meant clearly, "Heavens! what a narrow escape!" Narrow indeed. I think I had come creeping quietly as near insanity as any man who has not actually gone over the border.

Conrad's story has never been a particular favourite of mine—it lacks power since he insists too much (the reminder that the narrator's secret sharer is a "double," a "second self," and so forth, is laid on so thickly that one feels like telling Conrad after three pages that he has made his point). But the intensity of the situation *for Conrad himself* has to be conceded, or we do not know what he is saying. A young captain, assuming first command over an unknown ship in the Gulf of Siam, takes on board a swimmer who declares himself to be the mate of a vessel nearby who had actually murdered one of his hands for insubordination during a perilous storm. The readiness of the captain to believe this man's story, and altogether trust him, is quite unreal or unnatural, and precisely what Conrad wanted to emphasise. There is the usual Conradian dubiety about the ethics of the "murder"—as in Jim's famous jump from the *Patna.* The murdering mate Leggatt himself feels he was simply protecting his ship, and the lives of those on her. The hand gave him "cursed insolence at the sheet." So, as the storm menaced, he "felled him like an ox." The other then came at him and they fought until the sea crashed on them "as if the sky had fallen on my head . . . I was holding him by the throat when they picked us up. He was black in the face." No British jury, Leggatt thinks, remote from the tensions of the situation, would give him a chance. Conrad further interjects a doubt not only about the precise nature of Leggatt's crime—if it be such—but about a definitive order which the visiting captain of the *Sephora*, trying to find Leggatt, says he gave, but which Leggatt later denies that he did. There is no easy resolution.

This moral incertitude is the whole point of the story. Any jury today would acquit Leggatt without further ado; the visiting captain of the threatened *Sephora* admits, in Conrad's pages, that Leggatt saved his ship—

> "That reefed foresail saved you," I threw in.
> "Under God—it did," he exclaimed fervently.

The film makes of this captain a pious Welsh Presbyterian (a nice touch), but what it does not, cannot, effect is the true tension in the story, the terror and horror the captain feels. The film can give us the adventure of the original, suggest something of the moral crisis, but the camera cannot play depth psychologist. James Mason's muted rendering of Conrad's tormented skipper never approximates to what is going on.

And what *is* going on? It is, after all, a fairly irrational man who sees a swimmer like a large fish at the bottom of a rope ladder and who, when he hauls him in, immediately feels that "a mysterious communication was established already between us two." When he finds the man to be a fugitive from justice he shelters him as sedulously as if he had committed the crime himself. Leggatt has killed, there is no doubt about that; when he admits as much to the captain, the latter merely retorts, "Fit of temper." John Brahm's pedestrian approach quite misses the enormity of guilt involved in this night journey into the self; he has to compensate for its absence by enlarging the class level, which Conrad barely bothers with, and by such symbolic overtones as having Leggatt recount his "crime" behind rigging suggestive of prison bars to a captain whose sleeping suit is noticeably striped, like a convict's. Both the captain and Leggatt are upper-class "Conway" products—gentlemen. The groomed look of both James Mason and Michael Pate, playing Leggatt, is contrasted with the slovenly appearance of the two mates, Brown and Robinson. For some reason, too, Robinson is made to speak with an Irish accent, Brown with a Scottish, and the visiting Captain Archbold, played by Gene Lockhart, a Welsh.

For Lionel Trilling, one of the few critics to admit the Captain's genuine involvement with evil in the story, Conrad is presenting us with a little paradigm of authority; the guilty secret which has to be hidden from the crew is "the coercive *force* that lies concealed at the heart of all authority." This is a much more helpful recognition. Authority over one's fellows does have its ugly side, even in their own interest. Leggatt is Spenser's Talus reborn. Most critics forget that in *Heart of Darkness* (Welles's choice for his first film) the "honest" narrator Marlow feels a quite irrational attraction to the vile dictator, Kurtz. The orthodox liberal reader usually solves this dilemma by suggesting that Marlow, having had a horror image of the human condition at its lowest, ends up facing Kurtz's "Intended" a shaken and maturer man. This is not there in the text where Marlow explicitly observes that "I have remained loyal to Kurtz to the last. . . ." Brahm's film tries to account for this ambivalence at the end simply because it has to. Why, when all is said and done, does Conrad have the captain take his ship far closer to the island on which Leggatt is to be marooned than necessary? By doing so he endangers his own officers and crew, as well as his whole future career. Brahm accounts for this act of unreason by staging the abandonment of Leggatt near the island of Koh-ring in a high sea, to increase tension. The crew is seen on deck in a state of near-mutiny. Brown, terrified that they will founder with all hands, tries to push past Mason to get at the wheel, shouting "You're insane, man, you're insane!"* Mason grapples with Brown, while the leadsman's hail announces ever-impending disaster; as he shakes his mate by the throat there is a flashback to Leggatt's similar crisis and strangling of another "funk" or coward. At this the captain brings his ship round in the nick of time. Brahm then has him toss his cap over the side into the sea in some sort of jubilation, an over-conscientious answer to what happens in the original, for it establishes very little. In Conrad's story the captain had given Leggatt a floppy hat (his intellect or ego aspect perhaps) to protect him from the sun on Koh-ring; in fact, as Leggatt is swimming, he apparently sees the extent of the captain's foolhardy risk and throws his hat as a marker for the latter to use, in order to see when the ship was gaining way ("And now—behold—it was saving the ship").

In the film this moment has little function, and could have been dispensed with; Brahm would have found such an indication much too slow for his purpose at this point. Even as it is, we are hardly aware when the ship is clearing. Nevertheless, the words put into Brown's mouth as they head into open water, shortly after his Captain has nearly

---

* Aeneas MacKenzie's screenplay is conveniently reprinted in *Media for Our Time* (New York: Holt, Rinehart & Winston, 1971), edited by my colleague Dennis DeNitto; it is peppered with more sailing phrases than the whole of Conrad put together. It was clearly modified in the shooting: thus, for Conrad, Leggatt was naked when he came on board and the screenplay first has him so, yet tells us that as he climbs the ladder Leggatt is "clad only in a pair of seaman's short-length drawers."

throttled him to death and wrecked the vessel, are little short of ludicrous. He turns to Robinson with a smile, "Now you know what sort of a seaman he is, Mr. Robinson."

Conrad's captain is far from the lily-white naval cadet suggested by Mason's performance. This is a double legend, in the tradition of Poe and Dostoyevski, and to see one's moral existence outside oneself is a dreadful confrontation. The worst nightmares recorded from his hallucinations by Gérard de Nerval in *Aurélia* were those when he encountered a figure which turned out to be himself—"O terreur! ô colère! c'était mon visage. . . ." Pascal had earlier proposed this antithetical self of man, born out of anxiety and fear—Yeats's "anti-self," a soul-shadow that threatens our very identity. Poe's William Wilson meets his other self in one of these soul battles, and so does Conrad's captain who attains, however, that "perfect communion" at the end simply because he has been willing to acknowledge, as Trilling points out, his second self; he did so by risking conventional morality in the manner of Leggatt. When we are told of the latter that he had "crushed an unworthy mutinous existence,"—unworthy because it was mutinous—it would be jejune to take this literally. It is intended psychologically.

Conrad invites this reading throughout. He marries primitive superstition in the soul-double with contemporary psychological insight—before Freud. There is a note of magic in his story, certainly a transcendental level which Brahm's direction badly misses. Talking to Leggatt the captain imagines that if they were spotted by any of the hands, it would look like "a scene of weird witchcraft." Leggatt tells him, "No chief mate ever made more than one voyage in the *Sephora*, you know." Perhaps Brahm or his writer sensed the loss of something of this nature since the captain is given a fiancée whom he will marry "as soon as I'm anchored in the Thames." To which Leggatt is made to reply, "You get a ship and you get your girl." However, this may have been mere conventional padding, like the music poured in throughout or the scene in which Mason and Pate shave together in the bathroom, making a double image in the mirror (and violating all reality by shaving with cut-throat razors with one hand only).

Brahm's problem was principally one of narration, of point of view. The only way to handle a double story from within the perspective of one character is probably in the manner of Cocteau. His major film characters clearly externalise the split of a character into angel and demon, shown fictionally in Hermann Hesse's *Demian* (1919) and *Siddharta* (1923). In Cocteau's cinema the fissure is sometimes eventuated into and personified by other characters; the angelic or rational type in the arrangement, as in Rilke's lovely poem *Der Schutzengel,* must be a link between creature and creator; this drama is also presented by Mann in much of his fiction, as in the circus scenes in *Felix Krull,* hints quite lost in the film made from that delightful satire. Conrad's captain's double comes out of the sea and must be given back to it. Cocteau's play *Orphée,* produced by Pitoëff at the Théatre des Arts in 1926, contains the same theme in the guise of one Heurtebise, who also appears in a longish poem of lament called "L'Ange Heurtebise" (collected in *Opéra*).

When Cocteau was faced with filming *Orphée* some years later Heurtebise is again made the link; Jean Marais is directed to step into the underworld by piercing a mirror like water. This is no mere borrowing from the Alice books, for traditionally the soul-shadow lay behind mirrors and reflections, to break or step into which meant ill-luck. We remember, too, that Heurtebise was the name of a famous lift firm in France; in Mann's *Felix Krull* the Hermes-like hero takes a job in a Paris grand hotel as a lift-boy, an intermediary, no less, between our heights and depths. These charming puns on the human condition demand response in film, and are exceedingly hard to manifest there; Malle's analogy of *William Wilson* was banality itself, including a juicy whipping of Brigitte Bardot's back. Cocteau nearly always presents something of that "subjective interpretation" of objective reality desiderated by Dreyer.

In the play *Orphée* we meet Heurtebise as a glazier with his panes of glass around him (*viz.* as Baudelaire's "mauvais vitrier") suddenly suspended miraculously in the air when Orphée removes his chair from under him—for Heurtebise has the divine properties of elevation. Involving a multiplicity of arts cinema can do this much more effectively. We are not suggesting that Cocteau could have improved *The Secret Sharer* on celluloid; but a double story has deep implications and *Le Sang d'un poète* (1932) succeeds in being a more compelling, even if surrealist, psychomachia than Brahm's plodding version of a Conrad text of the second rank. In Cocteau's best films there is an imagination that has risen to cognition beside the viewer's own. In *Face to Face* we are constantly ahead of the filmic pace.

Conrad's little legend is a first-person story. By its end we cannot know if Leggatt really existed at all on the captain's ship; perhaps the latter is really suffering from split-personality hallucinations, going round the bend (as he himself confesses confusedly), but the film establishes Leggatt as existing. We see him in his hiding-place apart from the Captain. He is alive. And he is much less of a horror image by virtue of *not* being an hallucination, or evidence of autoscopy. "Are you a ghost?" Mason once inquires of Pate, but the question means little and when the latter tells us he is really "dead" we simply hear so many words.

Ultimately we learn that in its narrative aspect film depends on far more than visualisation. Such can be verified by strolling into a cinema and seeing the last ten minutes of some visually-powerful work. However arresting, the images remain empty; then, when we see the whole art work from the start, they acquire significance.

If film is to show "inner not outer life," as Dreyer required, how finally could it best present so thoroughly inner a story as Conrad's *The Secret Sharer*? By keeping the viewer on the wrong foot . . . guessing . . . until the very end, as in *The Spider's Strategy* (1973), the work of that cerebral director Bernardo Bertolucci, or in Elio Petri's brilliantly contrived *Investigation of a Citizen above Suspicion* (1970)? By an "absolute" point of view attempted throughout something like *Lady in the Lake* (1946)? I have mentioned that Robert Mulligan's *The Other* presented a teasingly brilliant exercise in such narrative integrity. Here the norms of narration were subtly fitted for film. The unprepared viewer could not know that Holland, the younger of twins who palpably exists on the screen in the first, lushly lit moments of the work is in reality a corpse. When you return to the novel, however, you are tipped off, at least to an extent. The unpleasant lad Russell (to die impaled on a pitchfork) comes upon the barn hiding-place of the twins Niles and Holland, and the novelist's secretion of the latter (who is dead) behind some baskets becomes so fictionally awkward as to be alerting. However, this film or its screenplay could be said to be a special case, perhaps the kind of fiction we shall see increasingly in the future, both on our shelves and on our screens. The author Thomas Tryon, who had worked successfully in pictures, was plainly thinking in filmic terms. Tryon surely constructed his narrative to accord with cinematic principles, if not Literary Guild values. Conrad was a novelist, commercially unsuccessful for the most part, and nothing evinces this more clearly than John Brahm's courageous attempt at filming him.

Three:
METHODS

Three Modes of Adaptation

Film, wrote Susanne Langer in a now famous Appendix on cinema to her *Feeling and Form*, is "a new poetic mode." It has "swallowed the photograph" and produced a new form of dream. Yet, she goes on to remind us, the camera itself cannot be a dreamer. The camera, accompanied by a soundtrack, is the manner of presentation of the dream whose agent must be the creative imagination.

A film is like a dream, as we have discussed above, since it exists in the present. In common with a good painting it should create and resolve visual tensions. It is called on to give form to the world; ideally it should be the unique expressive form available to its content. A great novel by Flaubert incorporates within it certain natural objects since these have been selected for the purpose of a unified abstraction and perception. Something is being exhibited to us; we begin to see through the dreamer's eye, just as we tend to see the objects in a painting in the way the artist saw them while at work on his canvas. A reverie, however, is not necessarily art, and cinema has had to be the most public form of reverie ever indulged in. The first nickelodeon theatres were often given names like "Dreamland" or "Bijou Dream." Theoretically, each new form of realism entering into cinema should have provoked greater possibilities of expressive form, by expanding the potential for art, rather than eliciting cries of philistinism from such as René Clair. It is surely for this reason—its proximity to the subconscious and its management of spatial illusion—that film relied so heavily on fiction that at the time Mrs. Langer was writing her Appendix over fifty per cent of a sample of pictures coming before the U.S. Production Code office were from novels.

George Bluestone calls fiction "a medium antithetical to film," and by being linguistic rather than visual it is so. But this is surely to miss the point. Far more than poetry, an intellectual mode, the novel is a dream in the sense that it has generally given us an exterior world as seen by the reflections of a character. Virginia Woolf told us that all "which is accessible to words alone, the cinema must avoid." In its *secondary* illusion it must; but its art is acting for a primary agent, the dreamer.

In a sense everything is accessible to words. Eisenstein saw Griffith, therefore, as a "pioneer, by his own admission, rather than an inventor." Griffith's techniques for presenting the secondary illusion which is set on the screen were all drawn from novels simply because the formulation of life in fiction resulted from the same formal relationships as exist in making a film. In both, as we have seen, a point-of-view is being created. "Using literary sources for such experiments," writes Gerald R. Barrett, "Griffith eventually produced all of the major film techniques." This may be a hard truth for *cinéma-vérité* and *auteurist* critics to swallow, but it is one. It is for this reason that good films can be made from indifferent fictions. Béla Balázs clearly realised this point in his *Theory of the Film*. A form, he saw, made its own content, an insight elongated from Flaubert:

There can be no doubt that it is possible to take the subject, the story, the plot of a novel, turn it into a . . . film and yet produce perfect works of art in each case—the form being in each case adequate to the content . . . It is possible because, while the subject, or story, of both works is identical, their *content* is nevertheless different. It is this different *content* that is adequately expressed in the changing form resulting from the adaptation.

To take the life of a man from Plutarch and make of it a great play is essentially, in this sense, to alter content. This is a happier way of looking at the process of adaptation than to say, as did Balázs elsewhere, that a film-maker may look on an existing work of art "merely as raw material."

Film has often performed the task of restoration on fiction. In the Forties one thinks of Max Ophüls's *Letter from an Unknown Woman* out of indifferent Stefan Zweig; of Ford's work on Richard Llewellyn's *How Green Was My Valley* after having superbly transposed weak O'Flaherty into *The Informer;* of the ennoblement of second-grade American thriller writers of the time, e.g. Huston's *The Maltese Falcon* from Dashiell Hammett or Howard Hawks's *The Big Sleep* out of Chandler (the screenplay being in this case co-written by Faulkner). In the Fifties Ford's *The Last Hurrah* refined a mediocre best-seller, with Hawks doing the same for A. B. Guthrie Jr.'s pot-boiling *The Big Sky.* It could even be said that, in the next decade, Robert Bresson improved on Bernanos in *Mouchette* (with the earlier *Diary of a Country Priest* earning more laurels for the same novelist) and Welles enlarging Isak Dinesen in *The Immortal Story.* It could be argued that this was a period when the number one best-seller was almost invariably docketed for the screen and since a high proportion of such fiction was commercial trash, it was not hard to make an improvement. Even so, subsequent films of consequence continue to come from relatively ordinary novels: James Agee's *The Af-*

rican Queen, The Graduate, The Last Picture Show, The Godfather, Goodbye, Columbus, Midnight Cowboy, A Separate Peace (as suggestive of Hesse's *Demian* as of its John Knowles original) —each could make up his or her list. The strain prevails.

Its true philistinism can perhaps be seen at its ripest in McLuhan and his followers (or predecessors) whose popularity was surely assured when young people who found "difficult" novels difficult were reassured that they were really inferior to films, e.g.:

> The film *Moby Dick* was in many ways an improvement on the book, primarily because of its explicitness. For *Moby Dick* is one of those admittedly great classics, like *Robinson Crusoe* or Kafka's *Trial,* whose plot and situation, as distilled apart from the book by time and familiarity, are actually much more imposing than the written book itself. It's the drama of Ahab's defiance rather than Melville's uncharted leviathan meanderings that is the greatness of *Moby Dick*. On film, instead of laborious tacks through leagues of discursive interruptions, the most vivid descriptions of whales and whaling become part of the action. On film, the viewer was constantly aboard ship: each scene an instantaneous shot of whaling life, an effect achieved in the book only by illusion, by constant, detailed reference . . . Unlike the book, the film gave a spare, hard, compelling dramatization, free of self-conscious symbolism. (From Edmund Carpenter and Marshall McLuhan, *Explorations in Communication*)

On the basis of Balázs' thesis, therefore, three types of transition of fiction into film can be considered here. The first of these will be the *transposition,* in which a novel is directly given on the screen, with the minimum of apparent interference. This has been the dominant and most pervasive method used by Hollywood throughout its history. We shall see that it has also been the least satisfactory precisely owing to what Balázs says: the same material can only successfully be put into a new form "if the terms 'content' and 'form' do not exactly cover what we are accustomed to call material, action, plot, story, subject, etc. on the one hand and 'art form' on the other."

The head-on Hollywood assault on classics of fiction, aspects of which we shall examine below, has been typically puerile. The film was envisaged as a book illustration, an effect frequently heightened by an opening in which the pages of the original are turned over. The "classic" comicbooks, in which *Hamlet* is reduced to a few wordless pages, mostly of the duel scene, is the ultimate *reductio* of this attitude; but even its more intelligent applications are more likely to dissatisfy than not. As Stanley Solomon has said, "What can a visual image do but repeat what Shakespeare has described?" Writing in *The Dial* in the Twenties an early film critic, Thomas Craven, paralleled what I. A. Richards was saying in semantics:

> I doubt if the most astute and sympathetic reader ever visualises a character; he responds to that part of a created figure which is also himself, but he does not actually see his hero . . . For this reason all illustrations are disappointing.

They usually are, except to children; and Hollywood was for long making films for children of all ages.

The second category of such translation I have loosely termed *commentary*. This is where an original is taken and either purposely or inadvertently altered in some respect. It could also be called a re-emphasis or re-structure.

Today our property concerns do not incline us to regard any tampering with an original as a tribute and, of the three types considered here, the restatement of an original novel is naturally in the minority. This seems to represent more of an infringement on the work of another than an analogy which may simply take a fiction as a point of departure. Yet film can make authentic reconstructions in the spirit of so many cinematic footnotes to the original: Visconti's *Death in Venice* might be considered one example of this kind of creative restoration, whose extent varies with directors. Ken Russell's work with Lawrence (*Women in Love*) or Huxley (*The Devils*) comes to mind in this respect, as does Schlesinger's interpretation of Hardy's *Far from the Madding Crowd*. And what of the indebtedness of Chaplin's *Modern Times* to Clair's *A nous, la Liberte*?

One telling instance of such filmic restatement might be Bernardo Bertolucci's operation on Jorge Borges's *Theme of the Traitor and Hero,* issued as *The Spider's Strategy* (1969, Italian TV). Bertolucci here quite reverses the role, or essential motivation, of the main character he is dealing with, an historical researcher in Borges's pages. It does not matter, for the film is successful, and this is all the more interesting in a director who, in adapting Moravia's *The Conformist,* had kept close to his original text. Indeed, Bertolucci's restructuring of the latter is almost a model of how to deal with an intransigently "inner" story. *The Spider's Strategy* might also lead to helpful comparisons here, but in neither case is an English text currently very available.

Sometimes a change in character or scene may actually fortify the values of its original on the printed page. In Richardson's *Tom Jones* the celebrated meal in which two bed-partners consume mountains of food faster and faster made a sexual pun that was fully in Fielding's spirit. It is when there has been a different intention on the part of the film-maker, rather than an infidelity or outright violation, that I would class the result as a *commentary.* An example chosen below is Wyler's *The Heiress* which knowingly embroiders on James's *Washington Square* in its ending.

Ending alterations vary. At times they seem forced on the director by the imagery he has previously exploited. Thus, in the story of *The Graduate* Charles Webb has Ben arrive split seconds before the wedding ceremony, uniting Elaine to the "square" Carl Smith, has been completed; Elaine then runs off with Ben. By this point in the film, however, Nichols is obviously stuck with the Dustin Hoffman image of Ben, a fairly incompetent youth despite his running prowess (which looks unlikely anyway, given that actor's waistline) and one considerably bedraggled in Elaine's eyes. Nichols thus cleverly shows yet another defeat for bumbling Ben, since he arrives after the ceremony is over. However, this serves to increase our satisfaction since we not only see a small guy getting his girl, as the couple board the bus, but we see marriage as a straitjacket institution defeated. The attendant songs of Simon and Garfunkel celebrate this sense of triumph.

Again, the successful Asquith-Howard *Pygmalion* of 1938 distorted its ending, admittedly from a play, even more daringly. In the film, as in the later *My Fair Lady* when Shaw's original was returned to the stage, so to speak, we are given a repentant Eliza going back to Higgins in the manner of a little girl who has had a temper tantrum, and being all the more lovable for such. Shaw himself does not give Eliza back to Higgins. True, Higgins assumes she will return, and the Epilogue treats their reconciliation, but it did not have to be staged and the play is stronger without it. When Eliza originally walked out, she meant it. It is true that Shaw wrote the screenplay, at Pascal's insistence, yet he was not a scenarist and had by this time heavily sentimentalised his earlier feminism. The film is prefaced by a few sweet words about Pygmalion and Galatea, but Shaw had originally written, "Galatea never does quite like Pygmalion: his relation to her is too godlike to be altogether agreeable."

Of much less importance Ronald Neame's 1972 restructuring of Paul Gallico's *The Poseidon Adventure* appeared to have been another case of re-emphasis due to strong plot changes required by imagery. The same happened to *The French Connection;* though not a novel, this was an authentic story of the attempt to smuggle some $32 million of heroin into the U.S.A. The film of it makes a fascinating study in the changes inevitable in cinema, when any verbal original is enjoined. Before any critic jumps on William Friedkin for directorial butchery here, or writer Ernest Tidyman for unscrupulous self-indulgence, several requirements involving imagery have to be taken into account. The book describes 1961; the film is set in 1971. Car styles changed considerably in the interval, and a car is the medium of heroin importation. In the book, Patsy (Sal in the film) has a brother called Tony (in both book and film), who is a longshoreman from the Bronx. The film has him a trainee with the NYC Sanitation Department. *Verb. sap.!* The film turns into a single chase, not too far from the ending of *Lord Jim* in the hands of Richard Brooks. Anyone, however, who knows the hypersensitivity of legal departments of major studios will more than sympathise with Friedkin's difficulties of restructure in *The French Connection.*

Finally, there is the *analogy.* Martin C. Battestin has written: "To judge whether or not a film is a successful adaptation of a novel is to evaluate the skill of its makers in striking analogous attitudes and in finding analogous rhetorical techniques." One might thus think of films that shift a fiction forward into the present, and make a duplicate story: George Bluestone's transposing of Melville's *Bartleby the Scrivener* to contemporary London would be a case in point. Wolf Mankowitz's loose use of Gogol's *The Overcoat* to characterise British Jewry, a short highly praised in its day, might be another. Norbert Carbonnaux amusingly advanced *Candide* in 1960. But the analogy can go much further than this, and also in different directions. Professor Robert Richardson has, for instance, ingeniously argued for *La dolce vita* as an analogy to Eliot's *The Waste Land,* both being "twentieth-century versions of Ecclesiastes." My colleague Professor William Herman was once faced with having to teach a film course in this field without funds; he had his students read novels and then sent them out to local movie houses to see "analogies."*

*e.g., *Jules et Jim:* Chaucer, "The Knight's Tale"; *8½:* Dante, *The Inferno; Pound:* Kafka, *Metamorphosis.* In fact, a film of the last was made in the Sixties for BBC television. I would myself further suggest comparing the life of Christ with Bergman's *Cries and Whispers.*

For our purpose here analogy must represent a fairly considerable departure for the sake of making *another* work of art. One analogous technique, as in the sex-as-gastronomy passage in *Tom Jones,* is not enough. Again, in *The Graduate,* we find techniques used to support the story by analogy. In Charles Webb's story the central character Ben admits his intimacy with Mrs. Robinson to her daughter Elaine on a sunny day. Nichols introduces heavy rain at this point, thus reinforcing the traumatic confession by a now soaked and thoroughly dishevelled image of Ben—as he promptly becomes in the girl's mind. The rain further serves as information, telling Elaine that her mother, equally soaked, has been with Ben. These are indeed rhetorical techniques, substitutions, one could say, inserted to urge the story along. In our sense, however, an analogy generally goes far further than this and so cannot be indicted as a violation of a literary original since the director has not attempted (or has only minimally attempted) to reproduce the original. In the old Hollywood transposition there was an implicit guarantee that you would see something of Dickens or Thackeray intact, or else you would be distinctly disappointed when you left the cinema. Both *Tom Jones* and *The Graduate* reproduce their originals with considerable fidelity and cannot be classed as analogies by our definition here.

Yet an analogy can still be a violation. Robert Bresson's *Four Nights of a Dreamer* (1972) took Dostoyevski's *White Nights* and transposed it from Nineteenth-century St. Petersburg to contemporary Paris—legitimate enough, if a slightly shoddy effort to pay court to youth-cult values, since hippies are lovingly photographed playing guitars *à gogo* throughout the streets of the once great capital of the intellect. Despite considerable fidelity in some of the dialogue, this film leaves so little of Dostoyevski, and at the same time so carefully distorts what remains, that one may ask why Bresson did not take another text altogether, perhaps something from Chekhov. Here Dostoyevski's withdrawn and poetic dreamer, who we know all along was in love with Nastenka, becomes a more than usually retarded version of Nichols's Ben, lacking all sensitivity. Instead of romantic speeches he gropes for a girl's breasts, thus substituting sexual desire for quietly desperate idealism. Bresson organises Jacques's love for his Marthe in a series of equally silly vignettes that do no more than pander to the so-called sexual rebellion, and make one wonder why this director is so adulated in the serious film press. Something like this seems to be violation with a vengeance.

Another such, reminding one that there can be no neat pigeon-holes in this area, comes all too readily to mind. Is Buñuel's *Belle de jour* (1967) commentary or analogy? I confess to having been tempted to include a consideration of this film, so recklessly praised, under the former heading, but relinquished the idea on two scores: first, Andrew Sarris, a Buñuel fan, had admirably performed the task already in *Village Voice* (reprinted in *Confessions of a Cultist* and *Film 68/69*), while, second, I could hardly be impartial since I was entrusted with the English translation, and resuscitation, of this dormant fiction, one that I had long admired.*

Kessel published *Belle de jour* in 1929. An attempt at a stage adaptation by Philippe Hériat proved abortive. Since the Thirties it remained relatively forgotten. Robert and Raymond Hakim invited Buñuel to film it and, though an alcoholic by his own admission, the celebrated director did so in eight weeks, editing it in twelve hours, and making a mint of money at the box office in the event. It is certainly a baffling translation. Elliot Stein called *Belle de jour* "a masterpiece" in *Sight and Sound*. But a masterpiece of precisely what? Certainly not of the transposition of a first-class thriller, of what the French call *de bonne mauvaise*

---

* My translation, which presumably Sarris and perhaps other critics have used, was published in America by St. Martin's Press (Dell in paperback) ; an English translation of the scenario is published by Simon and Schuster.

littérature, which is what the book turns into at the end;
for Buñuel deliberately eschewed a climax which in Kessel's
text is one of tremendous suspense—read "melodramatic"
(Sarris), "novelettish" (Stein).* Perhaps it is a masterpiece
of masochism? A pre-*Histoire d'O*? Buñuel fortified this approach at the start, in the scene where Pierre (Jean Sorel)
stops the coach and asks his wife Séverine (Catherine De-
neuve) to step down for a whipping by his servants. Yet
somehow this steal from de Sade is so banal and empty of
true sado-masochistic reverberation—"Pierre, I love you,"
she whimpers after the whipping—that it seems, when we
return to the couple's Paris apartment, so much cheap surrealism.

Other critics, other views. Sarris speculates that the empty landau at the end signifies that Séverine has now lived
through her cathection and, as it were, kicked the habit.
This is to deprive the story of all Kessel's social understanding and compassion. His Séverine is raped by a plumber at
eight. Her later inclinations are disallowed by society in the
way they would not be in the hyper-sophisticated and her-
metically sealed circle of Buñuel's depiction. Kessel gives us
a sensual outlaw, Buñuel a frivolous sensation-seeker. Such
is underlined by the fact that, rather than follow up
his sado-masochistic images, Buñuel tosses in a three-ring circus of sexual perversion—necrophilia, lesbianism, bondage,
fascination with scars, the usual shoe fetishism (even at the
end), degradation by mud, and love of leather. One male
masochist comes to the brothel and makes effectively ridiculous that touching need which Kessel's Séverine feels. The
threads are therefore so dispersed that the only way critical-
ly to tie them together is to say that everything is really an
allusion to a previous Buñuel film (Stein finding the end-

---

* The two critics seem here to be in almost alarming accord, Stein writing,
"The climax of his film is simply the most astonishing 'open ending' in
the history of the cinema," and Sarris, "The ending of *Belle de jour* is
tantalisingly open as narrative." The question arises as to whether it is so
"open" that it does not constitute any form of ending.

ing reminiscent of *L'Âge d'or*) or else to his collaborators. It was surely for this sort of sophistry that Occam perfected his razor. I incline to put some substance in the remark Buñuel made to two interviewers, Juan Cobos and Gonzalo S. J. de Erice, that "I don't like Kessel's novel at all, but I found it interesting to try and turn something I didn't like into something I did." To the comment that he did not like *Robinson Crusoe* either, one is tempted to retort that he made of it just as bad a film. What Buñuel does is to deprive *Belle de jour* of all tragedy; his ending admits as much. Kessel closes in mutism.

Analogy films may, however, take but the merest hints from their sources. Godard is notorious for this approach; for that reason I have included, and concluded with, a consideration of *Contempt* which exerts a very fragile hold indeed on its base, a Moravia story. Alternately, a film may follow its narrative fairly faithfully yet come under this head by offering "analogous rhetorical techniques." By making Mann's Aschenbach into Mahler Visconti perpetrated such an analogy in *Death in Venice,* a genuine critico-creative act.

Obviously, such a net could let in a very large number of fishes. It could be said that *Ma nuit chez Maud* (1970) is an equally interesting critico-creative commentary on Pascal. However, Eric Rohmer is to date an atypical director: there are surely few making films today with such an implicit lack of interest for whether or not an audience stays in the cinema. Furthermore, he seems to be atypical in being a cerebral type evidently supporting all the lost causes —piety, fidelity, even Catholicism, all those chimeras most intellectuals think ridiculous. Whenever Rohmer touches on a subject of intellectual suasion I, for one, find it hard to leave his films. He remains, however, tangential to this study until he develops some novelistic theme.

These three modes of phrasing fiction in film form may not be exhaustive; but they can help us clarify meaning in each, and appreciate the norms of both. We can become better viewers by knowing what is happening to us in this way. In a nutshell, the three modes of presentation can be identified in a single *genre,* namely that of the James Bond films, as follows: (a) transposition—*Dr. No, Goldfinger, On Her Majesty's Secret Service;* (b) commentary—*From Russia with Love, Thunderball;* (c) analogy—*You Only Live Twice, Diamonds Are Forever.**

---

* This is an admittedly over-schematic pigeon-holing, and omits the worthless *Casino Royale;* furthermore, it must be confessed that some of the restructuring was clearly forced by plot problems due to the reversed order of issue of *You Only Live Twice* and *On Her Majesty's Secret Service.*

A: Transposition
WUTHERING HEIGHTS (1939)

In many ways William Wyler's adaptation of Emily Brontë's one great fictional work (setting aside her inspired juvenilia) is the typical machine-made Hollywood transposition. The type persists to our own days, recently resulting in *Doctor Zhivago*. Wyler's film, moreover, marks a culmination of the transposition of a large number of fictional classics into cinema throughout the Thirties. *Kane* was shortly to be created, the war to come; after it Wyler moved on to the feminism of *The Heiress* and the scathing social criticism, ambitious for its time, of *The Best Years of Our Lives*.

Although he wisely refrained from mentioning the fact in his voluminous autobiography, Ben Hecht collaborated in the Emily Brontë screenplay; John Gassner considered that "in some respects the film play even improves upon the novel by concentrating upon the central drama in the lives of the possessed lovers." The film ran close on the heels of *Gone with the Wind* for an Academy Award, while subsequent similar transpositions, of which we consider as samples below *Jane Eyre* and *Madame Bovary*, were already showing signs of becoming "arty."

In the first of these Welles is seen by a huge fireplace, while he orders Joan Fontaine to play the piano, highly reminiscent of his lone epic; in the other the Vaubyessard ball scene, with chandeliers revolving as Jennifer Jones is whirled in the suggestive ecstasy of a waltz, was considered daringly original at the time. Finally, we shall reach the present period when the wheel is come full circle and a literal transposition can achieve high cinematic art, as in the film made of Hamsun's *Hunger.*

WUTHERING HEIGHTS (1939, Wyler): the typical Goldwyn "transposition:" the dour existence of the Yorkshire gentry of even Edgar Linton's rank at the time is turned into vulgar ostentation.

In the Goldwyn-Wyler *Wuthering Heights,* starring Merle Oberon, Laurence Olivier, David Niven and Geraldine Fitzgerald, the danger may be seen of taking too simply Béla Balázs's position that the novel should be approached "merely as raw material" for the screen. It is perfectly true that, as Balázs observes, Shakespeare saw in a story by Bandello "merely the naked event narrated in it." So did Shakespeare in some of Plutarch's *Lives.* We have already suggested, however, that in such cases he made new "content" by altering "form." He saw the bare bones of a story that could be fashioned for his purpose, which included the use of language as well as all the obvious stylisations and conventions of Elizabethan drama. There surely comes a point at which one wonders whether any prior "raw material" is needed at all in minds as totally opaque as those which have fashioned some Hollywood productions. Why bother with Emily Brontë when what you intend to produce is what Bluestone accurately describes as "the story of the stable boy and the lady?" Apart from the advantage of being able to flourish CLASSIC on the hoardings, and lure in some unsuspecting souls who will have the vague feeling that they have experienced *Wuthering Heights* by seeing it on the screen, the perennial answer seems to be that a love interest is held to construe to audience interest almost exclusively. More copies of the book have been sold since Wyler made *Wuthering Heights* into a film than in the whole of the near-century that preceded it.

In a now justly celebrated study Lester Asheim found that out of twenty-four adaptations of novels for films seventeen heightened (already high) love interest. *Madame Bovary, Jane Eyre, Great Expectations* (in all its many filmic forms), the Robert Z. Leonard *Pride and Prejudice* of 1940 which was, with *Jane Eyre,* scripted for the screen by Aldous Huxley, all these now period pieces were transposed as essential origins of heavy love stories. The front offices could only be made to listen to such. But for any admirer of Emily Brontë Wyler's approach to *Wuthering Heights* makes the end result absurd, and indeed suggests that the supposedly literal transposition may falsify an original fiction far more than an intelligent analogy.

If there is one thing *Wuthering Heights* is not, it is a love story in the received sense of cinema of its time. Unlike Jane Austen, Emily Brontë had little direct interest in constructing conduct in a Christian society—and even her sister Charlotte seems to have been lukewarm, in the extreme, to Austen. Nothing erotic exists between Catherine and Heathcliff, who are brought up as brother and sister and who both marry siblings. In the one scene of any passion in the book—the parting, conveniently witnessed by Nelly Dean—Heathcliff shows little male interest in Cathy. The important thing for him is that she is a force dying in the sense of disappearing from physical view. He is jealous of her essence being taken from the sensory world; and so when she is physically removed he is as much interested in her "absence," at the end, as in her real self when living. Sex, in sum, is a less divisive antithesis than that between life and death.

Each new film version of *Wuthering Heights* inherits this idea that it is a great love story. In fact, it has nothing to do with what the cinema-going public of the Thirties called sex. It is England's one outstanding ontological fiction. In *Aspects of the Novel* E. M. Forster moved toward this view ("no book is more cut off from the universals of Heaven and Hell. It is local, like the spirits it engenders . . ."), and Sir Herbert Read moved to the same view beside him. The cortège of comprehension was completed by Lord David Cecil who, in *Early Victorian Novelists,* wrote of Catherine Earnshaw as follows:

> She believes in the immortality of the soul. If the individual life be the expression of a spiritual principle, it is clear that the mere dissolution of its fleshly integument will not destroy it. But she does more than believe in the immortality of the soul

in the orthodox Christian sense. She believes in the immortality of the soul *in this world*. The spiritual principle of which the soul is a manifestation is active in this life: therefore, the disembodied soul continues to be active in this life. Its ruling preoccupations remain the same after death as before.

How to make a film of this? You would have to be Japanese to dare to try. Bragging that his scriptwriters had done "a brilliant job" Goldwyn had the second part simply lopped off, as Robert Stevenson's *Jane Eyre* omitted the intractable St. John material. It was not simply what the Wyler team cut out of *Wuthering Heights;* such may have been partially necessary to the exigencies of the medium. By Asheim's addition, thirty new scenes were scripted from a total of fifty. Once more: why take the original at all, but for the accreditation of a great name? Hecht was, in any case, far more at home with the contemporary American scene, having made his reputation with von Sternberg on *Underworld* (1927).

In fact, sex is what killed Catherine Earnshaw, who dies in childbirth, or "two hours after." And social custom also killed her. She had married "the first gentleman of the neighbourhood" and no sooner is she dead than Nelly Dean reflects what hard luck it was on Edgar to have been left without an heir! Nothing could be more categoric. "The latter's distraction at his bereavement is a subject too painful to be dwelt on; its after effects showed how deep the sorrow sunk. A great addition, in my eyes, was his being left without an heir." Too bad. The wife has meanwhile died. In the film Olivier is directed to lift Merle Oberon from her unspecified sick-bed, which she has been expressly forbidden to leave by Dr. Kenneth, and to carry her in his arms to some open French windows, so that she may see the heather. In a sense it could be said that Wyler's Heathcliff kills his Catherine.

What Emily Brontë was saying in *Wuthering Heights* is indeed closer to recent Japanese cinema, in which the dead are allowed to remain decorously "present," and persist as influences, than to a Thirties love story.

There is one line of criticism, espoused by Mary Visick in her *The Genesis of "Wuthering Heights"* which takes it that Catherine did love her eventual husband Edgar Linton. Miss Visick proposes that "Catherine loves her husband for the plain reason she gives Nelly; he is young and attractive, he is the first gentleman of the neighbourhood. . . ." Though understandably ignorant of this book, which was published by the Hong Kong University Press in 1958, Hecht and MacArthur espouse its interpretation, not seeing the latent sarcasm under Catherine's words to the ubiquitous Nelly. Thereby, the scriptwriters were led to reinforce and even, at times, introduce a totally spurious class consciousness. Instead of being a classless vampire Heathcliff is tamed to an underprivileged stable hand, a sort of pre-Mellors, whom Catherine (socially ambitious) wants to promote into an overprivileged landowner like Edgar . . . Catherine Earnshaw of all people! The transposition tells its own story. In the Thirties the tycoon could still be a hero. After the war he was generally democratised to a doctor or lawyer.

Wyler establishes this in a scene at Penistone Crag where the young lovers have their private "Castle," a poorly-painted set to the banality of which the incidental music makes fit reply. "Why aren't you my prince like we said long ago?" Catherine asks Heathcliff. She leads him in a scamper across the heath to watch an overdone ball scene in the Linton manor, at which she gapes enviously. Climbing back over the wall she is gored by two mastiffs who would, in the time accorded by the frames, have eaten most of her leg in real life. Next, she is helped into the house and Heathcliff, in his working clothes, kicked out of it.

Such class distinctions are not only unfaithful to the fiction—they would be acceptable if established as real—they seriously distort the society shown. It is true that in *Shirley*

Charlotte Brontë showed the cruel discrepancies between cotton-mill owners and their sweated workers of the time, but Emily was operating on another level, in another sphere altogether. In the Yorkshire of the time the landed gentry spoke with thick accents, regarded the industrialised south with suspicion, and in common with the Scottish laird (or Corsican count) worked their estates alongside their hands, from whom, I suspect, they were often physically indistinguishable. Look at the Yorkshire parsonage in which the sisters grew up, their brother drinking and doping himself while their father lectured them on the sexual differences when he was not burning their favourite shoes or scribbling indecipherable poetry upstairs.

The china-doll image portrayed by Merle Oberon thus responds to the stereotype of the pale consumptive handed down of Emily herself. Yet this was a girl who, according to Charlotte, half-beat her pet bulldog to death with her fists, was thought of as a man by Mrs. Gaskell, was mistaken as such by the local villagers, while later the Belgian schoolmaster M. Heger was explicit—"She should have been a man." Her fantasy world of Gondal was dominated by a ruthless Amazon called Augusta. Clifford Collins writes, "The love of Catherine and Heathcliff may be described as a life-force relationship, a principle that is not conditioned by anything but itself." We note that she can speak of Heathcliff as the same constant in her being even after she is carrying Edgar's child! Hecht and MacArthur might reply, How can we make a film out of that? To which one could equally legitimately retort: Why try? It is the ignorance that hurts.

And it is the ignorance that makes the film more than a reversal of even a high school text. Some such reversals, as we shall see, can be filmically effective, but total intellectual contempt for what a text says, as in this case, reduces it to so many purloined names. Catherine marries Edgar Linton out of social duty and so that she may earn a pa-

rental pat on the back. Actually, in the passage cited by
Miss Visick for support, Catherine is simply parrotting so
many social values. The girl of the manor marries someone who is "handsome, and pleasant to be with." In the
catechism to which Nelly subjects Catherine after the latter has revealed Edgar's proposal, given in Chapter IX, we
observe the many uses and misuses of the word *love*:

> "Why do you love him, Miss Cathy?"
> "Nonsense, I do—that's sufficient."
> "By no means; you must say why."
> "Well, because he is handsome, and pleasant to be with."
> "Bad," was my commentary.
> "And because he is young and cheerful."
> "Bad, still."
> "And because he loves me."
> "Indifferent, coming there."
> "And he will be rich, and I shall like to be the greatest woman
> of the neighbourhood, and I shall be proud of having a hus-
> band."
> "Worst of all! And now, say how you love him."
> "As everybody loves—You're silly, Nelly."
> "Not at all—Answer."
> "I love the ground under his feet, and the air over his head,
> and everything he touches, and every word he says—I love all
> his looks, and all his actions, and him entirely, and altogether.
> There now!"
> "And why?"

This is clearly intended to be a mockery of the manner in
which Merle Oberon delivers the answers, as of the way
she gives the famous "I *am* Heathcliff" passage, adduced in
almost every criticism, and where the language attains such
heights that it is hard for anyone to miss. But this actress
merely mouths so much English.

In the original, Catherine here knows the true terror of
her realisation, how alien it is to what the Goldwyn-Wyler
society calls love, so that in discussing the matter with
Nelly she appears to be conversing with some dull-witted
schoolchild who had been babbling something about her be-

ing separated from Heathcliff should she marry Edgar ("Who is to separate us, pray?") ; she then goes into the famous long speech which Merle Oberon utters as so many lexical units since she is another character entirely from Emily Brontë's. "Nelly, I *am* Heathcliff—he's always, always in my mind—not as a pleasure, any more than I am always a pleasure to myself—but as my own being—so, don't talk of our separation again—it is impracticable. . . ." Deep truth is often a dreadful joy. Heathcliff is not a "pleasure" to this Cathy, he *is* her.* Together the pair inhabit another level of existence, one in which there is no marrying nor giving in marriage, one thoroughly understood by Lord David:

> Emily Brontë does not see animate man revealed against inanimate nature, as Mrs. Gaskell does. She does not even see suffering, pitiful, individual man in conflict with unfeeling, impersonal, ruthless natural forces, like Hardy. Men and nature to her are equally living and in the same way. To her an angry man and an angry sky are not just metaphorically alike, they are actually alike in kind; different manifestations of a single spiritual reality.

Presumably a society receives the kind of films it wants. The quick social climbing and class mobility of America in the Thirties led Wyler to domesticate *Wuthering Heights* to soap-opera standards, and to make of its heroine a vulgar tease and common snob, the bitch-heroine luring her helpless male to destruction. To this end Wyler had to keep all the anti-clerical and vampiric elements sternly out of the screenplay. In the original Heathcliff tells Nelly Dean how he had dug up Catherine's coffin and tried to take her in his arms again; his spade scraped the coffin and he wrestled with its lid.

Given its context this is all perfectly conventional. Heath-

---

* In the novel Catherine is called Cathy less than her daughter by Edgar; the film reverses this nomenclature. It hardly matters, but it does make for confusion in any joint criticism of the two.

cliff is here the male vampire (or addict) demonstrating withdrawal symptoms and requiring his draught of blood (or "fix") —we note he is after her the night she is buried. Infected, Catherine too is of the undead. Aside from the Christian devil identity Emily conferred on Heathcliff, and which so disturbed Charlotte, we must remember that Catherine herself is anti-Christian. Buñuel understood this in his version of *Wuthering Heights,* a Mexican mish-mash of mis-casting which nonetheless visualises necrophilia better than *Belle de jour.* The Wyler film, on the other hand, suggests a Christian after-life. The book does not. In her famous dream Catherine tells Nelly she went to heaven but was forcibly flung out by the angels there. "If I were in heaven, Nelly, I should be extremely miserable," she confesses, adding that "the angels were so angry that they flung me out, into the middle of the heath on the top of Wuthering Heights; where I woke sobbing for joy." Sobbing for *joy.* This, she maintains, is her "secret." Catherine believes that some form of vitality persists, to which recognition Heathcliff comes at the end—"that the dead are not annihilated," as he asseverates just before he dies on the injunction that "No minister need come; nor need anything be said over me." Catherine, we learn, is buried closer to the moor than the kirk, and so on. The Wyler film could not possibly allow such anti-clerical intrusions.

The film finally has to excise the book's second half since it destroys precisely that easy conventionalising indulged in from the first. That is to say, Heathcliff is originally brutalised by the supposedly refined or civilised class in the book, and when he takes his revenge upon it we applaud. He is, however, attacking a hypocritical social code, rather than a class *per se* (in the book he becomes a considerable landowner by the end). The brutal expulsion of Isabella from the Heights—having been sent sprawling in Hindley's blood, she passes Hareton on her way out hanging puppies off a chair—repels us far less than the facts (the beating of a defenseless woman) rightly should. Wyler allows Heathcliff one, quickly-regretted, slap to Catherine's face (she is knocked about more, it is true, in the recent Robert Fuest version starring Anna Calder-Marshall as Cathy). By the end of the book Heathcliff has turned into a demon, the Heights (to which Catherine would return with "joy") housing a tyrannical would-be Dracula in himself, a slut for a maid in Zillah, a half-crazed evangelical clod in Joseph, an idiot boy in Hareton, and a drooling alcoholic in Hindley. The kailyaird school of fiction never improved the picture. Nor could Buñuel.

Hecht and MacArthur, on the other hand, clearly preferred the plaster-saint picture of a genteel society presented by the Lintons. If this was modern America, their script says, so would you. The condescension is illustrated in one determining manner in the film—by the treatment of its narration. Emily's novel is based on a great deal of improbable overhearing by Nelly Dean—it has been estimated that only a tenth of the whole is direct narration by the supposed narrator, Lockwood! As a result, Lockwood could well have been cut from the film altogether, allowing only for the loss of the brilliant Gothic opening of the tapping on the window-pane. In the film our reports come from the camera, an omniscient eye. True, we keep on dissolving gracefully from Nelly Dean's narration, but we soon lose her point of view, or herself as a centre of vision of scenes she could never have witnessed.

Accordingly, Nelly Dean is promoted *by technique* into ourselves, into a rational and impartial spectator, a position she is far from occupying in the text of the book. Most literary critics find the Linton ledger very feeble. Does the Edgar Linton-Nelly Dean axis really represent what Hecht-MacArthur give it as, and what Wyler's direction of David Niven as Edgar hints at, namely the "healthy" side of the book? Far from it. Any reader with emotions surely finds them enlisted on the side of the unregenerate rebels Heathcliff and Catherine, who are engaged in trying to break up just that society the scriptwriters seem to find so admirable.* There is even the suggestion made by Joseph at the end that Heathcliff may have murdered Hindley Earnshaw or put him out of his agony—"un he warn't deead when Aw left, nowt uh t'soart." Concerning Nelly's reliability as an impartial witness, John K. Mathison stated:

> In spite of all her fine qualities, nevertheless, she fails to understand the other characters and, more important, fails in her behavior in important crises of the action. From the emphasis on her admirable qualities, and from her final inadequacy, the reader is led to see that the insight of the normal, wholesome person cannot penetrate into all feelings justly.

Wyler's handling of how his story was to be narrated was thus operative. From it many of the defects spring. By it alone he was forced, or his writers were, into seeing the whole imbroglio as a "tempest in the soul," the actual title of a 1949 critical essay on the novel and virtually what the repeatedly revived Italian version of the epic dubbed it, wherein Catherine is an early Connie Chatterley—*La Voce nella tempesta*. The handling thus takes Nelly Dean at face value; the passion between the pair is a *coup de foudre* which time and convention, plus many chubby children, would have pacified, had not death intervened. These "ordinary satisfactions of life" (which Miss Visick claims to be why Catherine chose Edgar Linton) have little to do with that life of the imagination to which Emily Brontë's heroine was addicted and dedicated. Catherine did not choose Edgar. Her society did. And it was the society of the American Thirties that served up the Goldwyn-Wyler-Hecht-MacArthur vulgarity.

---

* Generally speaking, physical chastisement of females in films has been confined to those starring John Wayne. Usually such is scripted out, as it was for Ava Gardner in *The Little Hut*, Sophia Loren in *Boy on A Dolphin*, and Nancy Kwan in *The World of Suzy Wong*. In Germany novels by Siegfried Lenz and J. R. Becher can be seen to have retained such scenes in transposition.

JANE EYRE (1944)

Unlike *Wuthering Heights* Charlotte Brontë's *Jane Eyre* is a love story. Probably *the* love story. It is so archetypal as to have made fortunes for women novelists, like Victoria Holt and Mary Stewart, who have used it as source.

A girl of eighteen, small, plain and poor, reads a lesson in sexual equality to and gains the hand of a man in his forties, large, Byronically handsome (*viz.* ugly), and rich. The would-be bigamist Rochester, married to "a nature the most gross, impure, depraved I ever saw," a man with an illegitimate child and mistresses in many lands, is brought to order by a "Quakerish" schoolmistress—for in the original Jane underwent a period teaching at Lowood, omitted in the Robert Stevenson film.

Aldous Huxley's script left out all the St. John material in the latter part, though for some reason he gave the name to a warm-hearted doctor who appears to stand in for what Miss Temple (of the tender appellation) meant for the young Jane in the original. On the whole, the excision does far less harm than did the surgery performed by Goldwyn's butchers on Emily's masterpiece. It forces Huxley to leave Jane an orphan throughout; in the novel she gains relatives, and an inheritance. However, it seems highly unlikely to most modern readers that Jane should be as ready, after her period of impoverishment and dependence, to dower this about at once as she does in the book.

The truncation also has other odd effects. In the novel Rochester's banterings and anti-societal tauntings sharpened Jane's tools for her so that when she eventually meets St. John, an extremely unpleasant character for most women readers, she can stand her ground and resist his moral blackmail—"Again the surprised expression crossed his face. He had not imagined that a woman would dare to speak so to a man." But Jane had just so spoken to Rochester. Hence, her lover can now call her back to his side via the telepathic cry. They have become truly equal and she can say to him, "I love you better now, when I can really be useful to you, than I did in your state of proud independence, when you disdained every part but that of the giver and protector." The film leaves Jane at Gateshead after the death of Mrs. Reed (played with relish by the late Agnes Moorehead), with the house being sold. She has far less animus against her tormenting "Aunt" Reed on the screen and is seen seated at a table writing when a storm blows up, and in its thunder, developed by Bernard Herrmann's music, she hears Orson Welles calling—or groaning—for her.

Admittedly the St. John episode involves philosophical material; Jane's wandering over moorlands is fairly unbelievable, and the director was right to make these cuts, if he had to. Being a true love story, *Jane Eyre* could more sturdily resist the depradations of Hollywood than *Wuthering Heights*. All the same, one must strongly censure someone for the total and quite unnecessary suppression of Jane's intellect in the role played by Joan Fontaine.

It is highly likely that the nature of the star compounded this misinterpretation, for Fontaine was playing meek-and-mild plain Janes one after another at this time, in-

JANE EYRE (1944, Stevenson): typical of its time and taste, all realistic costumes and phony background.

cluding, opposite a moustached Laurence Olivier, a very similar role in *Rebecca,* itself a bold plagiarism of *Jane Eyre.** After the customary turning of the leaves of the book, whose opening passage Huxley saw fit to rewrite, the film begins with young Jane Eyre rebelling against the bullying of John Reed (whose sisters are well dispensed with). The child star is full of fire and very little like her grown-up image. In the book she rounds on John Reed and when the lady's-maid Abbot holds her arms and

---

* It is an irony of cinema that the star system was initiated by one of its principal aesthetic benefactors—when Chaplin demanded, and won, together with his Mutual Film Company. $67,000 for twelve two-reelers in 1915.

reproves her for striking "Your young master," she blurts back, "Master! How is he my master? Am I a servant?" The terminology is important since the characterisation is carried through by Charlotte Brontë and echoed at the end when Jane has found true equality with Rochester and can therefore, if she chooses, be subservient to him. Of Thornfield she muses, "it had a master: for my part, I liked it better." When she returns to the blind and maimed Rochester who is obviously anything but her master (indeed the reverse—the film wisely omitting Orson Welles in gypsy drag), she gloats, "I can single out my master's very window." There is, in the film, a distinct discrepancy between the independent child Jane and the later subdued woman who leaves to tutor Adèle; being much younger, Charlotte's Jane was more understandable a creation than that of Joan Fontaine. In fact, for Bessie (the kinder of the two Gateshead maids) to be able to recognise the grown Jane Eyre in the film considerable business about a brooch had to be added.

Nevertheless, since there is here a good deal else other than the love story available to a film-maker, *Jane Eyre* is much less wounded by the cliché-mind of its era than was *Wuthering Heights* or even the Garbo *Anna Karenina,* a truly strange film to re-see today since it completely revised the character of Karenin (probably through frank misunderstanding, since no such character could be approximated in Thirties America), not to mention Vronski, played by Fredric March, whose first distinction is literally to drink a crowd of Cossack officers under the table. Gateshead in *Jane Eyre* is faithfully transposed, with an admirable Reverend Brocklehurst whose Calvinist original, William Carus Wilson, lent also to Charlotte's portrait of St. John. The school scenes are tolerably faithful and well shot; in actual fact, in Lowood Charlotte strongly exaggerated the discipline of her model, Cowan Bridge School, the Brontë Society having usefully reprinted the 1830 Report of this establishment "for Clergymen's Daughters." We do not have the pleasure of seeing the young Elizabeth Taylor, playing Helen Burns, birched, though an excellent BBC radio transposition of the same period had made this character so suffer.

For the author of the novel Helen Burns was an extremely important character, her death (in love) forming a structural reply to that of Mrs. Reed (in hate) *. All in all, one feels that Huxley took care in rooting the chief character in reality. The fictional birching (as it may have been, in all senses) is rendered by a scene showing the girls having to walk in a ring in the rain holding up flat-irons in their hands. From this exposure Helen Burns dies in the film, rather than from that love of another world which Charlotte so beautifully rendered in her long speech concluding Chapter VI, her tribute to Emily in the book.

It is when we come to the love relationship itself that the film begins to become bogged down in the conventions of its time—stereotypes off which Daphne du Maurier's *Rebecca* had, on the other hand, thrived—just as it shirks the amputation of Rochester's hand or any actual vision of his insane wife Bertha Mason (we merely glimpse her back). A feminist apology was clearly out of the spirit of this Hollywood era, and it is ironic to consider how well *Jane Eyre* might have answered the temper of our present times in translation; in this respect, Stevenson's attempt barely advances the 1934 Monogram issue. The true Jane Eyre only marries Rochester when she can eventuate her full personality in a relationship of complete mutual respect.

It is precisely Rochester's anti-social tendencies, his rudeness and breaches of decorum, that stimulate the young

* Looking through the window during her visit to Gateshead, and reflecting on Mrs. Reed's death, the original Jane "thought of Helen Burns: recalled her dying words—her faith—her doctrine of the equality of disembodied souls."

Jane's own personality. He has recognised an inner life and is drawing it out to test it, as it were, against his. The references to *equality* on Jane's part start to increase with this skilful probing and they do so obviously much to Rochester's delight, until he stings her into saying in the garden, "Do you think, because I am poor, obscure, plain, and little, I am soulless and heartless? You think wrong!—I have as much soul as you—and full as much heart . . . it is my spirit that addresses your spirit; just as if both had passed through the grave, and we stood at God's feet, equal—as we are!" Rochester happily echoes "As we are," takes her in his arms, and proposes in these terms (*viz.* hers) :

> "My bride is here," he said, again drawing me to him, "because my equal is here, and my likeness. Jane, will you marry me?"

Later, he is to say, "Janet, by-the-by, it was you who made me the offer." She at once admits as much—"Of course I did."

This is far from the reading of the character by the histrionic, eye-rolling Welles, already inclining to fat (whose end-result is actually used as characterisation in the recent *Catch-22*). Again, it must be stressed that social convention, repression, really maims Rochester. Addressing Jane, he is pleased that this apparently insignificant little woman "mutinied against fate, and claimed your rank as my equal." In refusing to live as his paramour, Charlotte's Jane still has part of herself crying out that their relationship must be sanctified by religion, and society. Yet her inner self knows better and she has to wring herself almost physically clear of the shibboleths of Calvinism and pious heroics of religious self-denial in the St. John episode, before she can return to Rochester and marry him. The Orson Welles Rochester is a mis-reading of the intention of the original, due perhaps to self-indulgence by the actor. From the first scene in which his horse throws him in the snow he plays the bully straight, not with a purpose as in the original, where Jane confesses that "I like rudeness a great deal better than flattery."

Such is brought out in the proposal scene in the garden. In the film a ludicrous Blanche Ingram has been absurdly disposed of, and Jane and Rochester come together like any Hollywood couple of the time, when again one of those conveniently sudden storms that so assail England in cinema rises amain and splits the sullen chestnut tree. The filmic fissure is an image that contributes nothing to our understanding, for it is in no way symbolic. It is simply a repeat of what happened in a famous book, where, together with the ripped bridal veil, it advanced a telling bifurcation image.

The lesson is all too plain. Literary symbols cannot be repeated as so much visual imagery. They are part of what they arise from, a whole understanding or vision. Charlotte Brontë sees that Jane is forced by her society to be ambivalent to Rochester. She is fascinated by his physicality— the mention of amatory adventures has to take the place of what today would be repellent detail—and desires to submit to him, but her conventional side resists. No one of Jane Eyre's intelligence can allow such subservience to a man. Strip her of intelligence, convert her into the girl-next-door longing to marry (at that time), and the consequences of much imagery have to be abandoned.

Yet the equality idea is the essence of the whole book. Its loss in the Stevenson film frankly strands the images and makes us feel uncomfortable, rather than lacrimose, when the blind Orson Welles seeks Joan Fontaine in the ruins of Thornfield (another abode in the original). By this point there is scarcely much left of the man to dominate. Joan Fontaine appears destined for the task of that character sacred to soap-opera, the nurse.

In Charlotte's fantasy the maiming of Rochester was, as Richard Chase suggested, a minor castration. As that fine mind wrote of both *Wuthering Heights* and *Jane Eyre* "a relatively mild and ordinary marriage is made after the spirit of the masculine universe is controlled or extinguished." This is very nice. For Victorian or pre-Victorian England—the film is characteristically unspecific while the novel's reference to *Marmion* sets the action of *Jane Eyre* as prior to Victoria's accession—corresponds comfortably enough with Freud's final postulate of the Father-God or Man-God society, doubtless partially derived from it. The primaeval social order is here seen as duplicated in fact, with ruling males (all the more rigidly supported by a Queen) and inferior men plus, on the lowest rung of the hierarchy, as it were, useless, dependent, and/or frivolous women. We note the suggestion of incest in both Brontë books, a prime taboo in savage societies; in *Jane Eyre* the father-daughter relationship haunts that of Rochester to Jane until he becomes a cripple. Obviously it could not do so in a film of this pre-television era.

The Welles-Fontaine interpretation thus looks like a remake of *Rebecca,* Gothic romance seen through the eye of a woman. And a woman, in this very American version, on the make. The novel's awkward shifts in points-of-view (evidently induced by Anne's *Agnes Grey*) really matter very little this time round. In Robert Stevenson's direction we are nearly always with Jane, one way or another. However, she is far from the complete equal she is in Charlotte's book; there she forms with Rochester part of a mutual imagination, and can create herself as submissive if she so desires. Perhaps the Hollywood of the time could not countenance as frank a feminist statement as this, nor criticise so thoroughly so many social norms. In Stevenson's *Jane Eyre* we therefore find not the story of the stable-boy and the lady but that of the governess governed.

MADAME BOVARY (1949)

To take a book about nothing—"un livre sur rien" as its author defined what *Madame Bovary* was to be in a celebrated letter to Louise Colet—and to make a romance of it is to miss the point by a mile. For M-G-M Vincente Minnelli chose to make a child's colour-book of adultery, as seen through "emancipated" America's eyes. The oversimplification was such as to attain at times a kind of genius. "The kitchen drudge who dreamed of love and beauty," intones James Mason, playing Flaubert as framed in the 1857 dock. "What are dreams made of? Where do they come from?" Ah where, indeed? As Jean Domarchi said in a review of *Brigadoon,* "Marx would have liked Minnelli." In fact, it is via Marx's put-upon daughter "Tussy" or Eleanor Aveling that generations of English readers have come to the text in the first place.

A pictorial presentation of an adultery must concentrate on externalities. Who is adulterous with whom—and where, and how? The most resonant aspect of *Madame Bovary,* to which Flaubert organised structure, style, and even syntax, was its strenuous vision of the failure of erotic alongside social hope. For over one half of the human race this was the great betrayal, and that revenge for love which Emma must enact upon herself; it is that "bitterer poison" which rises to her lips with the bile of her eventual death-bed:

> Besides, nothing was worth the trouble of seeking it; everything was a lie. Every smile concealed a yawn of boredom, every joy a curse, every pleasure its own disgust, and the sweetest kisses left upon your lips only the unattainable desire for a greater delight.

How make a Hollywood film on this premise? Nothing could be more contra-cultural, the key word here being *unattainable*. Postwar optimism and confidence were at a high in America when this picture was made; indeed, George Bluestone has amusingly argued that filming *Madame Bovary* is a contradiction in terms since "to do so would be to expose the face of the industry itself." Emma is, as Jean Renoir's 1934 depiction tended more to underline, herself a victim of a "dream factory," in her case those trashy novels which preceded trashy films and now even trashier TV. *Bovarysme* is certainly the soil on which both bad cinema and cheap advertising have grown.

Yet there is another contradiction present since, as several critics have discerned, *Bovary* anticipates many cinematic techniques, certain scenes being scenarios in themselves. When Rodolphe makes his first approaches to Emma overlooking an agricultural fair—romance reigning, in this case, above the reality of prize pigs and manures—Flaubert daringly cross-cut dialogue in a manner wholly cinematic, yet which the essential commonness of Minnelli's mind missed.* Harry Levin has remarked also on the remarkably filmic cab ride around Rouen in which the narrative retreats, exactly like a camera, and watches the cab from

---

* As Joseph Frank points out in *The Widening Gyre,* there are three simultaneous or "parallel" actions being followed by Flaubert here, in a perfect anticipation of cinema's "spatial form."

without, as articles of clothing are tossed from it. The desecratory use of the Rouen cathedral as a sexual boudoir is equally suggestive of the same, while when a despairing Emma apparently offers herself to the town dummy (and army hero) Binet, Flaubert turns up the note of the man's silly lathe, and the scene is reported indirectly by a Greek chorus of nosy crones, one the Mayor's wife who would like to see her whipped. Flaubert everywhere most tactfully externalised his theme.

However, if you are giving the story of "the kitchen drudge who dreamed of love and beauty" you scarcely need such supports, nor indeed *Madame Bovary*. There were umpteen more or less consequential European novels of adultery available in the latter half of the Nineteenth century. Champfleury's is often said to have closely antici- pated Flaubert's, but it does not matter, the theme was in the air since it was an anagram of social betrayal. In Flau- bert all hope, all longings for anything beyond the self, are cut down in woman as in the society. Member of that class that is deceived daily, woman was the perfect vehicle for Flaubert's vision and the book, unlike the film, does not end with Emma's death, plus a few gratuitous platitudes from James Mason. It is framed in Charles, the betrayed, and at the very end there is a moment when he meets his cuckold Rodolphe and fierce life flares in him, only to die in stupor again. How much more telling this would have made the film than to conclude it with the cheap, and even faithless, complacence of Mason at having struck a blow for literary liberty ("Truth lives forever; men do not . . .").

In short, whatever *Madame Bovary* may be, it is not the story of a dreamy "kitchen drudge" (her father Théodore Roualt employed servants) nor of a provincial wife who takes lovers on the side: such could be found in the penny press of the time, the equivalent of any issue of *True Con-*

fessions. The doom of sexual hopes was a picture of the doom of social aspirations; this can be seen by comparing adulterous heroines in similar novels of power to come. In Theodor Fontane's German *Effi Briest* of 1895 or Eca de Queiroz's Portuguese *O primo Bazilio* of 1878 (a rewrite, from another angle, of *Bovary*) we find a far warmer authorial feeling. The same is also somewhat true of Zola's early and rather atypical *Thérèse Raquin*. But Flaubert insists: " '89 destroyed royalty and the nobility, '48 the bourgeoisie, and '51 the people." His *L'éducation sentimentale* ends on the same note of erotico-social apathy—"We were better off then." *Jules et Jim* is perhaps the nearest recent cinema has come to this inspired vision of anomy.

A film must begin with a spatial structure. As a rule we see an image before we hear a word. In fiction, the reverse is the case. It was essential to Flaubert's purpose that the spatial imagery provoke that longing for annihilation or "rien" which finally kills Emma. "What a look Rouen has," he wrote in a letter while composing *Bovary*: "Is there anything more heavy and depressing? At sunset yesterday the walls were oozing such *ennui* that I was almost asphyxiated as I passed!" Seen from postwar America, Minnelli's location for Yonville is, on the contrary, a charming French village in which many of us might like to live. Everyone seems very prosperous. When its characters are seen hurrying over the bridge to their daily occupations, each enumerated for us by Mason, we cannot find them nearly as monotonous as those faceless digits who rush to work every morning in any large city today. Yonville was intended to be a town of excruciating Norman boredom, surrounded by long flat empty fields; a paragraph like the following, so carefully worked by Flaubert, knocks the nails into the casket of every local hope:

Beyond this there is nothing to see at Yonville. The street (the only one) a gunshot long and flanked by a few shops on either side stops short at the turn of the high road. Turning right and following the foot of the Saint-Jean hills one soon reaches the graveyard.

In Flaubert's pages one does indeed, but Minnelli's Yonville is "romantic" rural France. Even the scene of Emma's abortive elopement, which Minnelli stages watched over by the usurer Lheureux (of the sarcastically chosen name), is far less desolate than it might be. We wonder why she is fleeing this rather pretty village.

So much for setting. It should have been far harsher, and was so in a group of indigenous French films made at about the same time, including the admirable *Jeux interdits*. But while Minnelli romanticises one side of his chosen masterpiece, he emasculates another. At the Vaubyessard ball, where Emma touchingly reveals her provinciality by rolling her gloves up into her wine glass in order to prevent the waiters from giving her champagne, elements are included clearly without being understood. After a successful mirror shot Minnelli ends his ball with a meaningless smashing of windows; in the original this was for Emma a telling and provocative aside. Someone at the party had called for more air and in this society the waiters could evidently smash a few window-panes to get it. They would presumably be repaired the next day. We can sense the country girl's intoxicated wonder at such affluence.

When it comes to plot we find the director quite inexcusably shirking not only the demands of his original but also those of "the existing work of art merely as raw material," in Balázs's famous predicate. As portrayed by Van Heflin, Charles Bovary is softened out of all recognition from the original, so much so as to make him Emma's victim rather than the cause of her suffering (the major initial alteration Flaubert made in the Delamare story, on much of which *Bovary* is based, was to have Emma

Charles's *second* wife, for whom he had originally, therefore, felt evidently legitimate adulterous yearnings—in a
male society). This emphasis is made stronger by Minnelli's casting of Jennifer Jones as Emma, with her thoroughly
American coquettishness, attitudinisings, and underlying female power. Jennifer Jones gives us a bitch-heroine of the
time; in accord with this the narration talks about "the
lives she ruined."

It is perfectly true that distinguished critics have found
this book about "nothing" unpalatably caustic. It was too
much so for Sainte-Beuve who, in his weekly book review,
asked, "Why did Flaubert not include a single character
who, by the spectacle of his virtue, would have offered
some comfort, some repose to the reader and become a
friendly presence?" This was partly why the book was so
revolutionary and why it was prosecuted. It was also why
Minnelli's film was so tame. Matthew Arnold was in accord. Flaubert's hatred of provinciality that made him observe as carefully as any Spaak thesis film resulted in un-
likeable material, in (for Arnold) "an atmosphere of
bitterness, irony, impotence; not a personage in the book
to rejoice or console us."

How could someone like Minnelli subscribe to this
cruelty to his own characters? Cinema of the commercial
type depends on warmth of authorial feeling. The novel
can remain cold, apart—as Flaubert, and his follower Joyce,
determined. You are not required to have empathy with
any of the strange characters of *The Brothers Karamazov*
for it to operate powerfully upon you. Any interpretation
of *Madame Bovary* on the screen is likely to lose at the
box office beside any version of *War and Peace,* let alone
Gone with the Wind. As a result, Minnelli softened his
Charles Bovary to a point where the character appears
rather pitiable, a dutiful country doctor frustrated by a
minx of a wife. We are sorry for Charles in a way Flaubert never permitted us to be; his Section XIII of Part

MADAME BOVARY (1949, Minnelli): Charles Bovary (Van Heflin) meets not so young Emma Rouault (Jennifer Jones); here costume and set decoration betray the care of the original novelist, for whom every object symbolised.

Two in fact concludes on an almost jeering note: "And, on top of all this, the poor fellow had money troubles." One direct result is to lose all the feminism Flaubert poured into the original.

In the Minnelli version Charles actually declines to perform the operation on Hippolyte, an act for which we must admire him, whereas Flaubert's intention was to indict provincial stupidity by having him horribly bungle the affair. The phrenological head in Charles's study is a permanent visual mockery of his aspirations to be a doctor, while the tapping of Hippolyte's ruined leg later serves as an auditory haunting of the failed doctor's days. The operation might have made a powerful visualisation for Minnelli, until one realises that it would have been far too cruel for the type of public he envisaged—which was maximal. Baudelaire saw this moment of failure as a psychological turning-point for Emma, who had egged her dolt of a husband on to the task and when he had made a mess of it, as Baudelaire says, "Her fierce anger, pent up for years, suddenly bursts into the open; doors slam; the awed husband, who was never able to give his romantically inclined wife the slightest spiritual satisfaction, is relegated to his room." It is important to the intent of this most seminal of fictions of "Moeurs de province" (as it was originally subtitled) that the dreadful mis-operation *be* performed, that its results should be a catastrophe equivalent to the loss of Emma's social hopes. What emerges rather more in the film, during the preparations for the operation, is the difficulty faced by medicine proper in the first half of the Nineteenth century.*

The interminable *ennui* that falls on French writer after writer in the second half of this century is really what *Madame Bovary* is about; to this end Flaubert would spend hours constructing a single sentence, his reiterative use of

---

* Emma's reading and Flaubert's allusion to the Rhône flooding situate the couple's arrival at Yonville l'Abbaye around the winter of 1840.

the imperfect tense having been shown to contribute forcibly to this effect. As Erich Auerbach summarises: "The novel is the representation of an entire human existence which has no issue." This is what makes the term *ennui,* only roughly translatable into English by "boredom," so reverberative within industrial capitalism. Baudelaire made of the emotion the cornerstone of his one poem collection, *Les fleurs du mal.* Dostoyevski used the term, in French, to denote the sickness of his underground man, just as Tolstoy accused his Ivan Ilych of it. Closer to home, Herman Melville's Bartleby declines to participate in a money-mad civilisation; we are led to the weakness of will to be found in so many modern intellectual figures—Mann's Kröger, Eliot's Prufrock, Valèry's Monsieur Teste, Huysmans's Des Esseintes. But to incorporate this sense into the film would have meant that Minnelli had to criticise himself, and all that we loosely call Hollywood stands for.

For *ennui* is the symptom of what Emile Durkheim called *anomie,* that gap between society's aims and its achievements which becomes so damaging as it enlarges under the impetus of a technology. It is a kind of profound psychological emptiness well personified by Emma Bovary, and indeed by Flaubert, who equated himself with her and surprised Jean-Paul Sartre by the intensity of the identification; Théophile Gautier remarked of Flaubert that his every line was "the coffin of a dead illusion." When all the social directives fail, all the promises and catchwords turn out to be empty, the human animal sinks into apathy, an *accidia* of the soul from which perhaps suicide can be the only escape of valour. So Emma's adulterous *ennui* has a resonance completely missed in any film version to date. It was a whole social issue in embryo. In her amusing *Adam's Rib* Ruth Herschberger writes: "It is precisely because women do nothing that they get so tired doing it. The cure is not rest and sedatives but the freedom to participate." George Bluestone is right: you cannot hope to

make a film about a subject you do not want to make a
film about. So you simply change the subject. Hollywood
was obviously not going to contribute to the criticism of
itself by being faithful to films like *Madame Bovary;* only
the dumbest calves, as the saying goes, select their butchers. The book's long litany of passages indicting the Christian religion as yet another great betrayal had also to be
sidestepped; there is a perfunctory nod to the text beside
Emma's death-bed. Extreme Unction is given. Of this passage Flaubert wrote to Madame Schlesinger that it was
"nothing but a page from the *Rituel de Paris,* put into
decent French." His parody, however, enlists our sympa-
thies on the side of the senses, rather than their repression;
stripped of authorial commentary, the priest's passage in
Minnelli's film is restored again to the *Rituel de Paris.*
There can be no *ennui* in Minnelli's dream factory. For
his purposes it would have been better to take Eça's Bazilio; but then it did not have the name (nor the same
part for James Mason). Flaubert was writing a revolutionary document. "In his total picture of the times," writes
Auerbach, "there appears something like a concealed
threat: the period is charged with its stupid issuelessness
as with an explosive."

LORD JIM (1965)

In common with *The Secret Sharer* and *Heart of Darkness*, Conrad's *Lord Jim* has had slightly excessive attention paid to it in academic circles. These works are perhaps easier to "teach" than something like the magnificent, complex *Nostromo* or the Slavophobic *Under Western Eyes*. Of the former Conrad planned a drama with his Polish friend, J. H. Retinger, and at one time he also hoped to make the latter into a play. *Lord Jim* was first made into a film in 1925, starring Percy Marmont. It is an interesting novel but, in the final analysis, far from satisfactory; Richard Brooks's cinematic attack on it represents the most ambitious attempt at a faithful transposition we shall consider here, one with an obviously large cast budget including Peter O'Toole, Paul Lucas, Dahlia Lavi, Eli Wallach, Curt Jurgens, James Mason, Jack Hawkins, not to mention hundreds of indigene extras.

The story as Conrad had it is extremely carefully evolved, with every action and character (even the narrator Marlow) acquiring metaphysical significance. Conrad had by this time collaborated with Ford—*Romance** was to appear in 1903—and he admitted to Curle that he wanted to cram a good deal of episode and action into the book. As remarked above, this is what has tempted director after film director to Conrad. Brooks further had the idea of making Paul Lucas, as Stein, look extremely like Conrad himself; critics have observed that Stein, the butterfly collector who recognises "romance" as Jim's affliction, and greatness, is the authorial stand-in. Conrad, however, only lets us meet Stein through Marlow's eyes, whereas he is a much more established, and even developed, character in the movie. Jim runs guns for him. He is altogether more powerful. To the Conrad devotee, there are even suggestions that Brooks was attempting a kind of anthological vision. Hints of *The Rescue* can be sensed, while the Patusan compound over which Eli Wallach is made to rule, and where Jim is tortured, reminds one forcibly of Kurtz's similar colony in *Heart of Darkness*. All in all, Brooks's attempt was sincere and deserved better than it achieved. For one thing, he put in much too much music and the colour was appalling.

The story is one of guilt and atonement. Gérard Jean-Aubry assures us that it springs from the seed of early sailoring on foreign ships where Conrad may have had language problems; Jocelyn Baines has now documented the actual incident, the abandonment by a captain of a pilgrim ship called the *Jeddah* in 1880, on which it is based. We find Conrad artfully constructing a hierarchy of decisions and indecisions which keep us morally off-balance; by a kind of Chinese-box distancing technique he makes it hard for the reader to judge too quickly. The extenuating circumstances are so contrived that we are compelled to ask ourselves what we would have done in the circumstances; so we can share in Jim's agonised questioning of Marlow

---

* *Romance* is an anti-Conrad fiction, with everything external rather than internal.

to this end. In the film we really cannot. The character is closer to a neurotic.

The training-ship rescue, when Jim shows himself a trifle slow in reacting, is omitted by Brooks, though it is the first in the chain of a number of events which led Jim finally to jump from the *Patna*. As a result, the director has to deepen the hypnotic paralysis Jim feels as he hears the cry to jump; he inserts a lightning flash and we hardly feel that the man is conscious at all.* In actual fact, Jim had been busy cutting the cables of what lifeboats there were so that they would float free when the ship sank and provide a haven for at least some of the pilgrims. He sees his skipper leaving and then a further complication intrudes, with the death of the "donkeyman" (or third engineer) of a heart attack. When Marlow says in Conrad's pages that "the real significance of crime is in its being a breach of faith with the community of mankind, and from that point of view he was no mean traitor," he is surely judging Jim, at least, over-harshly. He comes to a more liberal view of morality in the end. In his place Hawkins is unchanged, indeed lost about half-way through; he is the sea-salt cliché and through him Marlow is taken at face value.

This may not matter much. A good film could be made of the regeneration of a white neurotic at large in the Malaysian archipelago at the turn of the century, even it were not true to Conrad. To this end, however, much has to be altered: as evolved by Conrad, Jim's rehabilitation is not that of a redeemed neurotic. Brooks inserts one scene towards the end in which Stein acts like a psychiatrist, urging Jim to expose himself by returning to Patusan and "face the music" of having been a funk (Doramin having,

---

* Is there a Flaubertian echo here? Jim hears the cry "Jump! Oh, jump!" When she has read Rodolphe's cruel letter giving her up, Emma goes to her attic window, and "looked at the paving-stones, saying to herself, 'Jump! jump!' "

in this case, already found out). This is to turn *Lord Jim* into quite another character study, that of a man with some chronic neurosis, as depicted in that neglected British film, starring Maria Schell, called *The Mark*.

To change the theme is to make the old structure worthless. Conrad had deliberately distorted the chronological sequence of events, giving us, first, Jim seen as a water clerk, then some elements of the *Patna* voyage, then the Court of Inquiry, Marlow's entry into the story and finally Jim's jump. Brooks restored all this, more or less, to a "realistic" sequence, thereby making the film immensely long and unbalanced (the blowing-up of Eli Wallach's compound, after a lot of extremely obscure semi-western fighting, forms a crescendo, after which the film sags and it becomes hard to generate interest). Above all, the episode concerning Brierly is drained of any meaning and Brooks's writer has to push this important character into another position altogether. Big Brierly is an assessor involved in the Court of Inquiry; formerly a successful seaman, he drowns himself after the Court to the puzzlement of all. Marlow explicitly states that it was not because of money, drink, or women, and a fellow mariner called Jones, who discovered that four iron belaying-pins had helped keep Brierly down, tells Marlow it was not madness either. It was, rather, "one of those trifles that awaken ideas . . . with which a man . . . finds it impossible to live." In Jim's condition, that is, Brierly had looked momentarily into "the heart of darkness." He should have been omitted from the film, where he is only distracting; when we are shown the newspaper headline announcing his death, it is meaningless.

Brooks presents visual images of Jim's regeneration in two scenes on which he stakes a lot. Just as he had had Jim's imagination show him the possibility of water spurting from the bulkhead of the *Patna,* so he creates an apposite reply in a sequence during which Jim puts out a fire on a small boat carrying gunpowder, at loose in a port where "the community of mankind" is indeed royally threatened. Gunpowder is then secreted up a tree in Patusan, with the help of a graceful native boy. As Jim is tortured at a stake, Brooks stages a local boxing scene in the background and by its symbolism we know that Jim has won. He will not give in.

LORD JIM (1965, Brooks): an addition to Conrad in the interests of action.

The filming of *Lord Jim* is not advanced here as the betrayal of a masterpiece, such as we followed in *Wuthering Heights* or *Madame Bovary*. It is simply not a very good film in itself. It is, rather, a case of a novel-film being hindered by its source: Richard Brooks could have done far better with an original screenplay. The final scenes, showing "Gentleman" Brown (a fine characterisation by a bearded Mason) and his cronies brutally betraying the noble savages, are extremely well done, but they are well done in an external rather than internal manner. Together with *Lawrence of Arabia,* in which O'Toole had made his name, these were films of what historians call "the development decade," showing minority Third World cultures in need of some guiding force from the West. If anything, Conrad's message was the reverse of this.* For him the external journey into exotic places was a paradigm of the soul's searching into, as he calls it in *Lord Jim,* the "fundamental why."

---

* I tried to show something of his true liberalism in the colonial context in: "John Bull's Other Empire," *Modern Age,* vol. VIII: no. 3, Summer, 1964, pp. 284–290. For instance: Conrad would never have fallen into the cliché Brooks gives us at one point, when we see a wall-eyed native following Jim and assume he is evil because of his appearance. It is sad that films perpetuate the primitive idea of the cripple being sinister.

HUNGER (1966)

Henning Carlsen's Danish film made from Hamsun's rambling and experimental novel-autobiography of a man freaking out from hunger must surely remain one of the masterpieces of cinematic transposition of a literary source. Strictly speaking, *Hunger* might seem outside the scope of our comparisons since it is both more and less than a conventional fiction. It is, rather, in the words of one authority on Norwegian literature, Professor J. W. McFarlane, "the release in a new form of a body of thought that had been building up for the better part of a century; it was the expression in the literary mode of that same thing to which Freud was soon to give scientific formulation: speculation about the ways of the unconscious mind." On the surface, nothing would seem more unamenable to film. Thanks, however, in large part to the superb acting of Per Oscarsson as Hamsun himself starving in Christiania (winning Cannes Best Actor and National Society of Film Critics awards), Carlsen succeeded in creating a genuine spatial structure out of a linguistic medium—indeed, out of a somewhat wordy source. He can be said to have truly captured Pudovkin's "cinematographic essence" of a literary original; in common with Hamsun's agonised prose poem, the film contains relatively little conversation and almost no drama. Nothing much happens at all. The visual thus has a large and taxing task. Imagine a story conference at Paramount proposing *Hunger* as subject.

What happens? The book is loosely divided into four parts. In Part One a dishevelled, dirty and unlovable writer emerges from his garret, meets on a park bench an equally unattractive dwarf for whom he invents a ludicrous past, which is evidently acceptable and accepted; he sleeps out, comes across a painter friend, follows a girl, and finally learns the intoxicating elation of art as he completes his article and has it taken by an editor for ten kroner ("I knew, oh I knew so well, that the inspiration and holy breath I had just experienced and written down was a wonderful working of God in my soul, an answer to my cry of need of yesterday"). This moment is beautifully dramatised in the film as Oscarsson rhapsodically inscribes on the wall of his dismal room the pseudo-initials of the critic who had read the first fragment of Hamsun's *Hunger* that appeared anonymously in *Ny Jord* in 1888 and who was to write of it later: "With that little stump of prose, twenty-nine magazine pages long, Knut Hamsun had laid the foundation of a new literature in the North." This extra-cinematic and extra-literary allusion is about the only one in which the director indulges and, unlike those of Godard, it is both unpretentious and perfectly in place. Moreover, the touch reminds us once more of how film feeds off fiction; for to have a film made about a man writing the novel of which the film is itself made personifies Huxley's Quaker Oats theme mentioned.

Part Two takes place some two weeks later. The narrator is now homeless and becoming increasingly manic in his behaviour. He visits pawnbroker and editor in turn and begs 5 øre in a yarn shop. Part Three is a week later and characterises his sexual side; it concludes with his being taken in by the girl, confessing his hyperaesthesia and instability and being kissed—a scene much in the manner and spirit in which Dostoyevski's underground man had sought similar succour from the prostitute Liza. After an undetermined interval Part Four starts with an absurdly prolonged reckoning of the price of cheese with his landlady. The tone of the whole harshens as images of cruelty are contrasted, through the narrator's eyes, with the innocence of thwarted children. He watches a paralytic grandfather (straight out of Zola) tormented and sees the landlady's husband gleefully peering through the keyhole at his own cuckolding by an itinerant sailor—both scenes brought over with great tact in the film. Finally, our would-be writer takes a job on a Russian ship and leaves Christiania "where the windows of the homes all shone with such brightness." Here Henning Carlsen makes one rather puzzling addition. In Hamsun's text the narrator has just eaten some sweet cakes (without any real alleviation of his hunger) and seems to leave the city in a neutral frame of mind. Carlsen has Per Oscarsson smile as if in relief and inward anticipation. It is unclear why, unless the stint of manual labour will mean a relaxation of those intellectual pressures to which he had been so subject.

In any event, it can soon be seen that there is no "story." What we have is a series of psychological events, some of them surrealist; this is a miasmic world peopled with gibbering grotesques and culminating in total cruelty. Like sickness, drink or drugs, hunger here confers a new vision of society from beneath: "Nothing escaped my eyes, I was sharp and my brain was very much alive, everything poured in toward me with a staggering distinctness as if a strong light had fallen on everything around me," and again, "My poverty in fact had actually sharpened some of my faculties. . . ." Here filmic translation created some insuperable difficulties for the director.

In the book, as in Dostoyevski's *Notes from Underground* to which it is obviously indebted, the protagonist's masochism can be clarified; in the film, on the other hand, we do not realise the extent of his hunger for some time, and perhaps not even then (the actor himself appearing tolerably well fed, though he gnaws self-destructively at his own manuscript early on). Secondly, it is hard to understand his reasons for inflicting such recurrent pain on himself and generally so damaging his chances. He appears silly rather than tormented; a certain impatience with this self-willed misfit may result. He is certainly a much less likable character than Hamsun's, a person of no self-pity whatsoever. (Though both wear glasses, Hamsun's *alter ego* seems to have been a big man—he stops a wagon with his shoulder and has fists that could "grind a longshoreman into small bits"—whereas Per Oscarsson is small and frail in appearance.) Yet it is hard to see how any of this could have been helped.

Carlsen made his film in a splendidly stark black-and-white, not only reminiscent of early cinema but responding well to the harshness of the protagonist's lot and his sense of deprivation. It was also reminiscent of René Clément's *Gervaise* (1957), made from Zola's *L'assommoir,* printed black-and-white on colour stock (at least in its 35mm version) in order to catch the essence of old daguerrotype prints. In a dream sequence built to visualise the writer's hunger we see him on all fours in competition with a large dog for a fleshy bone—the sky is white and the cobblestones black. There are no sweet dissolves or cuts. The bleaching of the leaves in the park when the narrator first sees his dream-girl Ylayali admirably effects that lack of hold on reality from which he so desperately suffers, a lack of identity characterised also by his fooling with signals of time; he plays with a make-believe watch, repeatedly asks constables (unfailingly polite, like the pawnbroker and other "establishment" figures) for the time, is made anxious by numbers like 69 and totally confused by a shop-window showing differing clock faces. But we find that time agrees when he goes to Ylayali.

In common with the protagonist's, our eye is brutally arrested between non-congruent scenes by black-outs. This filling of the screen with blackness* not only forcibly reminds us of a first principle of film, the retina's retention of an image for one-tenth of a second longer than its physical contact, but replies to—condenses—the scene in its original when the narrator puts himself in prison for a night and attempts to deal with total lack of light ("The same darkness was brooding around me, the same fathomless black eternity which my intelligence fought against and could not grasp . . . God in heaven, how black it was"). This section, occurring in Part Two, is brilliantly written but legitimately excised from the film.

Internal with Hamsun, the story-line is externally minimal. Yet a film-maker has to show things happening to, or caused to happen by, his leading character: an eventless plot has to hang on a peculiarly interesting and convincing central figure. Dostoyevski's underground man was such since he presented an exaggeration of many tendencies we have nearly all, at one time or another, felt. Hamsun's, being more exceptional, cannot borrow any such empathy; in fact, the section in which he avoids paying a cab-driver makes the writer appear much more cruel on film than on the printed page.

Further, few modern viewers, barring those who have been in prisoner-of-war camps, can have known the extremity of hunger Hamsun depicted. His anti-hero reaches vertigo, he feels his head coming off ("it was balancing lightly and without content on my shoulders"), he hears his heart "like horses stamping," and at one point senses that "my eyes would soon be all the way through my head." At others he

---

* Strictly speaking, there is no true black in cinema since film and emulsion must be transparent to an extent.

talks to his shoes (an idiosyncrasy understandably cut short by Carlsen who may through it make allusion to Porter's last major film, *The Dream of a Rarebit Fiend,* in which a man's shoes walk out of a room on their own). Throughout the film the camera only once forsakes the narrator's point of view and that is to give us, briefly, Ylayali's —an aspect, when all is said and done, of his.

Carlsen tightens what plot exists, altering the order of some elements and condensing the writing of several articles by the narrator into one crucial case (possibly the essay "Kristofer Janson" which also appeared in 1888) ; and he uses his effective concertina to make various landladies into one. The only large intrusion—unexceptionable and unexceptional—is a passage in which we see a lip-reading school of the time, in which practitioners exaggeratedly enunciate "je vous aime." This brief episode, which disturbs none of the "cinematographic essence" of the original, is not unjustified: the narrator is suffering from a pathetic lack of communication and the final grotesque who mimes the words into the camera is a mocking gargoyle whose confidence is an accusation in itself.

McFarlane is right. In the final analysis the agony of hunger is secondary to "privation at a number of different levels—physical, erotic, social—and of an individual's struggle to build up an inner psychological defense against it." Hamsun's tortured pages tell us that hypersensitivity is an alien state. Passers-by stare at the camera (narrator) in the street, policemen are gravely suspicious, the writer's courtliness is broken down as grotesques haunt the edges of his every move, including one, faithfully-reported from the book, a seedy and apparently successful queer called Queeny; Carlsen integrates him as a suspiciously predatory figure throughout.

It is all so well done, since Hamsun's is a literature of symbolic detail, of the hidden depths of life, of the secret behaviour that lies behind our daily masks. Certainly, at least, this applies to the early Hamsun, the author of *Mysteries, Hunger, Pan,* and *Victoria,* all published (in book form) in the last decade of the last century. The absurdities of preposterous conduct—the hero of *Pan* shoots himself in the foot since he wants to look more like a rival and spits in the ear of another, a baron, at a ball—are like those of some terrible dream, in which trivialities can be revelations. In *Pan* the narrator finds that wrinkles on a woman's knuckles are "kindly" in appearance, or connotation, while a girl's thumb has a "chaste" look about it. This is true symbolism—presumably you deduce a girl's chastity by the state of her thumb—and the very stuff of cinema. In *Hunger,* as Ylayali turns from a window at which the infatuated protagonist is staring, "the expression of the shoulder as it turned was a sign to me." The Baudelairean echo is there, not only in a sequence in the film in which the hero's dreams are reduced to drab reality, but in a direct tribute to one of the most seminal of all prose poems, "Le mauvais vitrier." It is, meanwhile, rather to Dostoyevski that we owe the self-tormenting passage with the cab-driver, or the incident of mistaken change given the narrator in a pastry-shop.

The whole film is a triumph of transposition, since its director obviously understands literary metaphor. When Hamsun writes of his famished writer, "In front of a butcher's shop there was a woman with a basket on her arm, debating about some sausage for dinner . . . as she turned toward me, her eyes were still full of sausage," we are within the mind of a hungry man in a curiously possessive way. In the film we see this same woman through the narrator's vision, but it would surely have been a falsification of inner motive—Buñuel would probably have done it—to show actual sausages in her eyes on the screen. So many extraneous connotations would have become involved. Similarly, Carlsen correctly cut the more surrealist passages, such as the Burroughs-like conversation of the man with his shoes

("As I stared at my shoes, I felt as if I had met an old friend . . ."). It would surely be hard better to convey in near silent-screen images this parable of a man searching for values among so much . . . *meat*. It is curious how, by the end of *Hunger*, one has such an impression of well-fed characters; the constables, the editor, the pawnbroker, Queeny, all fill their clothes with an unpleasant complacence. Physical hunger is thus transmuted into spiritual.

This brings us, lastly, to the chief and perhaps only weakness in this otherwise admirable picture. The hero's sexual idyll-ideal Ylayali is a palindrome—her name can be said backwards as well as forwards. Together with other elements in Hamsun's work, she is thus a magic incantation like Martha Clifford for Joyce's Bloom. How real is Ylyali? She is part of that lie which is art. Hamsun says as much in his cabalistic numerologies and recurrent motifs of death, via cemeteries and shrouds. The narrator is an artist-impostor, inventing identities for himself—one of them Wedel-Jarlsberg, a celebrated Norwegian family which survived the Black Death—and he invents this ancestry to a girl who "stood still awhile, trying out this fantastic lie on her tongue." In the film, alas, Ylayali has to be so much flesh-and-blood. The narrator's last sight of her is in a mirage involving Queeny, perhaps over-faithfully reported from the original, where the hero is fearing the total loss of his mind and sees her as but a red dress. In the film she is played too much like a Strindbergian flirt, the capricious, fitful temptress Hamsun called Evarda in *Pan,* a girl who having impulsively kissed the hero at a picnic circles his hut all night like a bitch on heat and then licks his very footprints (she appears again in *Rosa* [1907], where she is still more dissatisfied and cruel). It is impossible to make a magic incantation into an image; Ylayali is invention itself. Once, when unable to sleep, Hamsun's hero sits up "to fight against the darkness." All at once he imagines a new word—"It is not in the language, I have discovered it—*Kuboaa* . . . by sweet Jesus, man, you have discovered a word!"

It is not easy to discover a word in cinema. Yet Carlsen's brilliant film takes a most difficult subject matter, filled with a Nietzchean *hauteur* guaranteed to make it "box-office poison," and goes far toward doing so. A classic of its kind, this is a stream of consciousness eventuated into "correspondences," far surpassing Joseph Strick's over-reverent attempt at *Ulysses.* Literalness is not fidelity in these transpositions, as can be seen in a whole line of such from Victor Sjöström's 1926 *The Scarlet Letter,* starring Lillian Gish at her best, down to Joseph Losey's 1971 *The Go-Between,* out of L. P. Hartley via Harold Pinter. Imagination has to play its part in order to make mere sincerity come alive.

LAST YEAR AT MARIENBAD (1961)

Though not based strictly on a novel, Alain Resnais's *Last Year at Marienbad* can legitimately be considered here since it represents the most faithful rendition of a novelist's conception put before us. And the novelist in question has expressed himself as delighted with the result.

Alain Robbe-Grillet had, by his own confession, never written a shooting script, so he was invited to try his hand at the approximation of one concerning "the story of a communication between two people, a man and a woman, one making a suggestion, the other resisting, and the two finally united, as if that was how it had always been"* (a description of *Marienbad* somewhat in conflict with its written ending). What we learn from this harmonious transmutation is what Robbe-Grillet remarks in his Introduction—"This is precisely what makes the cinema an art: it creates a reality with forms." In Resnais's film the visual image becomes more imaginative and suggestive for an open-ended purpose than the literary language. The word is specific. Robbe-Grillet's hesitancies—"Perhaps your hus-

---

* The text is published in book form by Grove Press.

band"—his reluctancies to commit himself—"Ackerson . . . or Patterson"—are rendered much more effective, and less artificial because more ambiguous, on the screen, where Resnais can, for instance, show two versions of the same scene.

Language must here be more explicit. In discussion, Resnais has always insisted that *Marienbad* can be open to almost any interpretation—or, at least, to a wide range. By virtue of its second eye, that interruption of the camera's selection between ourselves and reality, film makes this far more possible; we must interpret the camera's selection, trust or mistrust it. It can annul a reality very rapidly. Try as Robbe-Grillet may, he cannot with words be quite as inspecific as this. The amputation of the past, and its final translation into the present, of which he speaks in his Bergsonian Introduction, is the hinge of the whole; but it is qualified throughout his text by the connotative affects of language. On the printed page he tells us, for instance, that scenes take place "in the *imaginary* bedroom that have the raw light of day" (my italic). He has committed himself here far more than need the camera. Again, the character of X, given no patronymic so as to avoid any connotations, is specified when Robbe-Grillet writes of "a cold expression characteristic of him: hard, watchful but withdrawn, impenetrable." Most important, the ending is metaphorised in language as it is not in image: the girl A is taken off by X "as if she were a distinguished prisoner and he the guard leading her away."

Chosisme—the "new" school of fiction has been given many names, some of them distinctly unflattering—arose as a revolt against what was long ago termed the pathetic fallacy. As a typical example of the latter, Professor Josephine Miles cites *The proud fields laughed*. The metaphor has become a cliché, the lyric ratio turned tired. A discrepant group of writers grew up in post-war France, ranging from Alain Robbe-Grillet through anovelists like

Claude Simon and Marc Saporta, to more traditional experimenters like Michel Butor, and theorists such as Nathalie Sarraute—all evidently dedicated to eschewing metaphorical descriptions and banishing the pathetic fallacy. Nothing "intensional" should intervene between us and those fields which someone says are proud. The idea was surely to make the reader see again, much in the spirit of Conrad's belief that "art itself may be defined as a single-minded attempt to render the highest kind of justice to the visible universe."

The universe of the New Novel tries to be highly visible, or visual. We know by now that mere presence on a screen lets objects make their own statements. Physical facts are invited to speak their language, "uncontaminated" (Robbe-Grillet's slanting is significant) by the human. It is Chaplin's sense of the life of objects, as in the dream of *The Gold Rush* (1925) when two rolls on forks go into a little dance, that some critics feel accounts for his cinematic genius. This new, if scarcely novel, epistemology might however have been taken out of the aesthetic camp Robbe-Grillet opposes, that of Marcel Proust: "Perhaps the immobility of the things that surround us is forced upon them by our conviction that they are themselves, and not anything else, and by the immobility of our conceptions of them" (*Swann's Way*). The New Novel attempts to divorce objects from emotional states, especially clichés about them, such as mountains being "majestic" or fields "proud." "For Robbe-Grillet," writes his enthusiastic expositor, and film addict, Roland Barthes, "the function of language is not a raid on the absolute, a violation of the abyss, but a progression of names over a surface." In one of his essays in *For a New Novel* Robbe-Grillet best summarises his motives as follows: "Drowned in the *depth* of things, man ultimately no longer even perceives them: his role is soon limited to experiencing, in their name, totally humanised impressions and desires." How aptly this describes the condition of the girl called A in *Marienbad*. How admirably suited is cinema to an exposition of this philosophy, for, as Robbe-Grillet remarks, "The essential characteristic of the image is its presentness." Since the mentally disturbed or frankly schizophrenic live largely in the present, film is well equipped to depict them, e.g. *The Other* or *Images*.

It is in film that the object can best be cleared of the word, cleansed of all signals, especially those in any way oriented toward judgement (and, according to this credo, function is one form of pre-judgement). Let Roland Barthes describe it for us:

> A slice of tomato in an automat sandwich, described according to this method, constitutes an object without heredity, without associations, and without references, an object rigorously confined to the order of its components . . . For example, we would ordinarily say, "So-and-so's dinner was ready: some ham." This would be an adequate representation of the function of an object—the alimentary function of the ham. Here is how Robbe-Grillet says it: "On the kitchen table there are three thin slices of ham laid across a white plate." Here function is treacherously usurped by the object's sheer existence. . . .

This rephrasing of Heidegger ("The human condition is to be *there*") is a mirror put up to the devaluation of man in our days. This is the reality as seen by the technocrat or rabid engineer (roughly Robbe-Grillet's own trade, before that of New Novelist). Here, in this dissociation of consciousness, is the bomber pilot dropping his cargo of destruction over North Vietnam "like Rice Krispies." The world of the New Novel is that of (the more elementary or fanatic) engineering students, proceeding in a steady rote from Physics, Chemistry, Drafting back to Drafting, Chemistry, Physics, day after day—individuals who do not find Robbe-Grillet's fiction or films difficult at all. In this world man is *there* with a vengeance. In common with an object, he has no being beyond that of phenomenon. The methodological exposition of nuclear death given in Herman

Kahn's *On Thermonuclear War* makes Dr. Strangelove rational by comparison; and yet this was one who advised U.S. Air Force Generals. This is where Swift said we would end up if science was to solve everything.

The truth is that we do not remain engineering students all our lives and nearly all Robbe-Grillet's main characters are seriously disturbed, to the point of pathology. (A majority are involved in murder.) I first saw *Marienbad* in Switzerland before the critical brouhaha had begun and felt no difficulty with A at all.

If the film was "by" Robbe-Grillet, then its images were likely to cleansed of the cliché. The couple could not be lovers since this is precisely what the average moviegoer was obviously anticipating—some erotic interest by X in A. Despite one passage, when he briefly but abstractedly fondles her breast, this interest is not forthcoming. This moment, too, could be read as the analyst's often necessarily excessive commitment to his patient, in parallel with his excessive irritation with her at another point. The passages involving the statuary—a man making a protective gesture in front of a woman—reinforce this reading. X has seen something she has not seen, or recognized, as he explicitly informs her.

For *Bad* is where one takes a *cure*. At one point X tells A that maybe they had met elsewhere, yet in some other *Bad*—"at Marienbad, or at Baden-Salsa . . . "; his opening "once again," on which Robbe-Grillet put such emphasis, thus falls into place. Once more the therapist has to begin his journey "down these corridors, through these halls, these galleries, in this structure" of a disturbed mind. The last shot of the Nymphenburg palace, just outside Munich, is highly suggestive of a hospital. Resnais worked in Nymphenburg and Schleissheim simply because they were put cheaply at his disposal (as were A's Chanel costumes) ; yet he somehow managed to make both look clinical—from the infrequently seen exterior.

To those for whom the world simply *is* (to paraphrase Robbe-Grillet's own paraphrase on the subject), to those who have no past, as he assures us is the case of A (Delphine Seyrig), and the sinister M who looks "anxious" at the end (Sacha Pitoëff), the connection between symbol and symbolised, between word and thing, has been ruptured. This is the dissociation predicated in Sartre's *La nausée,* a work Robbe-Grillet has explicitly admired. Yet we must consult the footnote he accords to those pregnant first words from X, "Once again—." We read: "The dash represents a slight pause, more emphatic than the meaning of the text suggests." More emphatic, one might say, than it is possible for a text to suggest. X (Giorgio Albertazzi) enters the world of *La nausée* or even Faulkner's *The Sound and the Fury* where time is dislocated only by space and shapes carry their own meanings, or non-meanings. Here images are perfect cinematic frames, cut up, imposed beside and/or over each other. In Robbe-Grillet's *Le voyeur* the legs of one girl can adhere in the narrator's memory to the body of another. Time shifts are made by shapes, like O's and Y's and V's. In *La nausée* stones liquefy; in *Marienbad* balustrades crumble. It is the stuff of nightmare. Our ordinary assumptions about the universe suddenly fail. As Lionel Trilling has put it, though in another context, "The obsessive contemplation of the objectivity of objects, the thingishness of things, is a step toward surrealism, perhaps toward madness." Rather than the Gaelic "you" of yore, you become an "it." *He walked into the room. He picked up a piece of steel. He plunged its point into a chest. . . .*

I improvise, but Resnais's cameraman, Philippe Brun, exerts such excessive concentration on sheer objects at the start of *Marienbad* that anyone at all familiar with contemporary philosophy is soon tipped off. When servants are seen like statues, and statues like servants, in the hotel, when A "turns her head rather quickly left and right, like someone trying to find out the source of the phrase just spoken" and experiences other auditory and spatial difficulties (once trying to put a shoe on the wrong foot) , we surely need no further clues. A's state is well known to analysts. The static, almost hysteric, quality of the drama shown, the play "with a foreign, meaningless title,"* in which the actress's gesture, repeated by A, is "like that of a statue," further characterises the amnesic mind, so that when Welles jeered at *Marienbad* as reminding him of *Vogue* he was missing the point—or making Resnais's for him.

Resnais was a purist over sound in this film and his engineer, Guy Villette, a near-genius in the field. Not only in the disappearance of detonations, the crunch of footsteps on gravel in an hotel salon, the cut-off conversations and questions, but in the confused, non-communicative whisperings terminated by a suddenly exaggerated word like *"Extraordinaire!"*—in such ways the lack of spatial perspective in the mind of the central character is admirably accompanied. In this world man is simply *there* with a vengeance. Whether Resnais, who had made *Nuit et brouillard* in 1955, quite knew it or not, his film was by implication a deeply social document. When you reverse anthropomorphism, man is a digit, an "it." Bruno Bettelheim emphasised that it was the digitary "business as usual" existence that really betrayed European Jewry under Hitler. It is relatively easy to exterminate phenomena, end-products of capitalism. In our advertising, therefore, man is seen as a clothes dryer or "human engine," in T. S. Eliot's formulation; he is a "powerhouse," gets "turned on" or "keyed up" and the like. For Herman Kahn this meant that sixty mil-

---

* Unfortunately all too much meaning has been seen in this title, *Rosmer*, for Ibsen's drama does suggest some strange parallels. This is one of those curious coincidences of the creative mind. Resnais told me that, faced with a very strict shooting schedule, he had suddenly to think of a title for the play (without Robbe-Grillet on hand) since the poster had to be printed overnight; he wanted something as unspecific as possible and simply picked on the name of a childhood friend, Rosmer.

lion American "its" could be wiped out and there would still have been a successful "defence." The words of bomber pilots in Vietnam ring out of this nightmare of science, this extension of Huxley and Wells, which the New Novel has depicted, a world in which all crimes are forgiven in the amorality of attention to *things* . . . pardoned by the First and Second Laws. In this sense the New Novel suggests that if the human condition is simply to be *there,* we will not be here much longer.

It would be pressing the point too far to pretend that Resnais's *Marienbad* presaged Vietnam. However, the state of mind of its heroine has strong social reverberations when one considers that Resnais had made *Hiroshima mon amour* two years before. If A's actions are exonerated from the meaningful, then the universe has no meaning. Robbe-Grillet gave us the warning in his very first novel which concerned a private detective, a modern Oedipus, whose semantic relationship with the world, with things, had been fractured; Robbe-Grillet then followed up with similar parables concerning a homicidal watch salesman and a pathologically jealous banana-planter. As Trilling observes, any excessive concentration on objects is an unnatural activity for the human being, who must see one thing in relation to another. Thus, since A's world has no past, it is denied a future.

X, whose interest in her appears far more clinical than erotic (though the analysand must typically have some emotional involvement with the analyst), has to restore, if not her past in fact, at least some personality she can accept and live with. He has worked in this hospital before, been "down these same corridors, through these same empty rooms . . . these same thresholds, making my way as though by chance among the labyrinth of similar itineraries." For A herself this is a painful restoration ("she seems to be struggling against something, some inner threat"). She repeatedly begs X, "Let me alone. . . ." Her face is seen in "evident anguish." She screams before the pistol shot, there is the shock of the rape scene in which she must recognise and emancipate herself from her evil genius M (always the winner in the game within these walls), and then there is the tender relaxation of the ending. X has had to establish what the semanticists call an extensional world for A—via *things* (bracelets, necklaces, glasses), for things change less than people in Robbe-Grillet's world (his first novel is temporally staked out by the wearing down of an eraser or *gomme*). As A begins to exert a fragile hold on the pasts X suggests to her, so he retreats from his own suggestions ("no . . . that wasn't it . . .") —the choice must be hers. X has had to take her into reality "by force," as he confesses. The subconscious analogue is accomplished visually by the shooting of A (dressed and gesturing like the bird-victim of a hunter) by M, her Dionysiac demon.

There is a beautifully handled passage at the very end when A bids farewell to this side of herself, or perhaps pacifies it. We see the ruined balustrade (of her life) and return to her bedroom, which on this occasion is not bleached, as for a reverie or dream. She lies down on the bed and M enters. He knows he has lost her now:

M   *(sad, dreamy)* : Where are you . . . my lost love . . .
A   *(uncertain)* : Here . . . I'm here . . . I'm with you, in this room.
M   *(gently)* : No, even that's not true any more.
A   *(more urgent)* : Help me, please, help me! Give me your hand . . . Take my hands and hold them tight . . . Hold me against you.
M   *(makes a gesture toward her, but lets her arm fall back)* : Where are you? What are you doing?
A   *(with a cry that is scarcely contained)* : Don't let me go.
M   *(with emotion, but simplicity)* : You know it's too late. Tomorrow I'll be alone. I'll walk through the door of your bedroom. It will be empty . . . *(he moves a little away from the bed.)*

A (*desperately*) : No . . . I'm cold . . . No! Don't leave yet!
M (*simply*) : But you're the one who's leaving, you know you are.

LAST YEAR AT MARIENBAD (1961, Resnais): Delphine Seyrig as a wounded bird: a patent parody of the Travis Banton costuming of the twenties.

The simplicity of the dialogue, against the rococo of the décor, is immensely moving. Even M has his pathos. Overlapping their voices we hear X's soothing accents—"Yes, you felt better . . . yes, you're going to sleep now. . . ." It is thus an uncertain but courageous patient whom X takes into the world of reality, on the witching hour of midnight. When the clock chimes, and time suddenly becomes real, an index of existence, A stands up "like an automaton." She walks "stiff and expressionless," as well such a catatonic invalid might. The analyst follows, he must let her make her own way now. For a moment M appears, a sinister figure in his tuxedo against a screen of black, and the film ends with the slow reverse travelling shot outside the hotel.

Resnais wanted to make this film open-ended. Consciously or unconsciously he responded to an entire cultural condition. The human being without heredity suffers the embryonic anguish of the human race without heredity. In Balzac, according to Robbe-Grillet, things "belonged to a world of which man was the master." Technology threatens to reverse this ratio. It is thus all the more essential for man to *see again*. The painful effort is perfectly caught by Resnais's work, for in a sense we are all in Marienbad.

1984 (1956)

The outlines of Orwell's dystopia are too well-known to need rehearsal here. The story is virtually inexistent as such. The "fictional" side of the book is so weak as to be embarrassing when we meet the lower-class caricatures passing as characters ("Beg pardon, dearie . . . "). *1984* pales beside such sophisticated documents of the future as *A Canticle for Leibowitz* or *Giles Goat-Boy,* while in *Brave New World Revisited* Aldous Huxley exposed the shallowness of its reasoning more succinctly, and certainly more temperately, than had Wyndham Lewis earlier. Nevertheless, *1984* could still make a good film. As an example of what the French call *anticipation,* of projection into the future, it can logically conclude this section of cinematic transpositions. The book is an essay, yet Orwell's mind was such that an intelligent director could pull a telling visualisation from almost anything he wrote. When Orwell wrote this his last fiction he was dying of tuberculosis in the Orkneys as well as suffering from acute Russophobia of the *Partisan Review* variety.

None of this need matter to a film. Prejudice can often

make for visual sharpening—and Orwell had plenty of it. Toward the end of *The Road to Wigan Pier* (1937), with its superb opening picture of British mining conditions prior to the Second World War, there is a passage which threatens to undermine all the confidence placed in the author:

> there is the horrible—the really disquieting—prevalence of cranks wherever Socialists are gathered together. One sometimes gets the impression that the mere words "Socialism" and "Communism" draw towards them with magnetic force every fruit-juice drinker, nudist, sandal-wearer, sex-maniac, Quaker, "Nature Cure" quack, pacifist and feminist in England.

This is close to the gutter-journalism Orwell himself derides in this book, and others. Would he today, one wonders, publicly consider a feminist or nudist or pacifist or Quaker a "crank"? In issuing *Wigan Pier* for the Left Book Club, indeed, Victor Gollancz was unhappy enough about the nature of Orwell's prejudice to write a Foreword in which he took issue with this very passage: a "crank," Gollancz pointed out, then meant for Orwell "anyone holding opinions not held by the majority—for instance, any feminist, pacifist, vegetarian or advocate of birth control." Orwell's supply of vitriol in this respect was quite astonishing; he poured scorn on teetotallers, when he should have been encouraging them, as well as some luckless members of an ILP (International Labour Party) summer school at Letchworth who are described in terms worthy of the *Daily Mirror*—one old man is "obscenely bald," though why loss of hair should be indecent eludes reason. Orwell would probably have lost his.

All this is to say that Orwell was an untrustworthy witness at times—and perhaps, in *1984*, at all times. As a film the novel cries out for that sort of anagram or analogy we shall consider below. Michael Anderson chose to direct it head-on. This was a mistake; there is little predictive in the story line of *1984* as there had been in Huxley's *Brave New World* (anticipation of the pill via the Malthusian belt, of moronic TV, and the like). Orwell's satire, so-called, is set in a combination of post-war London and Stalinist Russia that was already dated when the book came out. The deliberate seediness of everything is Orwell's aesthetic revulsion to post-war Britain, one conveyed far better in Wyndham Lewis's *Rotting Hill*. In *1984* the word *dingy* occurs again and again—when Winston (parodistically named) wakes in the morning he seizes "a dingy singlet" for his daily physical jerks. One wonders why. It need not be dingy and in the film is not so. Moreover, the mass exercises now remind one of Red China, which has to date proved to be a singularly successful Communist experiment, and a contradiction of all Orwell's "thinking" of this time.

1984 is really not science-fiction at all, since it contravenes Asimov's useful principle that technology forms its own politics, from the Napoleonic to the Vietnam wars. In Orwell's vision, on the other hand, politics antecedes technology. He thus proposes that his Oceania will never be able to advance in science since impartial thinking is *per se* impossible to a fanatical socialism: "The empirical method of thought, on which all the scientific achievements of the past were founded, is opposed to the most fundamental principles of Ingsoc." If this is meant to be a serious statement about the nature of Communism, it is today made laughable by Russia's prowess in outer space. Anderson wisely realised that Orwell's strength was in the understanding of the relationship between politics and morals, not of something called science. The gadgetry of *1984* is weakly imagined, and of course far surpassed today; the torture section could be mediaeval.

The film thus opens with the A-bomb, which has already happened in fact, and a voice-over warning about what might happen to the human race, if. . . . Even at the time the film's technology could have been more advanced than it was; Anderson seemed to want to suit it to the drab mood of the book. The continual pap of neutral music pouring out from officialdom, as in some American bank, is accounted for throughout—there is even one operatically gifted prole washerwoman. Today the monitoring telescreens and dictating machines appear almost touchingly antique. They, too, have happened.

The film is set in bomb-damaged London, patrolled by a Fascist police. There are areas where only the (despised) "people" live: Orwell's pejorative term *proles* is avoided in the script, as is the name O'Brien for Winston's inquisitor (played by an unusually wooden Michael Redgrave). In the film O'Brien becomes O'Connor presumably because Winston is acted by Edmond O'Brien (another leaden performance). Goldstein's name has also been tactfully altered, though the Trotskyite appearance of the original crimethinker is maintained by the camera. Big Brother is invariably shown as a drawing (i.e. with an element of fantasy involved) and is made far less like Stalin than in Orwell's verbal description.

At first inspection, then, there seems little changed in the transposition, yet once again almost everything is changed. The nature of Orwell's satire is misinterpreted primarily since it is taken as narrative. The arrest of Winston and his Julia (Jan Sterling) via the treacherous antique dealer Charrington carries out in almost every detail the concluding pages of Orwell's Part Two. Yet somehow the extrapolation into reality, into a series of real scenes, tends only to point up the essential looseness of a lot of Orwell's thinking. For instance, the country idyll between the two lovers raises a host of questions. In contrast with the decimated city, the unbombed farmland looks so prosperous and well-tended—what is rural life like in Oceania? True, there is a brief explosion on a wheatfield, but then the ringing of the bell as an All-Clear signal in the abandoned belfry where the pair have taken refuge is simply so much more extension of wartime England, while the notion of executions being "a popular spectacle" to which "children always clamoured to be taken" is uncomfortably reminiscent of Kafka's famous penal colony. It is parenthetically interesting that Orwell's anti-feminism ("It was always the women, and above all the young ones, who were the most bigoted adherents of the Party") is avoided.

At the same time the film failed to—could not?—report Orwell's strength in this over-estimated "satire," namely his knowledge of semantics and his interest in how language could condition thought. Orwell knew that language is an integer of the human mind and its denial—seen here in erasures or rewritings of the past—an amputation of mind. In having his citizens "vaporised" rather than *massacred* he anticipated the dreadful euphemisms spawned almost daily during the Vietnam war.

Here Orwell's accusations ring true, give help, whereas his embittered gibes about the similarity of Nazism and Communism, one an intellectual creed and the other totally anti-intellectual, are faintly cheap. In any event, they are hard to visualise quickly. To say, "If you want a picture of the future, imagine a boot stamping on a human face—forever" is one thing, but to dramatise the cause of this effect in a fast-moving film is another. O'Brien's theory, considerably cut in the film, is really an extension of the Machiavelli of the *Discorsi,* a long essay within the book itself. The torture of Winston, and his final collapse in front of the cage of rats, is treated gingerly, generally offstage, the man's agony being watched by O'Connor on TV screens. Possibly this reticence was due to the concern with violence in films in England at the time; this was stimulated in the early Fifties by Gordon Mirams, the New Zealand Government Censor and Registrar of Films, who published a survey of acts of crime in feature films (an average per American film of 6.6, double Edgar Dale's Ohio State University sampling of the same in 1931). Mirams's concern resulted in British parliamentary action.

Only at the end of the picture does Anderson provide a telling touch, and an apt translation of an ideological implication into an image. Orwell leaves Winston boozing on Victory Gin in the Chestnut Tree Café, a wreck of a man. Anderson has him meet Julia on a seat under a tree in a London park. They admit their mutual betrayals. Winston then moves away to watch a crowd cheering Big Brother; when he turns back Julia is gone—or was she there at all? Despite the ineptitude of Edmond O'Brien's acting, the moment does suggest what has happened to the character's mind.

Basically, however, both book and film rest on shoddy thinking which wounds both. It is true that torture can coerce and intimidate, and perhaps even control, small populations for a time, but it is wasteful and expensive and finally less efficient than control by satisfactions. Dostoyevski's underground man had feared this direction in politics ("Shower upon him every earthly blessing, drown him in a sea of happiness, so that nothing but bubbles of bliss can be seen on the surface . . . "). These fears are surely very real by now. Lionel Trilling, for instance, sees that Marxist Herbert Marcuse "is apprehensive that, as compared with a traditional society, an affluent, permissive, and pleasure-oriented society will control the individual both more efficiently and more profoundly." This is the crux of the matter, a threat which the politically-embittered Orwell of the Labour-landslide period in England either missed or shrugged off. Thus, his celebrated *doublethink* is never nailed home to a social source that a film director could locate and use as foundation for his film. "The Ministry of Peace concerns itself with war, the Ministry of Truth with lies, and the Ministry of Love with torture, and the Ministry of Plenty with starvation." Smart journalism, the sentences slip out and seem to have said something, yet no idea has been advanced, though an oxymoron, in common with any healthy figure of speech, is generally an index to a social situation. "The key word here," Orwell tells us, as if discovering something, "is *blackwhite*." When Shakespeare's Timon said the same, he located the distortion in the accumulating cash nexus, money making "black, white; foul, fair."* Today American society often looks like a living oxymoron. "We will continue fighting in Vietnam until the violence stops," said Lyndon Johnson (cp. *The New Leader*'s headline of the time, "Vietnam's Democratic One-Man Rule"). While U.S. authorities poured aerial aid into a town battered by earthquakes in Nicaragua, they were busily plastering another peasantry with the bombs of the largest B-58 raids ever carried out. This is what makes for the rather slick validity of a work like *Slaughterhouse-Five*.

Orwell's Oceania has no thought-out dynamic on which a film director might get a grasp and which he could then pillory (the text admits the anarchy, "In Oceania there is no law"). The best choice for transposition thus veers toward a sort of Joe Orton farce, such as exists in Alan Sillitoe's imaginary Nihilon—either that or a power drama exchangeable with any gangster film. After all, political gangsters are still gangsters.

It was the second of these two possibilities that Anderson took for *1984*—which was a pity. For in *Brave New World* Huxley was able to generate considerable fictional energy from his understanding of the nature of mind, and his realisation of what egalitarian hedonism was doing to

---

* Or again,

> "Then let us say you are sad,
> Because you are not merry; and 'twere as easy
> For you to laugh, and leap, and say you are merry,
> Because you are not sad."
>
> *The Merchant of Venice*, I, i, ll. 46–49.

us. As he put it in his *Brave New World Revisited,* "In the light of what we have recently learned about animal behaviour in general, and human behaviour in particular, it has become clear that control through the punishment of undesirable behaviour is less effective, in the long run, than control through the reinforcement of desirable behaviour by rewards."

B: Commentary
THE HEIRESS (1949)

William Wyler's film of Henry James's *Washington Square* seems at first glance to disprove all norms so far advanced about the conversion of fiction into film. To start with, James's novels tend to be "stagey"; generally some confined cat's-cradle of relationships is modulated with great psychological intensity. Any illustrator of a later James fiction, let alone a film-maker, soon finds it hard to escape a sealed pattern of two or three people conversing together, usually without much movement and with any crowd scenes parenthetical. Furthermore, Wyler chose the added handicap of scripting a play made from the Jamesian original.

Yet the result was far from what Hitchcock derided as the camera simply looking at people. Although the important confrontation between Catherine and her father in Switzerland is omitted—reduced to a quick scene on a Paris boulevard—the film follows the novel quite closely, and does not balk at confinement in the mansion of its title. Indeed, by the end of it we find that the camera has utilised the interior of the house to suggest the claustrophobic pressures on Catherine's growing soul: Doctor Sloper, her father, effectively closes the sliding doors on his private study, as on his child's mind. So apt is the stylisation that the one directorial interpolation and expansion is the least successful part of the whole film, certainly its closest to *cliché*—the overlong ball scene at which Catherine meets the rotter, Morris Townsend. So does she in the novel, at Mrs. Almond's, but the film throws in a deal of unworthy business about dancing ability, or inability, and glasses of punch and so on. Here Wyler clearly desired to emphasise the theme of Plain-Jane-Up-Against-It, but he need not have done so. The book is not really about that, nor does the theme require it. The ball scene alone seriously lowers the intellectual level of what is otherwise a generally good, if not great, film, brilliantly acted by Olivia de Havilland, Ralph Richardson (superb in the part of Doctor Sloper), Montgomery Clift and Miriam Hopkins (the infuriatingly interfering Aunt Penniman). It was deservedly adorned with Oscars.

What is more, the play had accentuated what had been a very minor element in the novel, and the film followed suit; James gave the urbane Doctor Sloper a lost first child, a son, dead at the age of three. Catherine thus began life as "an infant of a sex which rendered the poor child, to the Doctor's sense, an inadequate substitute for his lamented first-born, of whom he had promised himself to make an admirable man." In short, this is a fully feminist fiction. In Doctor Sloper James presents a textbook case of sexism and in Catherine, his daughter, one of its most touching victims. She is confronted with the two males almost all women have to come to terms with sooner or later—father and suitor. She learns that both think almost wholly in terms of the cash nexus. Here the film's restructuring is unsuccessful, since it relies on some naïve psychology simply not equal to the thinking behind the original—the Doctor dislikes Catherine, we learn, since she is a plain and inadequate substitute for his beautiful wife who had died "a week after her birth." This is driven home at a number of points in the film, via photographs of the late Mrs. Sloper and so on, and the narrative impetus somehow slackens.

THE HEIRESS (1949, Wyler): part of the ball scene considerably expanded from the novel, in order to relieve the scenes in the house on Washington Square.

Austin Sloper had, in James's account, been "dazzled" momentarily by Catherine Harrington, yet never had regarded her as anything but his inferior, a member of the "imperfect sex." The alteration at the film's end is, however, far more successful; it is so since it results in a firmly visual scene, which rounds off the whole nicely, distorting James in its own best interests.

Catherine Sloper is deceived by a ne'er-do-well, Morris Townsend, to whom she gives her love. We soon suspect Townsend's approaches as not entirely disinterested, and the "geometrical proposition" that is the girl's father (by his own definition) reads the worst into them at once— "The position of husband of a weak-minded woman with a large fortune would suit him to perfection!" Sloper proceeds to crush all feeling from his daughter, to stamp out "the desire of a rather inarticulate nature to manifest itself," and by the end he leaves her an empty, forlorn husk of a woman, even—through his will—extending his dominance after death. In the last lines in the book Catherine, broken, takes up her fancy-work in the parlour—"for life, as it were." For James's purpose it is essential that Catherine should be so reduced. Toward the end, when Catherine has turned thirty "and had quite taken her place as an old maid," he inserts something omitted in the film, namely a suitor called John Ludlow who "was seriously in love with her." By this point Catherine cannot react; she has no emotions left.

Here, in some of his most pellucid prose, James is pressing on us genuine sociological insights. He had done the same in the very first paragraph of the book, warning about the true nature of "the light of science" when such alighted on the pecuniary, Puritan soil of the United States of America. Sloper is successful Science against Aunt Penniman's busy-bodying Romance, yet there is one dreadful scene in the fiction which reveals the fanaticism, the uncontrolled emotion, behind what we all too easily label the scientific mind. This takes place in "a lonely valley of the Alps" to which, *inter alia,* Doctor Sloper takes his daughter to forget Townsend; Wyler omitted it. The two alight from their carriage and walk among "the hard-featured rocks." Catherine senses "a great suffusion of cold red light" and when her father asks her whether she has given Morris up, she answers with a timorous negative. Sloper seethes. Admitting that "at bottom I am very passionate" he proceeds to

threaten Catherine with starvation "in such a place as this."
He has, he admits, "been raging inwardly for the last six
months." Figuratively, Catherine feels him "fasten his hand
—the neat, fine, supple hand of a distinguished physician
—in her throat." The ending of the film is quite different.
It makes no social insights, nor tries to; it shares with the
play in being principally an interaction of interesting characters. James leaves Catherine in the parlour with her fancy-work as a life sentence because, in a male-dominated ra-
tionalism of Doctor Sloper's kind, women will be eternal
victims. When the doctor interviews Morris Townsend's sister, hoping to elicit information about his proposed son-
in-law (and doing so) , he tells her explicitly: "You women
are all the same! But the type to which your brother be-
longs was made to be the ruin of you, and you were made
to be its handmaids and victims." When Morris Townsend
reappears, Catherine is effectively dead. She looks at him
and sees a man who "had made himself comfortable, and
he had never been caught." She *cannot* feel. "It was the
man who had been everything, and yet this person
was nothing." It is a touching moment since it is so true to
life. In the novel it is inevitable after what has gone before.
As Balzac repeatedly reminded his contemporaries (allegedly calling for one of his fictional doctors on his death-
bed) , there is a solidity of experience in the given universe
of a firmly-created fiction. We are, or should be, provided
with all we need to know within the compass of related
events.

It is scarcely relevant to say that the Wyler ending de-
tracts from James. It has nothing to do with James, *nor
was meant to have.* James showed a tragic victim. In the
film, however, Catherine's character strengthens after her
betrayals. When she realises that her father really hates
her, she hardens, and presides over his decline and death.
When Morris returns she is touched, yet tempered in the
fires of life. She arranges another elopement and, when he
arrives on time to pick her up, instead of abandoning her

as before, she turns the tables and leaves him battering on the bolted door, impotently crying "Catherine! Catherine!" to the empty square. The film then closes on this note as she proceeds up the stately staircase to her virtuous bed. It is visually a powerful ending, more especially so since the winding staircase had served as a central metaphor throughout the picture. Up these carpeted steps Catherine had joyfully bounded when Morris had been announced in the first days of his courtship; up the same had she wearily laboured with her lamp after the elopement betrayal. This ending reverses James: we scarcely feel sorry for a megaera who can revenge herself like this on both father and suitor. It must be admitted that this reversal originated with the stage play by Ruth and William Goetz, but Wyler's imagery, the movement of his camera, intensifies Catherine's strength at the end. We are able to look deeply into her face, as we are not on the stage, and we are told clearly the triumph she is feeling. She now has plenty of money, an enviable position in society, and there is no reason why she should not lead a full and fairly satisfying life.

Reversal of a narrative in this manner need not wound a film at all; in *The Heiress* it stiffens it. "Theatrical xerography" of James's original would probably have been less effective on the screen. Visually the rigidity of such relationships demands some climactic outburst. James provided his in the Swiss glen; Wyler uses the Goetzes, with the climax at the end, logically enough for his medium and audience. However, his re-structuring was kept within the organic growth of the whole. A reversal may not always do this; it certainly did not do so in the celebrated case of George Stevens's *A Place in the Sun* (1951), at the end of which Montgomery Clift goes to the electric chair accompanied by background music and haloed with a superimposition of Elizabeth Taylor's face. Compare the treatment of capital punishment in the filming of Truman Capote's *In Cold Blood*.

In common with Zola, Dreiser has drawn directors like

a magnet, the Laurence Olivier *Sister Carrie* being one of the more notable filmic interpretations of his work. As is perhaps well known, Eisenstein met Dreiser and scripted *An American Tragedy* for Paramount (originally Famous Players) in the late Twenties; the Russian appears to have planned a stark *reductio,* Dreiser's ten pages describing the lake scene reduced to ninety words. The studio (Jesse Lasky and B. P. Schulberg) were unhappy, hoping for "a simple, tight whodunit about a murder." In December 1930 the task of adaptation was then given to Samuel Hoffenstein and Josef von Sternberg. This scenario was completed in five weeks. Dreiser called it *A Mexican Comedy* and threatened to sue, which he in fact did after release of this version in 1931. Dreiser lost, but kept his integrity.

Given this background, one could scarcely expect Stevens, working in the hysterically anti-Communist Hollywood of the time, to bring out any very radical criticism of the American way of life. He concentrated on making a love story. Dreiser's characters were "creatures of circumstance," but the "circumstance" of America in the early Fifties, back to the wall against Russia, was sacrosanct.

Renaming Dreiser's Clyde—for some reason—George Eastman, Stevens had Montgomery Clift play another charming wastrel ditching, in all senses, his factory girlfriend Alice, played by Shelley Winters, for his own chance of "a place in the sun" alongside the rich patrician Angela (Elizabeth Taylor). Having abandoned Alice to her death in the lake George waits in death row; here, as always, the cinema's inevitably documentary eye cannot help but suggest social reform, and something of Dreiser's sombre message does seep through. But at this point Stevens has Angela visit George and express eternal love for him. This reverses Dreiser, who has Angela refuse to see George or have anything at all to do with him directly he is accused, thus showing the inhumanity of her values of class and rank. Yet the film's death-cell visit is successful, at least in the weepie genre. There is no time to think through the highly sentimental, indeed cloyingly jejune, values of the new story—if George had made it, after all, society was perhaps less unjust, while the love-conquers-all attitude of Angela considerably impugns her morality. What happens is simply good cinema; Dreiser's abiding social criticism is given a response as the lean Montgomery Clift leaves his death cell for the "hot squat" past a pot-bellied priest and laconically gum-chewing, equally portly cops. All the same, a reversal does not necessarily make a great film.

CATCH-22 (1970)

A hard-cover edition of Joseph Heller's sprawling war satire extends to 443 pages. It includes over fifty characters.
Although I have seen the blotter, or elaborate work-sheet,
for this novel,* it is essentially formless, cohering chiefly
in the verbal unity of the mind that gave it shape. If ever
there were a *verbal* novel, this is it. It is a brilliant exercise in general semantics.

Mike Nichols obviously had to cut out a number of characters and strengthen others. This resulted in a whole new
emphasis and inevitably altered what was going to be said.
Captain Black and Pfc. Wintergreen are eliminated in the
film, as are Kid Sampson and Corporal Whitcomb, Colonel
Cargill and Dr. Stubbs. The film is obliged to concentrate
on the development of Yossarian (Alan Arkin), who is important to Heller but not all-important. The scenes with
the dying Snowden—crying "I'm cold" as more and more
of his physical disintegration is shown in each shot—are
Nichols's attempt to try to account for the novel's looping

---

* Now published in "case-book" form by Crowell. alongside about thirty
essays and book reviews.

returns in plot. Somehow they do not work that way; Snow-den's death was meant to be the Rosebud of the whole, and simply did not come off as such.

Worse, by eliminating Wintergreen Nichols had to rein-force the role of Milo (Jon Voight). With the actor physi-cally suggesting an Aryan one-hundred-percent American ideal boy, Milo was made far more into a personification of Hitlerian villainy than a mere wartime profiteer. A scene

CATCH-22 (1970, Nichols): Jon Voight as Milo, an All-Ameri-can entrepreneur, driving into an Italian town as a little Hitler—a directorial addition. (No village in any European country at war was as unblacked-out at night as this.)

toward the end, when he drives into a small Italian square standing in his jeep, establishes him as controlling the local prostitution as well. In the same spirit, the casting, and playing, of Orson Welles as General Dreedle pushed that character to caricature. There are other further penalties for transposing a novel that is so essentially verbal. Heller had Yossarian win a medal for bombing a bridge at Ferrara; Nichols, forced to depict the target, a relatively innocent Italian town, finds himself thereby led into problems of locating compassion. He thus has Yossarian over-run the town to the sea and kill a lot of fish instead.

To my mind, Nichols obviously made an honest attempt to convey something of the book's spirit, but Heller was organising a coherent cynicism, an early example of black comedy in the American novel, which proved too intractable to translate. For one thing, his semantic insights were purely verbal, lexical; thus, in the Major Major joke— a character named Major also being a Major—we see Ernest Borgnine in a jeep surrounded by swirling winds and the whole point is lost in the invented visualisation. Nichols's ending, with Yossarian paddling to Sweden (which he obviously could never reach), verges on the ridiculous, whereas Heller was at some pains to stress Yossarian's final sanity in trying to come to grips with an insane world.

A CLOCKWORK ORANGE (1972)

Anthony Burgess's brilliant little "horrorshow" of urban violence attracted little attention when it first appeared in 1962. It seems to have been written with great intensity and Burgess himself admits that it was partially autobiographical—a point Kubrick concedes, rather pointlessly, by showing Alex's second name in the newspaper clips at the end of the movie as Burgess, a confusing change. The period is richly futuristic and invites imagery, though the reference in the film to a 1996 car is somewhat modified by the sight of unchanged cassettes and a Volkswagen. The principal feature of the book, however, or its chief originality was its dependence on an invented argot, a compound of Russian and Cockney rhyming slang.

This might be calculated to turn off a film director, rather than attract one: to "put a cancer in the rot" is not an image but has to be translated into one, namely to "put a cigarette in the mouth" (perhaps it helps to know that French *rot* can also be a belch). In fact, Burgess received very little money from the sale to cinema. On the release of Stanley Kubrick's film the book was reissued in American paperback provided with a Glossary, to Burgess's disapproval.

His annoyance was understandable. For a start, his invented language was phonetically raw and harsh, suitable to the theme; Kubrick's images, on the other hand, were generally smooth and graceful—despite his considerable fidelity to the slang on the soundtrack. In the slang the actions were implicit, transparent; their visualisation caused all to become explicit, apparent. Thus, the Burgess sublanguage was an important element in the whole, a kind of verbal mask (he described it once as a sort of fog you can walk around in). Such is dissipated even by a glossary of terms, but Kubrick's film from this text raises important aspects of any such transition. It is classed as a commentary here, not because it changed the story—all things considered, it followed it pretty faithfully—but because it put a different emphasis on the main theme, how a society accommodates violence. It drained the book of ethos.

After the release of the film and its reiterated success, Burgess himself was sorely tried, on TV and elsewhere, as a Sadean sponsor of violence. This was a sad irony, indeed, since his book clearly opposed it, being in part a reaction to youth delinquency in England of the same order as Wyndham Lewis's last fiction, *The Red Priest.** The usual charge made by first viewers of Kubrick's film is that his violence is far less detestable than Burgess's, just as his Alex is softened by the sympathetic features of Malcolm MacDowell. This seems a legitimate position. When Dim is knifed Kubrick goes into slow-motion, giving the action an elegant, balletic effect. Yet I have heard others argue that the film's violence is *more* disturbing than that of the book. The slow-motion slicing of Dim's hand (his wrist in the book) is more affecting than it might have been if giv-

---

* It is interesting that to date no novel has been made from the canon of this visual artist. Lewis expressed embitterment about this neglect to me at the end of his life.

en in normal time; certainly, the murder is far more explicitly violent in the film than in the book, where Alex is involved in an hilarious cat-fight as he kills the "very starry
ptitsa." He does so with a statue, just after trying to reach
a bust of "lovely Ludwig van in frowning like stone." Kubrick has Alex accomplish the action very deliberately, with
a phallic sculpture. Burgess's humour in this sequence considerably dilutes the violence enacted, as indeed it might
in the mind of the misguided youth concerned.

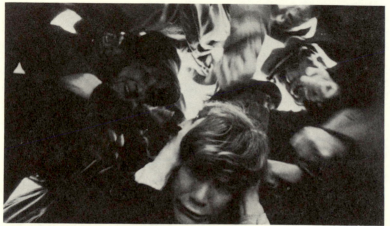

A CLOCKWORK ORANGE (1972, Kubrick): an **Expressionist**
visual to paraphrase a novelist's equally distorted language.

To give horror beautiful pictorial composition must be
to rob it of something of that horror. Assume that you have
seen newsreel shots of Büchenwald victims, and then
watch a director's carefully constructed re-creation of the
event—obviously, the intervening art has tamed, even sy-
phoned off, something of the crudity of the happening.
With a director as adroit as Kubrick we become more in-

terested in his compositional style than in the facts of the event. It can be answered that Burgess, too, cushioned his horrors in humour and an invented language; yet this is not necessarily to drain such of strength or trivialise violence. There are varying depths of responsibility, of seriousness, in art. Consequences (of being knifed, kicked in the groin, and so forth) are generally dimmed on film, often due to the time element. In *The Mackintosh Man* (1973) Paul Newman kicks a woman in the crotch as hard as possible; it is a shocking moment . . . but the moment passes.

In "The Cinema's New Language" (*Encounter,* April 1970) David Mowat writes: "In a straight fight the eye always beats the ear—movement kills words." In watching film we can become covert participants in a disturbing way —we do *commit the crime*. This helps to explain why distasteful or taboo elements can shock us so strongly. The new instrument for testing glaucoma—the non-contact tononmeter—spits a breath of air, an impulse, at the naked ball of the eye; though so soft as to be almost imperceptible to the fingertips or palm this impulse makes most people flinch, sometimes violently. Filmic stimuli are less absorbed, buffered, than are such verbal stimuli when reading. People faint in cinemas, though not when reading books (Dickens's *readings* may have made women faint, but his books did not). A recent Whitney Museum programme of "Outrageous Films" emphasised how visual shock is especially powerful since it has to be physiologically accommodated. Made to react in a primitive, pre-symbolic way, we feel intensely threatened. Furthermore, these filmic images are often enough not only staged like a dance today, they are also accompanied by music. In the case of *A Clockwork Orange* Kubrick can surely be charged with a certain ambivalence. Beethoven (suitably ferocious-looking) stands for Alex's vital spark, his imagination, even though he may want to use this in a perverted fashion—

knocking the nails into Christ himself, and so on. (He still was interested in what he was going to wear when doing so!) It is, however, more than uncalled-for, it is truly shallow, to track Elgar's "Land of Hope and Glory" music behind the visit of the Minister of the Interior to the prison (compare similar use of Elgar in *The Ruling Class*). Perhaps Kubrick felt he was being faithful in this way since Alex's mind is somewhat puerile and his slang often based on British schoolboy small-talk (eggiwegs, steakiweaks, fisties).

In Burgess's book we must remember that Alex enjoyed the violence of rape itself—he always chose ten-year-old girls in order to intensify this thrill. In the film the women he mauls are mature (the writer's wife, played by Adrienne Corri, extremely so), while the two girls in the music store, prominently featuring a record of *2001*, are consenting adults. Another re-emphasis of importance is that in the film only milk is drunk at the Korova milk bar; in the book, however, there are two vivid descriptions of the hallucinogenic experiences induced by imbibing at the Korova—there is even mention of a drug called synthemesc (synthetic mescaline?). At the end of the work, the writer F. Alexander (Frank to his weight-lifting henchman) remembers Alex by the latter's chanting "Singin' in the Rain." In the book it is the word *Dim* that gives Alex away. However, Burgess, a writer who (in his novel *M/F*) has put musical staves on a page, surely invites such a rendering.

In the final analysis it can be seen that there is a totally different approach to the nature of evil evident in writer and director. In Kubrick's film it is hard to find an ethos, so that the sense of Alex's choice is lost. Burgess, a Catholic, clearly feels that our society will only grow more violent if we continue to deny the original nature of aggressive impulses within us. Here he stands beside an analyst like Anthony Storr or a writer like Graham Greene.

Badness is of the self, the one, the you or me on our oddy knockies and that self is made by old Bog or God and is his great pride. But the not-self cannot have the bad, meaning they of the government and the judges and the schools cannot allow the bad because they cannot allow the self.

On the printed page Alex is a repulsive individual who has deliberately chosen evil; as a matter of fact, this presence of a strong central character makes *A Clockwork Orange* more amenable to filming than *Catch-22*. Kubrick symbolises this choice, fairly uselessly, by giving him a pet snake called Basil, once seen in a phallic superimposition over a woman's loins during the playing of Beethoven's Ninth. The prison chaplain (a "Roman," we note) tells Alex explicitly, "Goodness is something chosen." And Alex *has* chosen. "I was patronising the other shop," he states, in reference to *goodness*. And again, "What I do I do because I like to do."

All this could be written over the tombstone of any modern city today. In fact, it has been so inscribed. It was the Lisbon earthquake that made Voltaire avow, "Le mal est sur la terre." Alex is rather at one with the para-military discipline of his first curative establishment, or "reformatory," as he is with reveries of Hitler. It is the "liberal" attempt to institutionalise violence, to make it an effect rather than a cause (e.g. "He's sick," of some rapist), which Burgess surely sees as a modern disaster. However, his Alex is not clockwork. "Es irrt der Mensch, solang er strebt." A vital sinner is worthy of salvation; a socially-conditioned unit is not. And we see the robots in the shape of naked statues at the Korova bar (Dim talks to one as if it is alive since he is on no higher level of existence). After the Pavlovian deconditioning session Burgess gives his prison chaplain the following words:

"He has no real choice, has he? Self-interest, fear of physical pain, drove him to that grotesque act of self-abasement. Its insincerity was clearly to be seen. He ceases to be a wrongdoer. He ceases also to be a creature capable of moral choice."

Burgess's God is only interested in Alex if he has chosen freely. Unless you have choice you are subhuman, like the idiots and social units (including Alex's parents) who inhabit the edges of his consciousness, such as that is. Kubrick's final scenes show the nature of the re-emphasis or "commentary." Burgess had written a basically religious or mystical book, one about the nature of evil. His thesis is largely what Holy Church long considered as Manichaean, that good and evil co-existed, and that to know one you had to know the other. "Knowing God means also knowing His opposite," says the protagonist (eventually a priest) of Burgess's *Tremor of Intent.* The same character reflects elsewhere that evil "resides in the neutrals." T. S. Eliot seems to have felt the same, at least in his essay on Baudelaire: "So far as we are human, what we do must be either evil or good; so far as we do evil or good, we are human; and it is better, in a paradoxical way, to do evil than to do nothing; at least, we exist." Burgess's Hillier, of *Tremor of Intent,* thinks: "What counts is the willingness and ability to take evil seriously and to explain it."

Kubrick's interest in this situation is far less profound (though it is perhaps more socio-political). As his liberal, Lindsay-like politician leers over Alex's hospital bed in his mod suit one feels that a fairly banal statement is being made about political opportunism. Having once broken him down, the Minister will now build him up in the present government's own interest. There is no great insight here. Burgess probed far deeper; for that reason Buñuel called *A Clockwork Orange* "the only movie about what the modern world really means."

THE STRANGER (1967)*

By its nature philosophic fiction is both tempting and resistant to the intelligent film-maker; and the great writers of post-war France—Sartre, de Beauvoir, Camus (even Vailland) —were students or teachers of philosophy. Intellectually split during the war, France was forced to question basic values of the nation afterwards (Camus's Meursault is sentenced to be decapitated "in the name of the French people"). The glory of this group of writers was to universalise the predicament of their generation. To this effort of revaluation we must add the normative influence of philosophy on French life, but in general the period described by de Beauvoir in *The Mandarins* is the legacy of a small group of intellectuals suddenly brought brutally close to moral issues. In *Situations II* Sartre remarks on the

---

* Not to be confused with Orson Welles's film of the same name made from a Victor Trivas story in 1946, starring Loretta Young and Edward G. Robinson. The Gilbert Prouteau *Le dernier matin d'Albert Camus* is a twenty-five-minute documentary of the writer's days in general rather than of his last in particular; it does have, however, some eloquent and moving shots of his Algerian background, including of his birthplace at Mondovi and the Tipasa-Chenoua bay where *The Stranger* finds its climax.

proximity of torture and death as accelerative of the existential imagination, in small Resistance groups, at this time.

Though Camus's *The Stranger* was completed in May 1940, before the German invasion of France, it partakes heroically of this imagination. The first two sentences of his *The Myth of Sisyphus* read: "There is but one truly serious philosophical problem, and that is suicide. Judging whether life is or is not worth living amounts to answering the fundamental question of philosophy." This echoes Meursault's realisation when faced with the guillotine at the end of *The Stranger*: "How had I failed to recognise that nothing was more important than an execution; that, viewed from one angle, it's the only thing that can genuinely interest a man?" We, too, in this sun-drenched book "awaken" with that man and that tormented generation. The warden of the old folks' home to which Meursault has committed his mother tells him on her death, "One gets on better with people of one's own generation. You're much too young; you couldn't have been much of a companion to her." And what of the protagonist's very name? It occurs first (as Patrice Meursault) in a planned but unpublished novel called *La Vie heureuse;* but it is the name of a great Burgundy, a second growth. When I then came across a character called Figeac and another entitled Masson, on first reading this text, I was drawn to think of vintages . . . more or less great *generations.* Perhaps this is the last refuge of critical imbecility, for in fact Camus's *The Stranger,* the richest work of his early Algerian fiction, is crystal clear, blinding in its intensity. There are many kinds of philosophic fiction; Visconti, to whom Jean Renoir first gave work in 1936 (on Gorki's *The Lower Depths*) and who was led by that director to translate James Cain's *The Postman Always Rings Twice* into the splendid *Ossessione* (1942), has assaulted more than one mode, as we shall see below.

In *Death in Venice* Visconti had to deal with a philosophic apparatus to which he could put interpretive images. It had to be the other way around with Camus. The French author is here sternly realistic, his events creating a pattern of judgement. Camus saw fiction as a tool of conscience at this time, he was concerned in *The Stranger* with social sin. As in that presentation of him in *The Mandarins* (as Henri Perron) Camus seemed to want his fiction, of this time, principally to offer testimony; we are guilty of such social neglect that literature becomes virtually a suspect activity. Some critics, while admiring this honesty of approach, still feel it robs Camus's work of creative drive.*

It might be thought that this concentration on the physical in *The Stranger* would help a film director; in fact, it hinders him. Visconti faithfully inserts a sequence with the robot woman (inherited by Camus from Sartre's *La nausée*) who sits down in a café and eats "in a curiously jerky way, as if she were on wires." For Camus she is a representative of our digitary or puppet-like existence in big cities, but without knowing this the viewer of the film must wonder why we dwell on her so long. Similarly, the nurse with the tumour (sick medicine) is introduced, to no effect whatever on the screen. At one point Meursault reflects in Camus's text, "Never in my life had I seen anyone so clearly as I saw these people; not a detail of their clothes or features escaped me." One realises that, more than anything, this simply ties the director's hands. The screws in his mother's coffin are seen with unusual detail by Meursault, and Visconti reports this emphasis. Again, to no avail. He could be far freer when dealing imaginatively with *Death in Venice*.

Above all does this criticism apply to Camus's taciturn and withdrawn protagonist. Perhaps under Paramount pres-

---

* E.g. Irving Howe: "There is something attractive in Camus's resistance to the role of novelist, his feeling, as it were, that really there are more important things for grown-up men to do; but at any given point, as one is actually reading his stories, this usually comes through as little more than a lack of creative energy."

THE STRANGER (1967, Visconti): Camus's originally inert Meursault, here seen in vigil at his mother's deathbed, is wholly altered by the image of the sophisticated Marcello Mastroianni.

sure (the film was a Dino De Laurentiis production) Visconti chose Marcello Mastroianni for Meursault—a mistake of crippling proportions. At the start of the novel Meursault is an inert vegetable (a "stranger" to himself), caught up in the "machine" of human destiny without the semblance of revolt—"the machine," he reflects finally of the guillotine, "is on the same level as the man." He starts to achieve a vision of man's tragedy on earth with the shooting of the Arab, when the sun knifes into his eyes and "everything began." This *everything* is his transformation from a man who is as indifferent to the beating of a woman as of a dog, who readily complies to testify in favor of a pimp, Raymond, to one who acquires consciousness of the true guilt of the human condition and rounds on the priest in fury at the end for offering the opiate of religious solace. He discovers freedom in a prison cell, his "kingdom" in "exile," and as Camus wrote of him, he "dies rather than lie." To borrow another metaphor from Camus's existential vocabulary he has become solidary, *solidaire* (i.e. with the human race), by becoming solitary, *solitaire* (i.e. apart from their *clichés*). Like Sartre's Roquentin he "cheats" in this sense, and like that character he is *de trop*.

Half-way through my first viewing of Visconti's film I realised that, if anything, he should have cast Dirk Bogarde as Meursault and Mastroianni as Aschenbach. At any rate, someone relatively anonymous should have played Meursault. There are few intellectuals in Camus's fiction and absolutely no jet-set sophisticates, of which the international star Mastroianni appears here as a compound. He was totally wrong for the part and merely makes Meursault's moral obliquity at the start into so much sleepiness, sometimes induced by wine. To escape this problem of significant insignificance Visconti then re-emphasises the whole into a Perry Mason courtroom drama, with endless uncalled-for histrionics by prosecuting and defence lawyers. The film sags badly at this point and is only slightly revived in the death-cell confrontation with the priest.

Furthermore, as the story leads into the prison it turns into a thesis film against capital punishment. Many extraneous elements are intruded. In the "biggish room" where Meursault is first enclosed with "mostly Arabs" Visconti stages a colour composition worthy of Delacroix and turns the man who explains how to lay out a sleeping mat into a beautiful youth making a homosexual approach. Subsequently, when Meursault is in solitary, an exchange with the chief jailer is given a twist suggestive of masturbation while alone in prison. There is no hint of this in the original, where the jailer simply says, "Those fellows find a way out; they do it by themselves," and there is no need for it in the film.

The Visconti Meursault is barely pitiable. His shooting of the Arab on the beach becomes a brutal action; Camus's text is here wholly betrayed—"And just then it crossed my mind that one might fire, or not fire—and it would come to absolutely the same thing." For Meursault lives outside time. Sartre's essay on *The Stranger* entirely anticipates the kind of character Robbe-Grillet was later to deploy: "A Nineteenth-century naturalist would have written 'A bridge spanned the river.' M. Camus will have none of this anthropomorphism. He says, 'Over the river was a bridge.'" It is only in prison that Meursault acquires a time pattern, a human continuity: "Only the words 'yesterday' and 'tomorrow' still kept some meaning."

The Stranger has been examined here since it presents a curious paradox of commentary, one that can further our understanding of film. In his sensible *A Discovery of Cinema* Thorold Dickinson summarises what so many have said:

> The best of cinema, like music, is usually indescribable in words. The impact of film is instantaneous while literature to build up a picture has to use one damn word after another, over a period of seconds . . . The film, silent or sound, has no past or future tense, only the present. It is the nature of the image which tells you at which period of time you are now present.

It would thus seem that Camus's little masterpiece of human responsibility would be particularly amenable to filmic treatment, since it lives so palpably in the present. Sartre said as much, asking of Meursault, "Isn't he living completely in the present, according to his present fancies?" In Meursault's actions "causality has been carefully weeded out." So he is on trial as much for his indifference to his mother as for the murder. Since all the characters in cinema, however, are "living completely in the present" Meursault's actions are much less exceptional on the screen than in the book. In the book he is at first morally blind; he sees people as things. The sun, a premonition of vision and a life-giving force for Camus, both kills and awakens him. He starts to feel a feeling. In the film we once more confront ineluctable images. In the book Meursault kills an Arab; in the film he shoots a recognisable individual. In the book he has little but immediate physical feelings for Marie; in the film, since she is before us in the (over-glossy) form of Anna Karina, he appears cruel to her, certainly during the well-staged prison visit. Visconti's Meursault says he feels *ennui,* but we cannot sympathise with him when he does so. He looks upper-class, well-fed; we feel it is his own fault if he is dissatisfied. This is particularly the case when, in the film, Meursault's boss offers him a trip to Paris, and he declines.

The moral surely is this: if a film-maker wants to convert or reconvert a fiction, he must know *exactly* what his original was saying. Even though the latter may merely be used as a point of departure, he has to know its essence. Proceeding from idea to images is not the same as the reverse. In *The Stranger* Camus adapted his style perfectly to the needs of the book; as Sartre said, "There is not a single unnecessary detail, not one that is not returned to later on and used in the argument." The total form in which Camus expressed his thought makes that thought impossible to render by a direct filmic transposition. Visconti moved towards a restatement, but did not go far enough in the mode. He succeeded, as we shall see, far better with *Death in Venice.*

C: Analogy
CANDIDE (1960)

Norbert Carbonnaux's contemporary interpretation of Voltaire's 1759 satire, which this underestimated film-maker co-wrote with Albert Simonis, represents a little masterpiece of analogy, one much ignored since the film is not technically outstanding, the director remains little known, and the satire itself is uncomfortable to see today.* It is so both in France, where its blatant ridicule of Gaullism and the myth of the ubiquitous Resistance caused considerable local squirmings at the time, and in America, since Carbonnaux's Candide not only visits an inhospitable New York but finds himself finally shipped to the colonial wars in Indo-China where all sides are derided, including China. The Vietnam allusions—he sails for Saigon but the ship goes to Borneo by an error of navigation—are far too prescient today to be pleasant. Reality has by now overtaken

---

* I have seen it said that Lindsay Anderson's *O Lucky Man!* (1973) is a little *Candide*. This seems to me stretching the arms of analogy so far as to be of little service to either end of it; by this canon, almost any depiction of the miseducation of a young innocent is a minor *Candide*.

satire and the Lyndon Johnson of the David Halberstam memoirs, *The Best and the Brightest,* is more exaggerated and repulsive, with his genital and urinary jokes, than both Carbonnaux's Tweedledum-Tweedledee Generals, one French, the other English, put together. The film is not shown much; its 16mm version (U.S.: Contemporary Films) is little rented.

Like its characters, those human follies it is so hard to kill off, *Candide* has gone into many transformations, including an American operetta, with music by Leonard Bernstein and lyrics by Richard Wilbur. The resilience of *Pygmalion* to translation into various forms suggests that this is the day of "revivals" in new guises for new times; originally produced in 1919, *Irene* stormed back to the Broadway stage in 1973 as follows: "Book by Hugh Wheeler and Joseph Stein, From an adaptation by Harry Rigby, Based on the original play by James Montgomery." Somewhat in this spirit Carbonnaux starts off his contemporary *Candide* with a fancy-dress ball in Eighteenth-century costume in which the characters enact *Candide.* He ends it by having Pangloss suggest to Candide that he write his own autobiography. The work is made for analogy; a spoof of this sort can only be served by another spoof.*

Carbonnaux presents a delightful one, interspersing his narrative with cartoons, Second World War newsreel clips, and mirror flashbacks in which he accommodates some of the manifold stories within stories by means of which Voltaire mocked the tradition of galant literature lying just behind his own dark satire. In a preposterous lampoon worthy of its original the film has its Candide conscripted by both French and German forces, and then the Resistance, not to mention the colonialist military thereafter. Meanwhile, his beloved Cunégonde (played by Dahlia Lavi) is in the pe-

---

* Indeed, it is hard to draw borderlines for a filmic analogy; Claude Lelouch's 1973 *Money Money Money,* disappointing as it mainly was, could yet be read as a contemporary tip of the hat to the sage of Ferney.

cuniary care of the one-buttocked lady, whom Carbonnaux makes into a sort of cynical madame (via a thoroughly-buttocked Nadia Gray); the Jew and the Inquisitor who alternately participate in Cunégonde's delights, and are killed off by Candide, turn into a black marketeer and a Gestapo chief (enacted by that great comedian Louis de Funès), equally two sides of the same coin. It is, however, somewhat of a tribute to Voltaire that even a contemporary film-maker could not stomach the claim of the old lady to being a daughter of the Pope; Carbonnaux makes her father a Tsar.

Voltaire lived in a period of judicial injustice, a lot of which he personally tried to right. As Radoslav A. Tsanoff says in his book *The Nature of Evil,* Voltaire's final "dark scepticism" had none of the tragic piety of Pascal's; yet the former "never lost his faith in civilisation." This is what made it possible for him to insert into a world shot through with plagues, scaffolds, whippings, burnings, and diseases the vision of that happy state, where there is no money and everyone is a priest of love, called Eldorado. It is significant that this is the one part of the satire (over which so much ink has been shed) that Carbonnaux scants: there is a visit to a post-Lysenko Russia claiming to be a new Shangri-La, responsible for every invention, and the satire suddenly becomes dated. Indeed, Carbonnaux goes further. At the very end a bust of Voltaire is turned from the camera by Pangloss: as if to say, in Voltaire's day there was some hope of man organising a better society, today there seems none. The sage of Ferney should not be asked to look at ours.

Although the position does not seem to have been one of despair in Voltaire's case, he yet has his Candide harshen far more than Carbonnaux allows his. In the original, Candide is given a bitter outbreak as they arrive at Portsmouth and see an admiral shot—Voltaire had himself tried to intervene on behalf of Byng—and clearly changes after the visit to Eldorado: "What Demon exercises his power everywhere?" Shortly after this, "he admitted that Martin was right." Once again, the film-maker is a little conditioned by his imagery: Jean-Pierre Cassel was then a very bland-looking young man, while Pierre Brasseur as Pangloss so dominates every scene in which he appears that we tend to forget that he is the detestable source of his pupil's miseducation, this despite the fact that the filmic Pangloss is a *collabo* with all parties, not only with the new Russians, but with the old Germans, for we see him as Hitler, addressing ranks of Aryan soldiers with the Führer's voice pumping away behind him. The pessimist Martin, on the other hand, who had never expected to be dealt aces by life and whom Voltaire leaves at least believing in his philosophy while Pangloss merely moves his lips over his, is a minor character met in Borneo, in the land of the Oreillons.

We know that it was evidently the Lisbon earthquake which so shocked Voltaire and caused him, in turn, to shock all Europe with his poem attacking Divine Providence. From then on he seems to have taken almost a new view of evil, one de Sade was to accept and further. Unless we recognise the innate form of man's nature we shall continue to have wars, persecutions, killings, racism. *Candide* was written at white heat by a troubled Voltaire at the end of his life; concealing encyclopaedic learning and converting doubt itself into a positive force, it is something of an entelechy. Such is demonstrated by the failure to "continue" it beyond its own end, e.g. in that forged Part Two now usually attributed to de Campiqueulles (Thorel). In a sense, all one can now do is add so many corroborative footnotes.

In doing so filmically, Carbonnaux succeeded admirably. His Lisbon earthquake is the bombing of Lisieux, scene of miracles of faith. When a German officer absurdly discusses with his French counterpart where best to attack France, the decision is made for Sedan—and we know which "empire" will be ended. Jacques, the Anabaptist, a kindly but ineffective character, is converted into an equally ineffectual (and deaf) Red Cross doctor, who inspects prison camps, is shot down by German fighter planes, and parachutes into a lake where he is left to die by the eternally philosophising Pangloss.

Voltaire's *Candide* was a disputatious book. By having his characters argue endlessly on the brink of perdition Voltaire was, in general, accusing all hyper-scholarly rationalisations about man's condition of diverting our attention from a real look at the world; Carbonnaux has a similar philosophical debate between Martin and Candide tied to stakes in the jungle waiting to be put in the cannibals' pot. The film-maker, despite such purely verbal interludes, keeps his narrative movement alive since he knows that it is knit in with the development of Candide's own character, the acquisition of knowledge being accompanied by the loss of innocence. How can man, in the great chain of being, be superior to birds when he cannot fly? Obviously because wings would expose him to more imperfections than advantages. "Observe that noses were made to wear spectacles," says Pangloss, "and so we have spectacles. Legs were visibly instituted to be breeched, and we have breeches." In industrial terms, this is to say that man is simply there as a vehicle for technology.

It is tempting to fall into cliché oneself and conclude that this constant philosophising is, in common with the whole unity of conception, extraordinarily "French" (Baudelaire was bored in Paris because, he said, everyone there looked like Voltaire). Carbonnaux's film is full of good meals—as in Voltaire's Eldorado—lovely women, assorted chauvinisms, and no over-abundance of social justice. Corruption lies just beneath the apparent prosperity. The impression of Gaullist France is, as the French themselves put it, exact. The film-maker is penalised by topicality, however, the beauty of Voltaire's satire being its universality. This does not merely mean its internationalism; Carbonnaux reflects this excellently, notably in a delightful passage of *opéra bouffe* concerning the wooing of Cunégonde by a series of rapidly assassinated Latin-American military dictators. Voltaire's reference is always wide. He particularises the butt of his attack, Leibniz, only once, at the end of Chapter XXVIII. He pays off only a very few personal scores—against booksellers, for example. The Pococurante chapter is, too, a little personal and literary and Carbonnaux was wise to omit it.

On the other hand, some of the film's mockeries seem already to have dated or to be purely local. There is one sequence that takes place after Candide has killed the Gestapo boss and the black marketeer. Two French detectives come in and dispute *ad infinitum* over the corpses until one shows the other what he concludes must actually be a clue, and the pair leave for Spain in pursuit. It is all very pleasantly done, and one recognises the self-serving nature of police officialdom parodied; but it is somehow particularly French. The derision is *sui generis*. One could not envisage American detectives acting this way. Similarly, when Candide goes to America itself and is forced into a shotgun marriage with the daughter of a Mafia leader, under the eye of a complaisant priest, the whole level degenerates. We do not so much see satires of Americans or of American optimism, as of what the French of the time conceived to be Americans—gum-chewing, trigger-happy, Coca-Cola-swilling. Indeed, Pierre Brasseur as Pangloss had previously explained that, if it were not for Columbus, there would be no chewing-gum, Coca-Cola, or—syphilis. Directly Candide is married to his American floozie, she demands a divorce. A marriage court judge (made to resemble Eisenhower*) encumbers Candide with an astro-

---

* The political references are too localised. The film Pasha into whose harem Cunégonde is at one point sold is called Fourak (i.e. Farouk). What student recalls Farouk today? What student, indeed, remembers Eisenhower?

nomical alimony. This word has, until quite recently, been hard to translate into French. When I was living in France at the time this film was made, I remember the hoots of derision one received at the idea of actually paying any support to a divorced wife. Mention of alimony could reliably double up a dinner table of males. Here, it seems to me, the shoe is on the other foot; possibly more Frenchmen are drinking Coca-Cola than Americans—I don't know. Yet, all in all, the *Candide* of Carbonnaux represents a splendid, if topical, example of what filmic analogy can do for a literary original.

THE TRIAL (1962)

Kafka's name has by now become a household word for a certain kind of literature, as indeed film. A recent British-made television series called *The Prisoner* was, we are told, "Kafkaesque," as also the Warren Beatty vehicle, *Mickey One.* What we first notice about these is that they are not realistic. Is this literature, therefore, a kind of dream or surrealist world? If we are to believe Max Brod, Kafka once considered ending a story, "Enchanted by the sight, he woke up." But he never did. He was not writing *Alice through the Looking-Glass,* similar as some of Carroll's externalities seem to his work at first glance. In fact, he explicitly disallowed this easy solution in one of his most fantastic tales, translated as *The Metamorphosis.* Gregor Samsa awakens one morning "from uneasy dreams" into the reality of his salesman's life, and Kafka quickly puts into his first reflections the following: "What has happened to me? he thought. It was no dream." It is with some gloom, therefore, that as Orson Welles's version of *The Trial* opens we hear a narrator booming away off-screen about "the logic of a dream, a nightmare," and shortly afterwards find the writer causing Fräulein Bürstner (Jeanne Moreau) to say to K., "Are you sure you were awake?" This is to approach the problem from the wrong end of the telescope altogether.

Welles's film was a courageous, and on the whole faithful, attempt to make an analogy of Kafka's original. The locus of the picture is vague, ranging from ornate buildings that, once certainly, limb Prague to vacant modern lots with high-rise buildings, to ruins that suggest bomb damage (thus tying in with the ending). Chiefly, the film was shot in and around an abandoned railway station Welles had been lent by the French government—adroit at putting such gifts to use, Welles puzzled many critics with his killing of Cassio in a ruined Turkish bath for *Othello*, until his Iago reported that the idea arose merely from locale, an Italian *castello* Welles had been lent for a while. In *The Trial* the men wear modern suits, the women mostly drab black, with Leni dressed as a hospital attendant.

Alas, Kafka's dream *is* our reality. One is reminded of Goethe's comment that *what is* is only real in so far as it is symbolic. The Welles film starts with the Parable of the Law, which is, in effect, a useful key to the whole and the least realistic part of it, but he saw fit to have this grossly rewritten, omitting for some reason reference to the third Guard, the growing disparity of size involved, and having the light streaming through above rather than below the door. Are these mere quibbles? Recent Kafka research has certainly questioned the present chapter order, Professor Herman Uyttersprot requiring them to be drastically rearranged; but this revision was based on internal time sequences and, above all, the hero's state of mind. To begin with the most theoretic moment of all in *The Trial* is to trap it into being some arcane allegory. It would surely have been far better an analogy to have established a reality, and then arouse us to speculate about the abstractions behind it. Such was accomplished by Nanni Loy's *Why* (*Detenuto in attesa di giudizio,* 1972).

The world of *The Trial* happens; it exists; and it is, on the first level, quite literally our world, that of corrupt bureaucracy, bottomless accusations, petty spites, sexual jealousies, above all a perpetually suspicious, distant authority. Even *The Castle* can be read, in one sense, as an anticipation of a totalitarianism to come, a world of gnostic demons, personal insecurity, obscene and whimsical officials. Imprisoned in an actual castle after the Hungarian revolt, and treated with alternate bouts of brutality and *bonhomie,* the Marxist critic Georg Lukács, who had long resisted Kafka's appeal, finally said of him, "So Kafka was a realist after all."

In brief, Kafka writes a real story, one which helps us to "see" certain things happening about us; Welles gives us an interpretation of reality. In interviews after the film had been shown, Welles himself tried to get off the hook, or Morton's fork, of this dilemma, by claiming that he had used the original to dramatise certain autobiographical obsessions of his own. As if there were not some Kafka in all of us. Heinz Politzer has well called Kafka "a realist of unreality." Alain Robbe-Grillet has put it this way:

> If there is one thing of which an unprejudiced reading convinces us it is the absolute reality of the things Kafka describes. The visible world of his novels is certainly for him the real world, and what is behind (if there *is* something) seems without value, faced with the manifest nature of objects, gestures, words, etc. The hallucinatory effect derives from their extraordinary clarity and not from mystery or mist. Nothing is more fantastic, ultimately, than precision. Perhaps Kafka's staircases lead *elsewhere,* but they are *there,* and we look at them, step by step, following the detail of the banisters and the risers.

Thus Erich Heller can call Kafka "the least problematic of modern writers." It may be hard to recognise a picture of ourselves but Kafka writes a real story, forcing the reader to see certain images and not others. In *The Trial* there is a deceitful, incalculable bureaucracy, a seedy system functioning through modern machinery and mathematical computations—in short, any governing body of today. Leaving the Priest's Parable of the Law to one side, *The Trial* remains a uniquely realistic novel, obviously reminiscent of the political arrests of this age.

Welles obscures this aspect from the start. The man sent to arrest K. cannot at first be clearly heard or even seen. An interminable argument continues about misheard words like *ovular* and *pornograph;* a dentist's chair has apparently at some time been screwed into the floor of the bedroom (Frau Grubach's husband being a dentist). Subsequently, Fräulein Bürstner's voice, as dubbed for Jeanne Moreau, is far too loud for necessity, and so on. These audio-visual disturbances suggest K. as an incompetent neurotic, which is precisely how Anthony Perkins plays him. In his hands K. becomes younger and fluttery, so that when later he falls into interrogatory roles himself, as Kafka has him, he seems somewhat absurd, a posturing fairy who tries to avoid marriage for very different reasons from his original. Though Welles gives a briskly up-to-date ending, with K. killed by dynamite that mushrooms into an atomic explosion rather than dying "like a dog" (as K. exclaims in the fiction), he does not succeed in universalising the story. For *The Trial* is a trial of our whole philosophy. The surface of our world is recognisable, yet the abstractions behind it have ceased to function (or are else related to total evil). Our thought-system seems to have fallen apart, there is nothing beyond human judgement. One of Kafka's aphorisms summarises this:

> The crows maintain that a single crow could destroy the heavens. There is no doubt of this, but it proves nothing against the heavens, for heavens simply mean: the impossibility of crows.*

---

* There is another—"A cage went in search of a bird."

Thus, the painter Titorelli has a Goddess of Justice in one of his paintings, but it is a very insecure abstraction, seeming to be set in motion even as K. watches it. The Goddess of Justice turns into the Goddess of Hunt, flying along, in another allegory of how the Court contradicts itself. So Kafka puts the Law itself on trial. Welles assumes K.'s guilt from the start and has him kill himself with the dynamite at the end. What Kafka says is that man is a "dog" when his symbol-handling mechanism breaks down or is betrayed. Welles tries, but somehow his tricks never really seem to convince. The Titorelli episode is good, but the whipping scene over-extended—with Perkins as K. later pulling the door on one of the victims' fingers in a way that is comic rather than agonising. His K. becomes a victim of computer technology, he walks in the opposite direction to the vast crowd of stenographers leaving for the day and he is duly dwarfed by Orson Welles as his Advocate. But there is too much in the writing that is simply flippant. For instance: Perkins mounts the dais of the empty interrogation chamber, struggles for a second (needlessly, we feel) with lack of space in front of the table there, and picks up the "dirty" books. He dusts one off and opens it saying, "Gee, these really are dirty books, aren't they." The pun is wholly unworthy; it is not how Kafka's mind works at all, nor do such touches make good analogy.

It is perfectly true that there is a level of neurosis in Kafka's original. Like Gregor Samsa of *The Metamorphosis* K. feels isolated from fresh air at crucial moments, suffers vertigo, failure of vision, misjudges distances, hears people too loud; there are nightmarish transformations of rooms and buildings. Declining the class level (Kafka's accused all being from the better sections of society) Welles does his best to report the Kafka who predicted the Second World War. He gives us a very Jewish Block, concentration camp allusions on the way to the Interrogation Commission, and a sexily Aryan Leni (Romy Schneider) making love to K. on piles of dusty documents. But somehow it does not come off; the direction is not sharp enough. Once begun, the analogy should have been pushed much further. The scene with Fräulein Montag limping with her trunk over waste-land to a railway line is both over-long and unnecessary. Yet anyone making *The Trial* is going to come up against the difficulty that most of the characters in it are functions or social instruments (The Manufacturer, The Commercial Traveller); it is at first sight an insuperable task, certainly one that requires intense filmic concentration and unfortunately the later Welles can become pretentious at the drop of a hat.

Two crucial scenes, on which Welles rightly concentrates, show K. as standing at a different metaphysical or semantic ratio to anyone else in the society. Both show the paradox that the Court is guilty of having violated itself or, to resort to Kafka's pregnant aphorism, that the heavens have killed the crow but have thereby ceased being heavens. In the whipping scene the functionaries being chastised do not question the system at all; they simply hope one day to be promoted to whippers themselves. K., however, says: "I had no idea of all this, nor did I ever demand that you should be punished, I was only defending a principle." There is no sense of this level in the film where Welles only distracts by having a rather inefficient whipper repeatedly striking the light shade in the room (lit by a candle in the original) and making cymbal-like clangs. The other scene is the closest the film ever comes to the Court in the novel, namely in the Cathedral, where a "prison Chaplain" gives the only statement that is more than a mere guess. Welles does not make his authority at all clear, and after the Talmudic tergiversations about the parable, Kafka's K. says flatly, "It turns lying into a universal principle." Perkins's K. has by this point lost all dignity before our eyes and cannot make such a statement meaningful or tragic.

At the end of Kafka's original, on the other hand, K. summons up his dignity. He achieves strength, refuses the aid of a policeman on his Calvary, drags his guards with him and leads the way to his final revolt—which is a refusal to die ritually by suicide, but rather to make them kill him. " 'Wie ein Hund!' sagte er, es war als sollte die Scham ihn überleben." To say that you are dying like a dog is in fact to die like a man; a dog is unaware that it is dying like a dog. This is K.'s final dignity, to retain his human nature. It is the shame of the Court that lives on, and the death of the Law. That is why K. could say with meaning what Perkins's rendering of him could not, that it is only a trial if we recognise it as one. Kafka had a very great mind and only another, as in Nabokov's *Invitation to a Beheading*, can seem but inferior when laid beside it.

CABARET (1972)

Another attempt at analogy, Bob Fosse's *Cabaret,* based on Christopher Isherwood's novella *Sally Bowles,* made perhaps the greatest rift with its original of any film examined to this point. Yet it was one of the finest works of its year, even though critical opinion was divided ("too much traditional Hollywood musical gloss" for William Wolf). There was even one semi-learned attempt to show that *Cabaret* was a compound plagiarism of *Across 110th. Street* and the Maggie Smith *Travels with My Aunt.* One here confronts another picture which had a successful Broadway play interposed between it and the printed page of fiction.

All the more credit to Fosse, in a sense, for making his film so strikingly visual. He did not simply put a play on screen, but instead restructured the entire idea to create a compelling musical which, in the tradition of *On the Town,* made its point by its own rhetoric. Roland Barthes is quite mistaken, in my opinion, in dismissing this organic rhetoric of the American musical *Gesamtkunstwerk;* Barthes saw the U.S. musical as inevitably prey of the cultural cliché ("New York-ness" in the case of *On the Town*). Not so. In

Cabaret Fosse organised a style in the manner of a true *rhetor*, or *makar*, to convey a central metaphor with urgency, here the sense of political perversity in terms of sexual distortion. It should be added that, as ringmaster of the cabaret, Joel Grey was collected from the play to serve him brilliantly in this respect.

Nazi Germany itself is now becoming a *cliché*. To one like the present writer, who travelled in it, some recent filmic servings of what went on seem ludicrous. Fosse wanted to make a certain statement and needed musical shorthand with which to do it. He therefore took extreme liberties with the Isherwood original—most of them in the sexual sphere. Isherwood focussed on two characters, the author and Sally Bowles, trying to relate to each other in a climate of impending chaos. He was interested, as are all good novelists, in the reciprocal relationship between character and environment, how each shapes the other. To meet this Fosse suggested the lunatic night-club, to which all *Cabaret's* characters escape (except Sally), as a kind of crazy or even courageous sanity. The world outside is meanwhile going mad. He reminds us of this throughout in a number of intercalated scenes, culminating in the lakeside café just outside Munich where, in a rising crescendo of song, an entire group of placid Germans join an androgynous blonde soldier in vocal paean to the Nazi movement. (A scene reminiscent of *La grande illusion*, which Renoir co-wrote with Spaak). This unthinking acquiescence to the mechanics of sheer sound in our political semantic was a brilliant reference to the method of the man who (it was alleged) took Austria by radio, and it says far more than the whole of *The Damned*.

The film took over the catchy music of the play and even resuscitated characters (like Fritz and Clive) dropped from the novel, but the basic change was to make the young English writer Chris (Michael York), who does not seem to do a great deal of writing, a homosexual. Read by anyone knowing nothing of Isherwood, the novel yields not a hint of this. Nor can it be said that at that time Isherwood was constrained from being frank; *Death in Venice* was in active print in England when he published *Sally Bowles*.

At first glance this might be thought to damage *Cabaret*, making it a special case, with its own brief that could be otherwise more tellingly dramatised. Isherwood does not give us Sally and the narrator as lovers. She leaves him thanks to her innate restlessness and instability—to euphemise some plain selfishness. The outside world is beginning to intrude. The film has Chris leave, presumably imagining his homosexuality would constrain them from any "meaningful relationship," and hating her for aborting their child. This scene on the bed is perhaps the only thematic flaw, for while the director appears to throw sympathy on Chris, that of many women today might be to side with Sally in her courage to abort and take her career into her own hands. Once again superstimulation covers up such reflections; after all, this need not be so important. The two are succeeding far better than most couples, it seems, and Sally is not repulsed by Chris's sexual revelations. Here Isherwood awkwardly intrudes: his couple's asexual love was both pure and intense; it would be hard, however, to visualise this—fast. The temptation is to read "Professor Unrhat" for "Sally Bowles" and suggest that the union between a decadent, farded night-club singer with green fingernails and a refined writer is impossible—the anima is too far from the ego.

DEATH IN VENICE (1971)

Philosophic fiction, novels in which the author's chief concern is to project ideas, are clearly just about the contrary of what cinema normally expects to be. One can sympathise with German directors trying their hands at *Buddenbrooks, The Confessions of Felix Krull,* or even that delightful irony, *Royal Highness.* But Mann's prestige is such by now that leading film-makers have sought also to convey his stories of inaction, or stasis, like *Death in Venice* and even *Tonio Kröger.* It is significant that when Alfred Weidenman attempted *Buddenbrooks,* a familial saga or *roman-fleuve* to end all such, he issued the result in two parts in 1961. Mann's work resists compression with peculiar energy. He has always insisted that the creative act has its own laws and that the fiction of *Bildung* (the German word holds within it *becoming,* as well as *development, education*) is subject to all sorts of conflation unsuspected by the uneasy author:

> The Krull memoirs, however, were a difficult feat of equilibrium; I could not hold the note for too long a time without relief; and it was this seeking for variety, as I remember it,

which produced the idea which afterwards developed into *Death in Venice.* The immediate occasion of the tale was a chance stay on the Lido; it was conceived as modestly as are all my enterprises, a kind of improvisation, to be written as quickly as might be, and serving as an interlude to work on *Felix Krull.* But creation has its own laws. *Buddenbrooks,* planned with Kielland as a model for a novel of merchant life, to run to some two hundred and fifty pages at most, displayed a will of its own. *The Magic Mountain* when its turn came was to be quite as headstrong; and the story of Aschenbach, the heio of *Death in Venice,* proved persistent well beyond the terminus which I had fixed for it.

When tackling *Buddenbrooks* as, largely, a Nadja Tiller vehicle, Weidenman must have been surprised by the spread and grasp of ideology over all. In most of Thomas Mann ideas are still ideas—not symbols, least of all images. Long debates, even in relatively active novels like *Budden-brooks* or *Krull* or *Faustus,* presuppose a readership on the same plane as that of the omniscient author and one equal-ly inclined, with that author, to sense philosophic truth as carrying aesthetic value. Much of Mann's work, it is well known, is exposition in fictional form of philosophic con-cepts, chiefly those of Schopenhauer and Nietzsche. The Apollonian-Dionysiac conflict postulated in the latter's first great work sustains almost too many stories by Mann, from the early *Kröger, The Dilettante, Death in Venice, Gladius Dei, A Man and His Dog* (a preposterous rendering of the quandary!), to the 1929 *Mario and the Magician,* and be-yond. It could be called Mann's inhumanity to man.

The importance of Mann's anti-decadent work at the turn of the century is that its emphasis expanded, burst open, the gates of fiction in a way perhaps only Hamsun, before him, had succeeded in doing—for Northern litera-ture. The author writes about what he is interested in writ-ing about. The famous leitmotifs in *Kröger*—the inclined head (of reflection, repeated in Aschenbach as elsewhere), the fountain, walnut-tree, and rusty gate—are pre-Proustian markers in what Erich Heller has suggested that all of Thomas Mann's work boils down to, a parody of the Fall of Man. We acquire "knowledge," or aesthetic refinement and sophistication, that is to say, at the expense of our innocence (of knowledge Aschenbach saw at the end that "it *is* the abyss") ; this is what Heller calls a "tragic consciousness," that also of Goethe's *Wilhelm Meister,* Gottfried Keller's *Der grüne Heinrich* and *Der Nachsommer* by Adalbert Stifter (an author alluded to in *Kröger*). These parables of aesthetic rootlessness, of poetic apartness, of art as critical of the social fabric, ring perhaps as platitudes today, yet Mann was prescient rather than platitudinous (certainly in the racial undertones of his early work), and felt he was writing in the decline of European culture, and economy.

As a fiction, *Death in Venice* is obviously many things. It is at times an application of Nietzsche's *The Birth of Tragedy* and *The Genealogy of Morals* (some of whose *Abhandlungen,* indeed, are given us almost verbatim by Tonio Kröger). The Marxist Georg Lukács saw it as a predictive statement of the barbarous underworld of the German psyche, a *Geistesgeschichte,* as it were, or what Albert Thibaudet formulated as the "roman brut." In correspondence Mann said that it also originated in an interest in Goethe's elderly passion for Ulrike Levetzow; certainly, Aschenbach's moderation is destroyed as was Goethe's Eduard of *The Elective Affinities.* The upright, disciplined author of a work on Frederick the Great, whose life is symbolised by a fisted hand and whose favourite motto is *Durchhalten,* has become altogether too Apollonian, it is plain; together with Heinrich Mann's Professor Unrhat, he has grown over-stiff a *persona* and fails to recognise his irrational instincts. Venice, which Nietzsche equated with the musical, "this most improbable of cities"—art built on the unconscious sea itself—"relaxed his will." Licence overtakes discipline. Aschenbach rises each morning "as early as though he had a panting press of work" and yet the only writing he does on the Lido would seem to be a Dionysiac or frankly pornographic eulogy of Tadzio that leaves him spent and exhausted "as it were after a debauch" (the orgasmic suggestion is also given, though at a different point, by Visconti). *"Death in Venice,"* Mann has written, in a necessary over-simplification, "portrays the fascination of the death idea, the triumph of drunken disorder over the forces of a life consecrated to rule and discipline."

Clearly, Visconti was forced to concentrate on one aspect of this extraordinary *Liebestod,* of what Heller calls "invalid love rising from the invalidity of life." He did so by seeking into another Gustav's life, that of Mahler, who is said to have met Mann in a railway carriage utterly broken by a similar infatuation. Writing prior to the best of Proust and Gide, Mann suggested that *Death in Venice'*s "musical affinities may have been what endeared it." Whether Mahler did, in fact, transvalue an erotic entanglement of the sort into great art or not (he died in the same year that Mann's story was published), Visconti's response to it seems, at first sight, legitimate enough.

It has often struck me also that something of the horror with which the European intelligentsia watched the collapse of Oscar Wilde—Gide's Ménalque—before a similarly worthless symbol of Eros-Thanatos may lie in the mists behind Mann's masterpiece. Wilde indulged at the end in that rouging and powdering which was for Aschenbach a mock-Faustian rejuvenation; we remember Wilde's allusions to the natural corruption of Venice, while Sebastian (though not explicitly Sebastian Melmoth) is once cited by Mann, in *Death in Venice,* as "the most beautiful symbol, if not of art as a whole, yet certainly of the art we speak of here." Visconti therefore took Mahler as an anagram of Aschenbach (=stream of ashes) beset by his Dionysos (=Tadzio). He drenched his images in a soundtrack of, largely, the plaintive *adagietto* of Mahler's Fifth Symphony, made Dirk Bogarde* look like the composer, and gave him via flashbacks an associate called Alfred, a young man with curly hair. This automatically invited certain reactions. To start off, scholarly purists pointed out that for the Mann of this moment music—as in *Tristan*—is used for the Dionysiac and, if not the disordered, at least the suspiciously non-verbal. As in *The Magic Mountain* (its title taken from *The Birth of Tragedy*) words are associated with control, music with rapture. In that charming depiction of *fin-de-siècle* dilettantism mentioned, the *Tristan* of 1902, it is Gabriele Eckhof's expressly forbidden playing of Wagner that brings on her death. You can say that she woos death through art, but it is *this sort of* beauty that causes her to die—"death and beauty had claimed her for their own."

Visconti replies to and organises this sense of desperate and ecstatic pessimism with considerable integrity. It is true that he starts his story with Aschenbach on the steamer arriving at Venice, rather than introduces the (fictionally important) first death figure, that of the wanderer with his rucksack by the cemetery who so irrationally arouses Aschenbach's latent unrest. He makes an effort, however, to interlink this new beginning with his general theme. In his film the visit is evidently motivated, we later learn, by the composer's collapse at a concert, and the ship is called *Esmeralda,* which is the name of the innocent-looking, almost boyish prostitute Visconti has Aschenbach take, to his own disgust, in a brothel (this flashback is initiated from a moment in the present when Tadzio is playing on a piano). The first abortive visit Mann has his protagonist make to an Adriatic island is omitted; in the original it is

---

* This conscientious actor has often been cast as an intellectual perhaps since he is one; his real name is van den Bogaerde and during World War Two, as an officer in the Queen's Royal Regiment, he published poetry in *The Times Literary Supplement*. He seems to lack filmic intensity, a deficiency apparent when he is not cast as an intellectual (e.g. *The Night Porter* of 1974).

not Dionysiac enough for Aschenbach's mood—"it annoyed him not to be able to get at the sea." Yet the episode is not all that important. The real difficulty is the appearance of Bogarde, looking like an absent-minded professor who is in reality a lecherous fag. Vincent Canby aptly described him here as "a fussy old man who develops a crush on a beautiful youth." This happens because Visconti has no time to insinuate Tadzio into Aschenbach's consciousness as gently and delicately as does the original author. He has to throw the image at us, via the handsome Björn Andresen, and make what story he has at his disposal move. Tadzio's glances, which Mann only lets us notice through the filter of Aschenbach's point-of-view, now seem explicit, the boy almost propositioning Aschenbach. As Paul Zimmerman put it, "He and the boy exchange lengthy glances, whose sexual explicitness turns Aschenbach into a foolish dirty old man, and the boy into a pretty little tease."

Visconti's original intentions seem to have been far from this. In an early interview with Guy Flatley he declared that he was making a story about "love without eroticism, without sexuality." One of the errands of Mann's work, which came out before Freud's Leonardo essay, seems to have been to emphasise the nature of love rather than the love object as primary—hence the Platonic references in the text. He at one point mentions Aschenbach's "paternal affection" for Tadzio. But images are not implicit; and they led Visconti into certain contradictions which he tried to resolve through the extraneous matter thrown in. Thus, Stuart Byron saw in Aschenbach and his associate Alfred that relationship between men which society condones; we move from Alfred's encomium of the senses to an image of Tadzio, in the present, lifting an orange and smelling it—and the suggestion is that society still deems any other relationship between two males illegitimate.

One further cover-up Visconti indulges in is to expand Aschenbach's fear of old age. In Mann's text we read: "The presence of the youthful beauty that had bewitched him filled him with disgust of his own ageing body." This longing for youth is enlarged by the film's imagery. In the first flashback there is an important speech when Aschenbach mentions the hour-glass in his father's house (an hour-glass is seen on a table by the couch), and how one does not notice the sand trickling away until it runs out: then all the questions that one has not asked spring suddenly to mind. Visconti maintains the vanishing sand metaphor right through Aschenbach's death on the beach at the end. Unfortunately, Bogarde is too young to need the barber's rejuvenation, it merely feminises him. After this he has a journey through the underworld following Tadzio, as a beckoning figure of youth and beauty. Disinfectant is seen squirted like semen, fires burn in the streets, and there is one emphatic background of balustrades that repeats the hour-glass shape. Here Aschenbach has a greenish pallor similar to the later face of the mountebank, one of Mann's many death figures. Behind a rank of candles in a church there is a twisted Byzantine column to the right of the frame (showing Tadzio's praying face) whose glittering greenish bands suggest the serpentine nature of the voyeur's passion.

The sense of the ominous, narcissistic* and corrupt is what needs to be conveyed, the lulling of a great critical and creative faculty by fascination with the "abyss." The susurration and overlapping of voices at the table of Tadzio's mother (played by Silvana Mangano) is almost flattering to Mann's uni-referential ascription of Dionysiac qualities to Polish or generally Slavic characters (cp. Clavdia Chauchat of *The Magic Mountain*). Visconti gains a good deal of analogical power here by the lovely music:

---

* The famous "mirror and image" passage in Mann's original is a superbly confident exposition of narcissism; what would Mann have felt, one wonders, reading Paul Zimmerman on Visconti as follows: "It is narcissistic direction, in love with its own beauty, a tour of the set instead of film"?

for, as Stanley J. Solomon noted, "What Visconti tries to achieve here is an emotional response to the total impact of the narrative that in some way resembles what readers derive from the Mann text."

The narrative of the original is so undramatic that all these auditory additions seem quite justified and, indeed, one blenches a bit when Visconti encroaches on his stylisation by the over-dramatic flashbacks to Aschenbach's past, notably that involving the prostitute—which I can only find suggested in the text by the words, "He had been young and crude with the times and by them badly counselled." For some reason, also, the Visconti re-telling has Aschenbach's daughter die rather than his wife (the death of youth?).

All this is needlessly distracting to a genuinely "felt" texture. The film is so strongly expressive in its own right that when Bogarde sits at table, at the Hôtel des Bains, looks over the menu and says to the waiter, "Soup, fish, that's all," one is suddenly brought down to earth, as one is when he breathes out, much to our discomfort, "I love you." There has been an interference with, a reduction of, the obtaining stylisation. When an objective reality interferes by itself like this, we realise what a remarkable feat it is for any film-maker to preserve surface order for a long time, as does Bergman, in the absence of overt narrative action.

A cinematic analogy like Visconti's cannot be a treachery since it does not presume to be the original. We have by now broken away from the book-illustration approach, the xerography, of early transposition, studied above. Whether or not Visconti's assault on *Death in Venice* is a great film is open to opinion; but it surely succeeds in complementing its wonderful original, in the manner of some richly visual footnote.

Art is seen to heighten life: Tadzio is first glimpsed by Aschenbach as the sole object of beauty in a gloriously vulgar *fin-de-siècle* hotel gathering punctuated by fantastic fe-

DEATH IN VENICE (1971, Visconti): Dirk Bogarde, made to resemble Mahler, turns into a Peeping Tom in a decaying Venice —a tactful instance of filmic xerography.

male hats, a masterpiece of set decoration. And yet, this passion is "like crime." The man's love-role quickly declines. He is identified by the knowing governesses. He eats the over-ripe strawberries and becomes the true author of *The Abject,* in fact his own subject. Visconti handles the difficult point-of-view well. Since Tadzio is never seen except by Aschenbach "for us," as it were, he may never exist; all Tadzio's actions are, within the Mann text, intensional, a result of compulsions and passions inside the viewer himself. The refraction, that of the reader being psychologically a step ahead of the main character, is fictionally gripping and has been often copied (as in *Lolita*). Visconti has to stabilise the boy beyond the narrator's vision, yet he does so fairly tactfully, and indeed faithfully. A passage in which Aschenbach walks to the beach is cleverly threaded with some semi-balletic movements by Tadzio, nearly touching him, which one soon realises are imaginative. The more common entry of reality into this film is what really disturbs it, rather than any departure from its original. The overlong, almost tedious scene of the entertainers at the hotel is one such example: here Mann's fourth death figure, who receives the overlarge payment due to the illegal gondolier representing Charon earlier, is exaggerated and over-insistent. The trickles of black dye down Dirk Bogarde's face at his deck-chair death are also uncomfortably extraneous.

All in all, however, this analogy has to be respected. It struggles inside a work of great original vigour and resonance. As Aschenbach is lured towards the subconscious ocean at the end, in front of which the sturdy youth Jaschiu performs a surrogate homosexual act on Tadzio (more explicit in Mann than in Visconti), "a camera on a tripod stood at the edge of the water, apparently abandoned." This literal image, entirely natural in its surroundings, stands in for the tripod before the Delphic oracle, and makes a perfect synonym with that helplessness life feels in front of cinema, without the controlling transmutation of Apollo.

CONTEMPT (1963)

If Godard was at all serious when he said, "The object of a film is to produce another film," we are surely authorised in concluding our study with one that is an analogy of a novel itself also an analogy of an original. Alberto Moravia's *A Ghost at Noon* (1954) was on one level a careful study of a jealous man, bearing a relation to his whole work of Colette's *Le Pur et l'impur* to hers, while being on another level the story of how not to make a film: it concerns an attempt to put the *Odyssey* on the screen and may have had its inception in Moravia's disgust with the absurd Paramount *Ulysses* (1955), starring Kirk Douglas and Silvana Mangano, a film in which, I observed, the Cyclops is put to sleep on grape juice (the grapes are trampled and he is given the juice to drink, without fermentation intervening, whereas in the original the mariners had of course imported their wine into the cave).

It is quite unfair to state, as do Marsha Kinder and Beverle Houston, that this book takes a "condescending attitude toward film." Moravia, who had already seen pictures

348

made from his fiction by this date, and who was writing regular film reviews for a Roman newspaper, simply puts a variety of approaches into the mouths of his main characters. To take them as his own is ridiculous.

There are three main approaches to the *Odyssey* in *A Ghost at Noon*. The most obvious is that of an extroverted, "animal-like" producer for "Triumph" films called Battista. His crass philistinism, alas all too familiar, is expressed as follows:

> "What struck me above all in the *Odyssey* is that Homer's poetry is always spectacular . . . and when I say spectacular, I mean it has something in it that infallibly pleases the public. Take for example the Nausicaa episode. All those lovely girls dressed in nothing at all, splashing about in the water under the eyes of Ulysses who is hiding behind a bush. There, with slight variations, you have a complete Bathing Beauties scene. Or take Polyphemus; a monster with only one eye, a giant, an ogre . . . why, it's King Kong, one of the greatest pre-war successes . . . let it be quite clear that what I want is a film as much like Homer's *Odyssey* as possible. And what was Homer's intention, with the *Odyssey?* He intended to tell an adventure story which would keep the reader in suspense the whole time . . . a story which would be, so to speak, spectacular. That's what Homer wanted to do. And I want you two to stick faithfully to Homer. Homer put giants, prodigies, storms, witches and monsters into the *Odyssey*—and I want you to put giants, prodigies, storms, witches and monsters into the film. . . . "

So he instructs his young writer, Riccardo Molteni, and such is Moravia's characteristic amphiboly that one cannot altogether dismiss Battista's view with "contempt." Godard does so. He calls his producer Prokosch (Jack Palance) and makes of him a sandwich of Carlo Ponti and Joseph E. Levine, pillorying economic pressures on the industry. There is a hinted equation between this sort of financial pressure and Nazism, as when Prokosch revises Goebbels to say, "Whenever I hear the word culture, I reach for my cheque-book." As against this barbarism, the director Fritz

Lang, playing Fritz Lang, supposedly a victim of Nazi suppressions, quotes Hölderlin.

So far this seems an interesting analogy. The elongated credits for Godard's film suggest a distortion of reality of the type to be attacked. But the trouble is, he takes himself so seriously—Richard Roud has compared him to Joyce and even Vermeer. Here the Moravia original, the structure on which the filmic analogy is based, is far tighter: Battista's rape of Homer is paralleled by Moravia with his seduction of the writer's wife, Emilia (Camille, played by Brigitte Bardot with Godard). We are involved in matters of moral health and civilisation, in this attack on the Classics. Godard provides his Prokosch with an attractive, polyglot secretary/mistress called Francesca who makes multiple translations throughout (Godard refused to let his name appear on those copies which were entirely in Italian), and who carries a little red book about with her, presumably of aphorisms from Mao. At one point Godard alludes to *Les Liaisons dangereuses* by having Prokosch write a check on Francesca's back, after which she changes her yellow sweater to red, endures an endless story about Ramakrishna from the writer Paul (Moravia's Molteni), whom she then starts seducing.

Godard involves so many elements by these knowing allusions that it is hard to concentrate on any genuine thematic drive. Perhaps none exists. His characters wander from room to room, endlessly talking, and one loses interest in a way one does not, cannot, in far more adventurously static sequences from Rohmer. Godard apologists like Kinder and Houston surely confess this inadequacy when they write, "We suddenly find ourselves more interested in watching the movement of the camera and seeing whether the lamp is switched off or on than in listening to what they are saying." *Verb. sap.!*

Moravia, on the other hand, is quite clear about what he is doing. Battista, the producer, is with him a philistine who does enjoy a tangential, if vulgar, grasp on a degree of truth. His director is much less likeable, a German called Rheingold who may or may not be a spoof of Max Reinhardt; Moravia's Rheingold represents precisely what that author has explicitly eschewed, namely psychological interpretations of a reality which are, in a sense, just as much a rape of that reality as is Battista's. "It's repulsive," the writer Molteni exclaims at one point, with surely something of the author's intensity behind him, "this desire of yours to reduce, to debase the Homeric hero just because we're incapable of making him as Homer created him, this operation of systematic degradation is repulsive to me, and I'm not going to take part in it at any price."

Moravia's Rheingold produces that hoary Viennese chestnut, resurrected from a hint in Hesiod, that Ulysses was subconsciously avoiding a return to Penelope:

> "Ulysses did not wish to return to Ithaca and was afraid to go back to his wife. In the meantime, however, I should like to stress first one important point: the *Odyssey* is not an extended adventure through geographical space, as Homer would have us believe. It is, on the contrary, the wholly interior drama of Ulysses . . . Ulysses, in his subconscious mind, does not wish to return to Ithaca because in reality his relations with Penelope are unsatisfactory."

To this elaborate exposition Molteni objects that "if we don't believe in Homer, I really don't see who we are to believe." They might as well shoot the whole thing in a room in Rome, instead of bothering to go to Capri. He finds a complete falsification in Rheingold's view: "Your interpretation—if you will allow me to say so, my dear Rheingold—runs the risk of making him into a man without dignity, without honour, without decency. . . ." In short, the figure you make of Ulysses is that you make of yourself and of your own world. Molteni feels drawn to suicide shortly after this outburst; he decides to abandon the absurd job of being a middle-man between two extremes, one physical, the other mental. He delivers an impassioned diatribe against Joyce's treatment of the same legend, in which, it must be said, there are some serious mis-readings of that author's *Ulysses* (at one point Molteni calls Molly Bloom "a retired whore"—she is not a whore, and she is certainly not retired). He then apostrophizes a passage from Dantë seeing Ulysses as a shaking flame in the *Inferno;* the implication is clear—unless we take on some of Ulysses's qualities, his great voyage to the West, his legacy to our civilisation, will have been in vain.

The analogy Godard makes with Moravia's Rheingold is what upsets the balance of the film. By casting Rheingold as Lang-Lang, Godard makes the director admirable rather than detestable (indeed, the lines from the *Inferno* so dear to Molteni are given to Lang, who also quotes Brecht). Apart from Lang himself being, at his age then, a distractingly rigid actor, the whole turn of characterisation stunts the narrative drive. In Moravia's novel Molteni is desperately, despairingly, jealous of his sensual Penelope, and thereby drives her tragically into the arms of the crude Battista, arms which prove to be those of death. There is a logic created by the structure: the motif of sexual jealousy shadows that other jealousy we should feel for what something called culture has given us, a civilised past. Is there room in the modern world for an Attic or genuinely Hellenic figure? Riccardo Molteni has visions of his Emilia as immense, more than human, godlike. . . .

I do not think myself that Godard here has anything certain to say, so he substitutes for this lack by saying many trivial things. Bardot is directed to play Godard's wife, Anna Karina,* puts on a black wig (mourning?), red bath-

---

* The mode of allusion becomes infectious, or should one say incestuous? The Jean-Pierre Léaud character in Bertolucci's *Last Tango in Paris* was confessedly a parody of Godard. In Truffaut's *Day for Night* (*La Nuit Américaine,* 1973), yet another in a long line of films about the making of films, there are references to Welles, Vigo, Fellini, Buñuel, and several others; they don't make the film any better.

towels (Greek robes?), and shows lots of backside in what is apparently meant to parody the cinema of sexual exploitation but which really only succeeds in being sexual exploitation. "In" jokes abound: red and blue filters try fran-

CONTEMPT (1963, Godard): one character (Michel Piccoli) wears what we learn to be the director's favourite hat, while another (Brigitte Bardot) puts on a black wig to resemble the director's wife. How much better does this make the film?

tically to confer spurious symbolisms; Greek statues replace understanding of any theme. Aphorisms multiply, as do allusions to other films and other film-makers: one learns that certain scenes are in reality parodies of such important works as *Some Came Running, Rio Bravo,* and *Hatari!* On the wall of a projection room in Cinecittà there is a sen-

tence by Lumière. One does not really want to deride Godard, but the sense one gains from *Contempt* is contempt itself, a sixth-form schoolboy's clever showing-off in knowing
digs to his circle of five friends. When at the end Camille/
Emilia is killed in Prokosch's scarlet Alfa-Romeo, provok-
ing true tragedy in the Moravia fiction, we are supposed to
understand that now Lang can continue making a film
("The object of a film is to produce another film") ; as the
Kinder/Houston team of apologists put it, "The accidental death of Camille and of Prokosch finishes the writer's
story, but the film-making process, directed by both Lang
and Godard, goes on and becomes an epilogue."

How very convenient. What you say in the film is not
really what you say in the film. Surely this is to shirk all intellectual responsibility. So, *Contempt* is just a film about
film-making. To which one can justifiably retort that it still
remains a rotten film.

It is, however, interesting as an analogy, owing to how
it loses all the agonised moral investigation of the Moravia
original (a far better novel than it has been given credit
for, at least in Anglo-Saxon circles) . I have suggested that
Moravia did not side with any of the three points-of-view
attacking the original Homeric art work. Goethe prefaced
Faust with a bevy of almost blandly self-interested attitudes of the same nature, the Director, Dramatic Poet,
and Clown, in "Prelude in the Theatre." In both cases the
writer inevitably sided with the writer. So, pressed back
by the viscerally analysing Rheingold, Molteni presents his
own view, which is surely somewhat that of Moravia, and
certainly that of Camus. The visible "bright and luminous"
world is what we have been given to inherit, and this world
is populated by people first and foremost, not by a mass of
psychological dramas. Molteni breaks out:

> "The *Odyssey* consists precisely in this belief in reality as it is
> and as it presents itself objectively . . . in this same form, in fact,
> which allows of no analysis or dissection and which is exactly

what it is: take it or leave it . . . the world of Homer is a real world. Homer belonged to a civilisation which had developed in accordance with, not in antagonism to, nature . . . That is why Homer believed in the reality of the perceptible world and saw it in a direct way, as he represented it, and that is why we too should accept it as it is, believing in it as Homer believed in it, literally, without going out of our way to look for hidden meanings."

I can think of no more succinct statement of how the best cinema finds its image in reality. Godard is cinema's Narcissus in love with himself, and this is a declaration of defeat. At its best film is that medium of redemption which Schopenhauer saw in true art—"a pure medium." Almost more than any art we have developed to date it transforms reality into "pure appearance," and so helps us to see, and live.

In the ultimate analysis the new vision cinema has given us should result in a heightened moral and social awareness. In his *First Discourse* Rousseau felt that it was literature that made men more "social." Today this onus, following on T. S. Eliot's famous dictum that the novel is dead, has obviously fallen with some weight on cinema, equally an art—as we have tried to emphasise—designed to please. Thus, Bertolucci (a Communist, of sorts) has said: "I think the greatest cinema was Hollywood cinema during the Twenties and Thirties. It was a collective cinema, a collective experience. In Europe, because we were different, we were for the *auteur* politics, the politics of the director, but cinema *is* collective experience."

Yet film has tended to make of Rousseau's "social" man the "sociable" man, one who "knows how to live only in the opinion of others." Generally speaking, and until fairly recently, cinema has shown us how to succeed, how to advance ourselves in given situations, how to avoid pitfalls. This is, I suppose, likely to happen when you inject a composite form into a society, and thus force on it a certain betrayal of the individual aesthetic agencies of which it is composed. Film is usually much simpler than fiction. Film music is not music in the old sense of the term at all. A photograph is not a painting. The cinema was designed to please, but since life is not invariably pleasurable, film has all too often been driven by its nature into a false morality the novel could not afford if it were truly to exist, operate, and be read for generation after generation. Such, it seems to me, is perhaps the only really valid sense in which cinema has corrupted fiction. A novel can be translated into another novel with more or less accuracy; but a film requires to be changed not merely for another century, or even decade (look at the remakes of *Lost Horizon*) but for another coeval culture, Margaret Kennedy's *The Mechanised Muse* demonstrating how another ending had to be put on Sagan's *Mädchen in Uniform* for an English public.

In the final analysis there can be no real betrayal of a fiction by a film. What distortion may happen is not essentially formal, but results from a basic self-deception common to both modes at their worst, something that falsifies and lies at the root of the defection of all art today when it becomes more impersonation than creation, when Hollywood found "high art" corruptive and hewed the classics into shape. *"Rebecca,"* gloated Samuel Goldwyn, "reads like a scenario. But not *Wuthering Heights. Wuthering Heights* we had to cut. And Ben Hecht and Charles MacArthur did a brilliant job." They did a brilliant job, we have seen, in attenuating the autonomy of an aesthetic vision, and eventually perhaps losing it since copies of the Wyler version (at present writing) are threatened with destruction. Which might be called "high art"'s final revenge on film.

Cinema seems now to have somewhat declined the role of purveyor of public opinion, and licenced mode of our time. It can only pick up aesthetic energy thereby. Will it do so? Alongside generations of students by this time we tried, at the start of this work, to wrestle with some problems incurred by regarding pleasure as integral to an art form. Yet of all the arts cinema requires pleasure of a sort, else we walk out. This has certainly not been the case with the novel whose pedagogic intention was partly its charm. Schopenhauer is more palatable through the pages of Thomas Mann than through most of his own, but pleasure, immediate entertainment, still conditions and sanctions cinema. It still has to tell some form of story even though this be that of a psyche.

In *Sincerity and Authenticity* Lionel Trilling put his finger on "the drastic reduction in the status of narration, of telling stories" that has occurred today. Our time is "uneasy with the narrative mode," which assumes that "life is susceptible of comprehension and thus of management." Willy-nilly, film is forced to be a narration; one frame follows on another, with rather more insistence than one page follows on another in a novel. Externally, a film is scheduled over a rather tight time-span; even if within this we travel backwards in film-time, we go ever forwards in human-time. Experiments to the contrary, though interesting at their best, still remain eccentricities. We check our watches for the next appointment as we depart from the emporium. One notes that even Andy Warhol charged good money to those happy few who wanted to watch his hours-long depiction of the Empire State Building.

Narration, then, involves *per se* a continuity. The past is causal. Although film lives in the present, as so many have observed, and lacks tenses, it joins hands with fiction here in safeguarding a sense of identity and civilisation and in sharing a necessary activity of the human mind.

A Select Bibliography of Some Relevant General Books in English

Agee, James. *Agee on Film*. Boston: Beacon Press, 1964.

Armes, Roy. *French Cinema Since 1946*. 2 vols. New York: A. S. Barnes, 1966.

Arnheim, Rudolf. *Film as Art*. Berkeley and Los Angeles: University of California Press, 1957.

————. *Visual Thinking*. Berkeley and Los Angeles: University of California Press, 1969.

Baddeley, N. Hugh. *Documentary Film Production*. London: Focal Press, 1969.

Balázs, Béla. *Theory of the Film*. New York: Dover, 1970.

Bardèche, Maurice and Robert Brasillach. *The History of the Motion Pictures*. New York: Norton, 1938.

Barry, Iris. *D. W. Griffith: American Film Master*. New York: Museum of Modern Art, 1965.

Bazin, André. *What Is Cinema?* 2 vols. Berkeley and Los Angeles: University of California Press, vol. 1, 1967, vol. 2, 1971.

Bluestone, George. *Novels into Film*. Berkeley and Los Angeles: University of California Press, 1957.

Bobker, Lee R. *Elements of Film*. New York: Harcourt, Brace and World, 1969.

Bogdanovich, Peter. *The Cinema of Orson Welles*, New York: Museum of Modern Art, 1961.

Brownlow, Kevin. *The Parade's Gone By* . . . . New York, Alfred A. Knopf, 1968.

Casty, Alan. *Development of the Film: An Interpretive History*. New York: Harcourt, Brace, Jovanovich, 1973.

Ceram, C. W. *Archeology of the Cinema*. New York: Harcourt, Brace, Jovanovich, 1965.

Clarens, Carlos. *An Illustrated History of the Horror Film*. New York: Capricorn Books, 1967.

Coke, Van Deren. *The Painter and the Photograph; from Delacroix to Warhol*. Albuquerque, N. M.: University of New Mexico Press, 1964; revised and enlarged, 1972.

Cowie, Peter. *Seventy Years of Cinema*. New York: A. S. Barnes, 1969.

Crowther, Bosley. *The Great Films*. New York: Putnam's, 1967.

Dickinson, Thorold. *A Discovery of Cinema*. London: Oxford University Press, 1971.

Donner, Jorn. *The Personal Vision of Ingmar Bergman*. Bloomington, Ind.: Indiana University Press, 1964.

Eisenstein, Sergei. *Film Form*. New York: Harcourt, Brace, Jovanovich, 1949.

———. *The Film Sense*. New York: Harcourt, Brace, Jovanovich, 1942.

———. *Notes of a Film Director*. Moscow: Foreign Language Publishing House, 1958.

Eisner, Lotte. *The Haunted Screen*. Berkeley and Los Angeles: University of California Press, 1969.

Everson, William K. and Fenin, George M. *The Western*. New York: Orion Press, 1962.

Fielding, Raymond. *Special Effects and Cinematography*. London: Focal Press, 1965.

Fulton, A. R. *Motion Pictures*. Norman: University of Oklahoma Press, 1960.

Geduld, Harry M., ed. *Filmmakers on Film Making.* Bloomington, Ind.: Indiana University Press, 1967.

————. Harry M. and Gottesman, Ronald. *Guidebook to Film.* New York: Holt, Rinehart and Winston, 1972.

Gibson, Arthur. *The Silence of God.* New York: Harper & Row, 1969.

Gish, Lillian. *The Movies, Mr. Griffith and Me.* Englewood Cliffs, N.J.: Prentice-Hall, 1969.

Gottesman, Ronald, ed. *Focus on "Citizen Kane."* Englewood Cliffs, N.J.: Prentice-Hall, 1971.

Graham, Peter. *A Dictionary of the Cinema.* New York: A. S. Barnes, 1964.

Griffith, Richard and Arthur Mayer. *The Movies.* New York: Simon and Schuster, 1957.

Guback, Thomas H. *The International Film Industry.* Bloomington, Ind.: Indiana University Press, 1969.

Halliwell, Leslie. *The Filmgoer's Companion.* New York: Hill and Wang, 1967.

Hampton, Benjamin. *A History of the Movies.* New York: Dover, 1970.

Henderson, Robert M. *D. W. Griffith: The Years at Biograph.* New York: Farrar, Straus & Giroux, 1970.

Higham, Charles. *The Films of Orson Welles.* Berkeley and Los Angeles: University of California Press, 1970.

Houston, Penelope. *The Contemporary Cinema.* Baltimore, Md.: Penguin Books, 1963.

Huaco, George A. *The Sociology of Film Art.* New York: Basic Books, 1965.

Huss, Roy and Silverstein, Norman. *The Film Experience.* New York: Dell, 1968.

Jacobs, Lewis. *The Rise of American Film.* New York: Harcourt, Brace, 1939.

————, ed. *The Emergence of Film Art.* New York: Hopkinson and Blake, 1969.

————, ed. *Introduction to the Art of the Movies.* New York: Noonday Press, 1960.

————, ed. *The Movies as Medium*. New York: Farrar, Straus & Giroux, 1970.

Jinks, William. *The Celluloid Literature*. Beverly Hills, Calif.: Glencoe Press, A Division of Benziger, Bruce & Glencoe, 1971.

Jobes, Gertrude. *Motion Picture Empire*. Hamden, Conn.: Archdon Press, 1966.

Kael, Pauline. *Going Steady*. Boston: Atlantic-Little, Brown, 1970.

————. *I Lost It At The Movies*. New York: Bantam Books, 1965.

————. *Kiss Kiss Bang Bang*. New York: Bantam Books, 1965.

Kauffmann, Stanley. *A World on Film*. New York: Dell, 1966.

Kinder, Marsha and Houston, Beverle. *Close-Up*. New York: Harcourt, Brace, Jovanovich, 1972.

Knight, Arthur. *The Liveliest Art*. New York: Macmillan, 1957.

Kracauer, Siegfried. *From Caligary to Hitler*. Princeton, N.J.: Princeton University Press, 1947.

————. *Theory of Film*. New York: Oxford University Press, 1960.

Kuhns, William. *Movies in America*. Dayton, Ohio: Pflaum/ Standard, 1972.

Lawson, J. H. *Film: The Creative Process*. New York: Hill and Wang, 1967.

Lennig, Arthur. *Classics of the Film*. Madison, Wis.: Wisconsin Film Society, 1965.

Leyda, Jay. *Kino: A History of the Russian and Soviet Film*. London: Allen and Unwin, 1960.

Lindgren, Ernest. *The Art of the Film*. New York: Macmillan, 1963.

Lindsay, Vachel. *The Art of the Moving Picture*. New York: The Macmillan Company, 1922.

MacCann, Richard D. *Film and Society*. New York: Scribner's, 1964.

MacDonald, Dwight. *On Movies*. Englewood Cliffs, N.J.: Prentice-Hall, 1968.

Maltin, Leonard. *Behind the Camera*. New York: New American Library, 1971.

Mannogian, Haig P. *The Film-Maker's Art.* New York: Basic Books, 1966.

Manvell, Roger. *Film.* London: Penguin Books, 1950.

———. *The Film and the Public.* London: Penguin Books, 1955.

———. *New Cinema in Europe.* New York: Dutton, 1965.

Mast, Gerald. *A Short History of the Movies.* New York: Bobbs-Merrill, 1971.

McBride, Joseph. *Orson Welles.* New York: Viking Press, 1972.

McGowan, Kenneth. *Behind the Screen.* New York: Delacorte Press, 1965.

McLuhan, Marshall. *Understanding Media.* New York: McGraw-Hill, 1964.

Metz, Christian. *Language and Cinema.* Translated by Donna Jean Umiker-Sebeok. The Hague: Mouton, 1974.

Montagu, Ivor. *Film World.* Baltimore, Md.: Penguin Books, 1964.

Moussinac, Leon. *Sergei Eisenstein.* New York: Crown, 1970.

Murray, Edward. *The Cinematic Imagination.* New York: Ungar, 1972.

Neergaard, Ebbe. *Carl Dreyer.* London: British Film Institute (New Index Series, No. 1), 1950.

Nicoll, Allardyce. *Film and Theatre.* New York: Crowell, 1936.

Nilsen, Vladimir. *The Cinema as a Graphic Art.* New York: Hill & Wang, 1959.

Nisbett, A. *The Sound Studio.* London: Focal Press, 1963.

O'Dell, Paul. *Griffith and the Rise of Hollywood.* New York: A. S. Barnes, 1970.

Payne, Robert. *The Great God Pan.* New York: Hermitage House, 1952.

Pechter, William. *Twenty-Four Times A Second.* New York: Harper & Row, 1971.

Powdermaker, Hortense. *Hollywood, The Dream Factory.* Boston: Little, Brown, 1950.

Pudovkin, Vsevolod. *Film Technique and Film Acting.* London: Vision/Mayflower, 1958.

Quigley, Martin, Jr. *Magic Shadows*. London: Quigley, 1948.

————. *New Screen Techniques*. New York: Quigley Publications, 1953.

Ramsaye, Terry. *A Million and One Nights*. New York: Simon and Schuster, 1964 (originally published in 1926).

Reisz, Karel and Millar, Gavin. *The Technique of Film Editing*. 2d ed., enlarged. London: Focal Press, 1968.

Rhode, Eric. *Tower of Babel*. Philadelphia: Chilton Books, 1966.

Richardson, Robert. *Literature and Film*. Bloomington, Ind.: Indiana University Press, 1969.

Robinson, William and Garrett, George, eds. *Man and the Movies*. Baton Rouge, La.: Louisiana State University Press, 1967.

Rotha, Paul and Griffith, Richard. *The Film Till Now*. New York: Funk & Wagnalls, 1949; reissued, Feltham, Middlesex, England: Hamlyn House, 1967.

Sadoul, George. *French Film*. London: Falcon Press, 1953.

Sarris, Andrew. *The American Cinema*. New York: Dutton, 1968.

————. *Confessions of a Cultist: On the Cinema, 1955–1969*. New York: Simon and Schuster, 1970.

————, ed. *Interviews with Film Directors*. New York: Bobbs-Merrill, 1967.

Scharf, Aaron. *Art and Photography*. Baltimore, Md.: Penguin Press, 1969.

Schickel, Richard. *The Disney Version*. New York: Simon and Schuster, 1968.

Seldes, Gilbert. *The Great Audience*. New York: Viking Press, 1950.

Shales, Tom *et al*. *The American Film Heritage*. Washington, D.C.: Acropolis Books, 1972.

Sheridan, Marion C. *et al*. *The Motion Picture and the Teaching of English*. New York: Appleton-Century-Crofts, 1965.

Simon, John. *Private Screenings*. New York: Macmillan, 1967.

Slide, Anthony. *Early American Cinema*. New York: A. S. Barnes, 1970.

Solomon, Stanley J. *The Film Idea*. New York: Harcourt, Brace, Jovanovich, 1972.

————, ed. *The Classic Cinema*. New York: Harcourt, Brace, Jovanovich, 1973.

Sontag, Susan. *Against Interpretation and Other Essays*. New York: Dell, 1966.

Souto, H. Mario Raimondo. *The Motion Picture Camera*. London: Focal Press, 1967.

Spottiswoode, Raymond. *A Grammar of Film*. Berkeley and Los Angeles: University of California Press, 1950.

Stephenson, Ralph and Debrix, J. R. *The Cinema as Art*. Baltimore, Md.: Penguin Books, 1969.

Talbot, Daniel, ed. *Film, An Anthology*. New York: Simon and Schuster, 1959.

Taylor, John Russell. *Cinema Eye, Cinema Ear*. New York: Hill and Wang, 1964.

Thomson, David. *Movie Man*. New York: Stein and Day, 1967.

Tyler, Parker. *The Three Faces of the Film: The Art, the Dream and the Cult*. New York: Yoseloff, 1960.

Wagenknecht, Edward. *The Movies in the Age of Innocence*. Norman, Okla.: University of Oklahoma Press, 1962.

Weinberg, Joseph. *Joseph von Sternberg*. New York: Dutton, 1967.

————. *The Lubitsch Touch*. New York: Dutton, 1968.

Wollen, Peter. *Signs and Meanings in the Cinema*. Bloomington, Ind.: University of Indiana Press, 1969.

Wood, Robin. *Hitchcock's Films*. New York: A. S. Barnes, 1965.

————. *Ingmar Bergman*. New York: Praeger, 1969.

Wright, Basil. *The Use of the Film*. London: Bodley Head, 1948.

Zierold, Norman. *The Moguls*. New York: Coward, McCann, 1969.

Index

365